IMAGES
of America

ALLIANCE
NEBRASKA

IMAGES
of America

ALLIANCE
NEBRASKA

Knight Museum Board and Partners

ARCADIA
PUBLISHING

Copyright © 2000 by Knight Museum Board and Partners
ISBN 978-0-7385-0831-3

Published by Arcadia Publishing
Charleston, South Carolina

Printed in the United States of America

Library of Congress Catalog Card Number: 00107786

For all general information contact Arcadia Publishing at:
Telephone 843-853-2070
Fax 843-853-0044
E-mail sales@arcadiapublishing.com
For customer service and orders:
Toll-Free 1-888-313-2665

Visit us on the Internet at www.arcadiapublishing.com

We would like to dedicate this work to the late Hugh Bunnell. His love of history and the Knight Museum still serves us well. We were amazed at the wealth of information he possessed. As we perused his extensive files of research data for help with facts about Alliance, we missed his gentle voice and guidance. Our written word can never match his, but we know he would applaud the intention and be proud of the effort.

Cover Image: The Orange Tea Room was Alliance's best known eatery. Located in the corner of the Thiele Jewelry Store by George Milburn in 1925 and later moved to Thiele Drug Store next door. Back in 1947, or the "nickle-a-cup" days, when Dick and Bessie Becker and Merrill Averill took over, it soon became one of the most popular spots in town. Clientele included businessmen, ranchers, professionals, railroaders, housewives, travelers, and high school kids ordering sodas, full meals, or the daily special. When it closed in 1971, it was the end of an era in Alliance.

CONTENTS

ACKNOWLEDGMENTS

We would like to take this opportunity to thank the following individuals for their assistance in the creation of this glimpse into the rich past of Alliance. That true pioneer spirit is still alive today!

Thanks go to the Knight Museum board for their continued support. The Museum Partners, for the funding of the project. Our superb typists, Elaine Moore, Nathaniel Watkins, Aaron Watkins, and Carolyn Shannon, without whom you would not be reading this! Sherri Fry, for the tremendously valuable help with the research, narrative writing, and sorting, not to mention treats! To Gary Watkins and Shana Brown, for their expert photography skills with the newer pictures. Steph's Studio, for her patience with "needed it yesterday." Lou Chleborad, for his willingness to share the only picture of the American Legion in Alliance. Carrie Kelly, Diana Martinez, Charles and Ellen Lierk, and Polly Steinman, for their help locating, sharing, and describing many early photos. To Fern Wickham and Eleanor Dill, our RSVP volunteers, for their help with keeping the museum running smoothly. Barb Bignell, Mindi Keeley, Jim Girard, Pearl Mason, and Trent Benzel, for help with "do this and do that." Ellen Christensen, for the valuable help writing and tracking down little known facts. This project would not have been completed without the help of these wonderful people. Please forgive us if we have forgotten anyone.

Please note that with the exception of six photos, the rest come from the extensive collection of over three thousand at the Knight Museum. They are part of the research collection available for viewing in the Grace Spacht Library. For a more comprehensive look at Alliance, we would invite everyone to visit the Knight Museum at 908 Yellowstone. With the museum now open throughout the year, we welcome you and encourage you to call for more information at (308) 762-2384. "Come be part of Alliance history!"

Becci Thomas, Director
Rose Watkins, Assistant

INTRODUCTION

Once known as the Queen City of the Plains, Alliance is located in Box Butte County in the Nebraska Panhandle. It is situated on the west edge of the Sandhills, where there are thousands of acres of rich farmland. Located about 30 miles south of the Niobrara River and 30 miles north of the North Platte River, Alliance receives an ample supply of clear water.

Originally part of the Nebraska Territory, Box Butte County split off Dawes County in 1886. The first towns were Hemingford and Nonpareil. When rumors of a railroad junction started, the race was on to find a location. A small tent city called Grand Lake sprang up 18 miles south of Hemingford. It had four banks, two newspapers, several hotels, a livery, a saloon, a blacksmith, and some tarpaper or tent homes. When the commissioner of public lands held a land sale, the Lincoln Land Company and investors Sigafoos & Weston purchased 160 acres of land.

The railroad reached Alliance in 1888, but was not sure which direction to head from here. Should it go north to the coal fields in Wyoming, or to the gold mines in South Dakota, or even westward? Eventually Alliance developed into a division point linking the three states. The name Grand Lake was changed because of the confusion with Grand Island. The choice of Alliance has many versions, and today no one is really sure why it was picked. Those acres of land picked up by earlier investors were now worth a premium. A city had been born.

Homesteaders, businessmen, professionals, and families flocked to claim the land provided by the Kincaid Act. Alliance became a hub for shipping to transport the people and goods pouring in. By 1890, over eight hundred people lived here, and the population grew to over two thousand by 1900. Alliance expanded so rapidly that the city was incorporated on April 8,1893. In 1899, a lively controversy resulted in Alliance "stealing" the courthouse from Hemingford, and actually moving it by rail approximately 18 miles south. It took 45 men five days to accomplish this, and Alliance continues to be home of the county seat today.

As Alliance moved into the 20th century, it was a bustling city led by energetic people. Many of those same families have descendants living here today, and many have businesses still in the same hands. The pioneer spirit that brought many of those original homesteaders here kept them going through the lean early years, the "Dirty Thirties," two world wars, and the blizzard of 1949. They seemed to be always looking ahead. In 1921, Alliance became one of the first cities to adopt the city-manager form of government, which we still have today.

During World War I, a booming potash industry arose east of Alliance in Antioch. When the boom was over many of the homes and dismantled plants were moved to Alliance and are still in use today.

During the 1930s, Alliance had a new moniker of "Cattle Capitol of Nebraska," as the Nebraska Brand Office was moved here, and the Alliance Livestock Auction witnessed millions of dollars worth of cattle flood through their sale ring on a weekly basis. Ranching was a flourishing industry, and it seemed that every major businessman in town owned a small property with a herd of cows.

The 1930s also saw one of the most impressive park systems in Nebraska completed with a WPA work force. The 135-acre park system is still one of the most unusual around, and adds to a pleasurable way of life.

The greatest impact in the century was the development of the United States Air Base in 1942. This base for training paratroopers and glider pilots caused a flurry of activity that Alliance has never seen since. Over five thousand workers constructed 775 buildings, ran 35,503 feet of runways, and 12,332 feet of taxiways that became home to more than 14,000 soldiers. Over 66,000 people came from all over the area to view the dedication in 1943. New housing was needed in town to accommodate young military families, and businesses already struggling with rationing did their best to feed and care for a burgeoning population. The air base was deactivated in 1945, and 1,055 acres eventually became property of the City of Alliance. While the air base is just a memory, it brought many families here to stay and left a deep feeling of patriotism that Alliance had helped a noble cause.

During the years after the war, many changes occurred in Alliance. The growth could be seen in the railroad, which eventually became the largest employer. With the energy crisis, coal became a precious commodity that poured through Alliance like black gold. Young families expressed a need for larger schools and more housing. Incoming industries wanted more comfort features to draw in a work force.

With the arrival of the 21st century, Alliance tries to maintain one hand on the past to preserve the way of life brought here by the pioneers, as it looks toward a future filled with technology. The Knight Museum, with its slogan of "Come Be Part of Alliance's History," is preserving that history. New businesses and industries utilize features such as the Alliance Library and Attendance Center to help their employees obtain a college education without leaving town.

The Chamber of Commerce has a catch phrase stating, "We want to be your hometown." Most here will tell you that from the beginning of Alliance's history, a hometown is what it has been and hopes to continue to be . . . a hometown in Nebraska. Enjoy your walk down this path of memories.

One

The Early Years

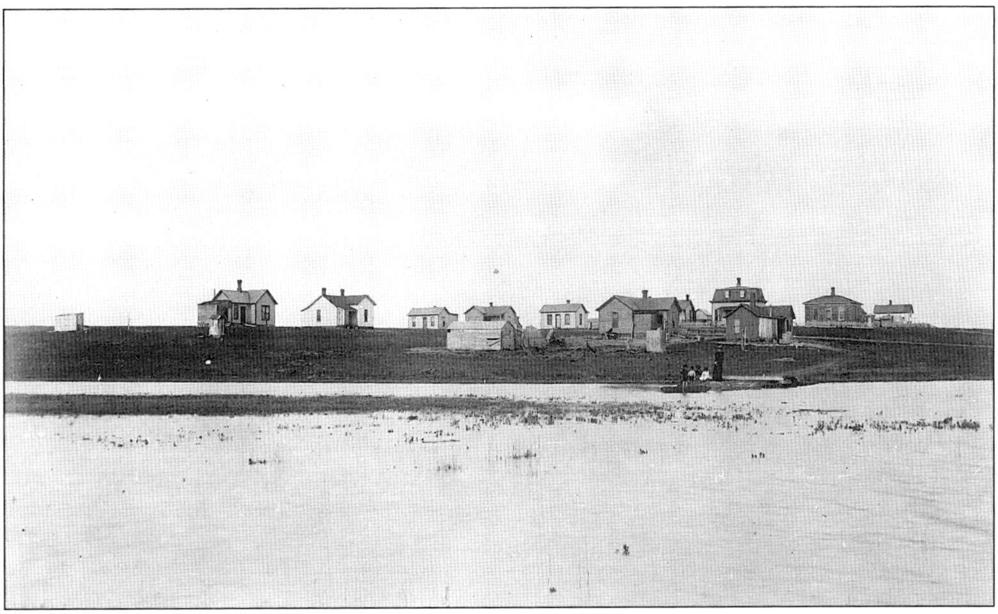

Grand Lake village, a collection of tents and frame buildings, had mushroomed on land just east of the Lincoln Land Company's Section 36. The name Grand Lake was not suitable, because it may have been confused with Grand Island in mail and train orders. Besides, there was no "grand lake." The village had first been named Bronco Lake for the nearest lake, 6 miles to the southwest, before it was changed to Grand Lake.

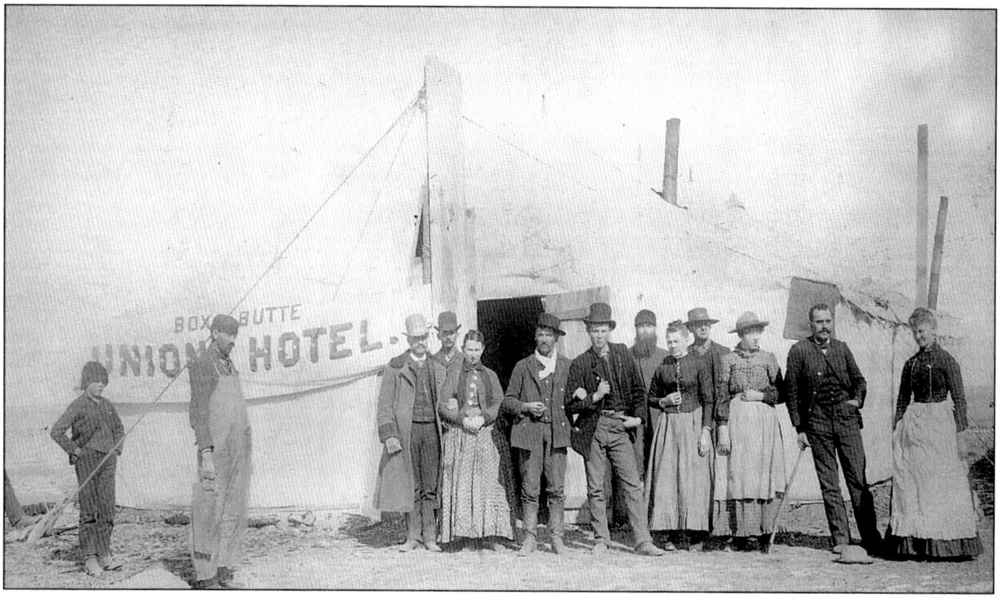

The Lincoln Land Co. sold the lots at this lot sale in Grand Lake, 1887.

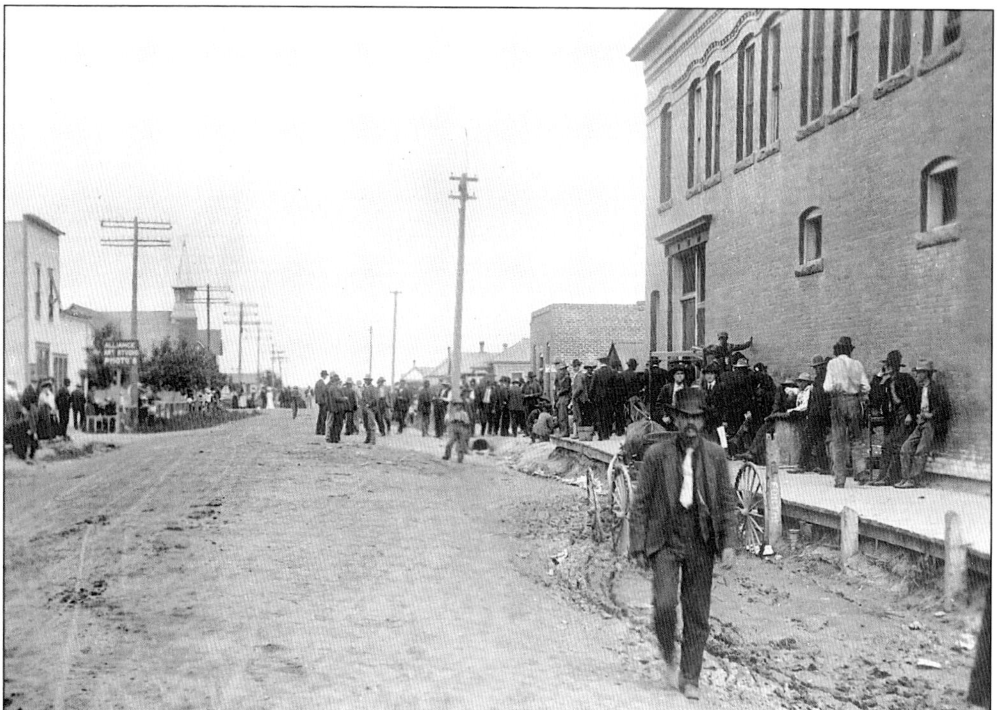

The lines were long in 1904 to sign up for the Kincaid Act for 640-acre homesteads. Henry Clayton is walking in the foreground.

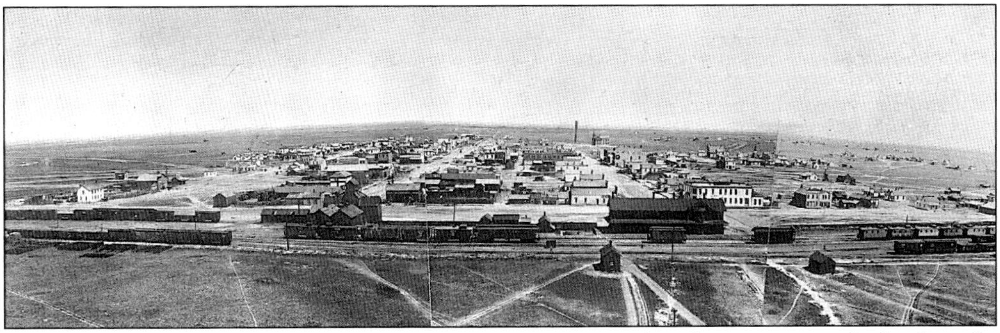

In 1898, Alliance had a population of over one hundred people. The caption on the back reads: "Alliance 1898—not a tree for 30 miles."

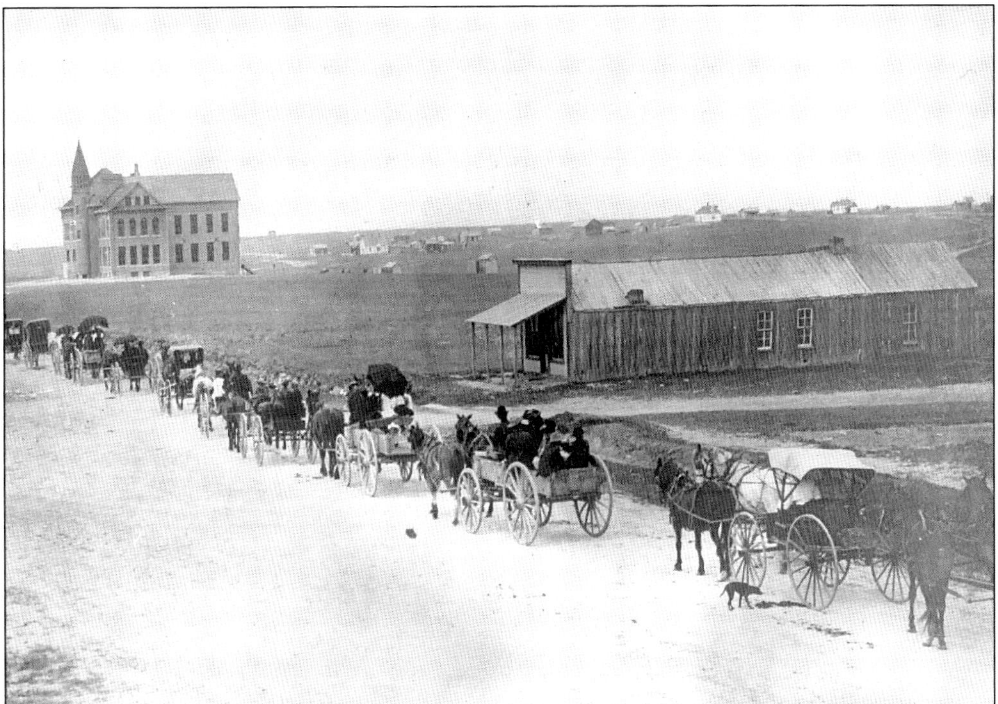

A Fourth of July parade in 1892 shows the area between Fifth and Seventh Streets on Box Butte Avenue. The building with the spire is Central School, and the wooden building sits where the courthouse is today.

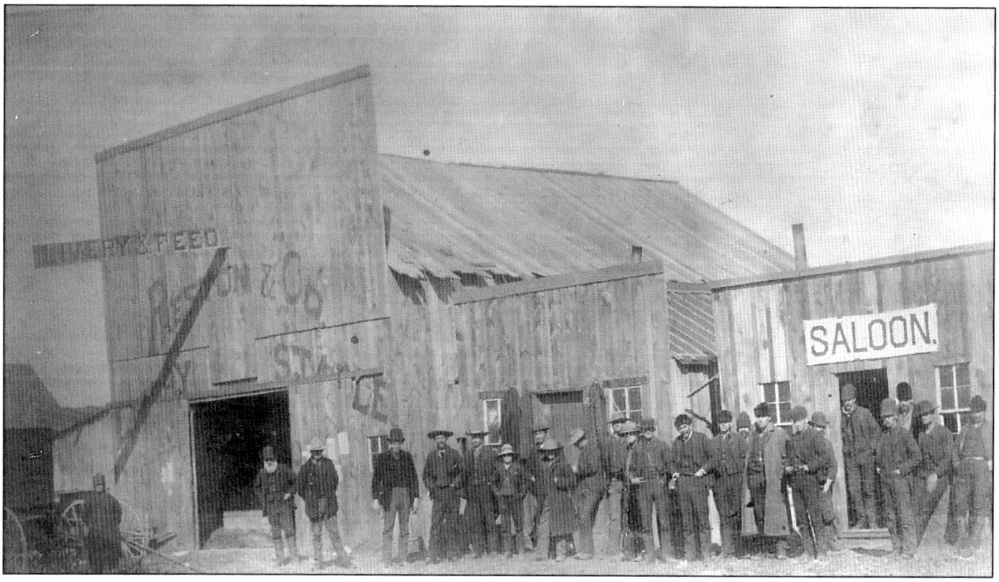

Shown is a photo of Preston and Co. Livery and Feed. After having one's horse taken care of at the livery, a drink could be procured at the saloon next door!

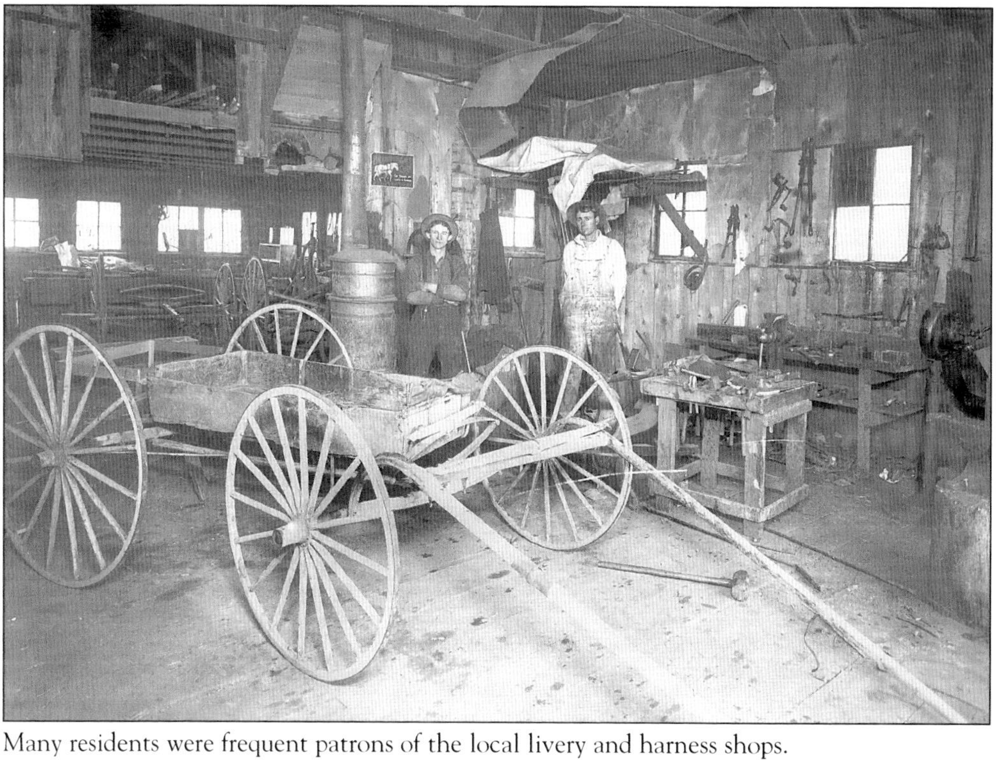
Many residents were frequent patrons of the local livery and harness shops.

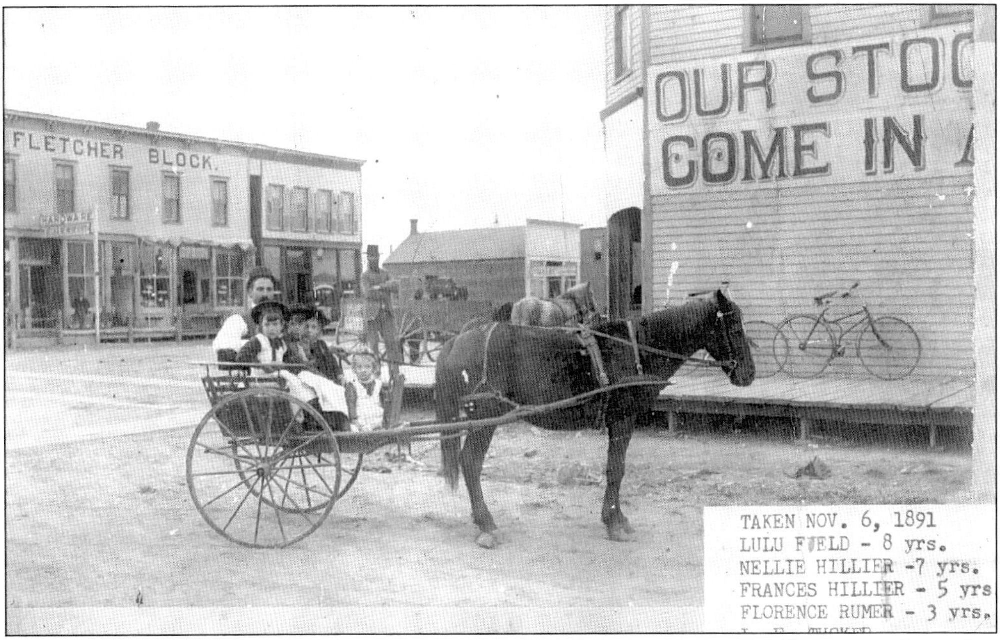

This local group is riding in a horse-drawn buggy on the main street of Alliance in November 1891. An early-day bicycle also is shown in the picture standing against the building.

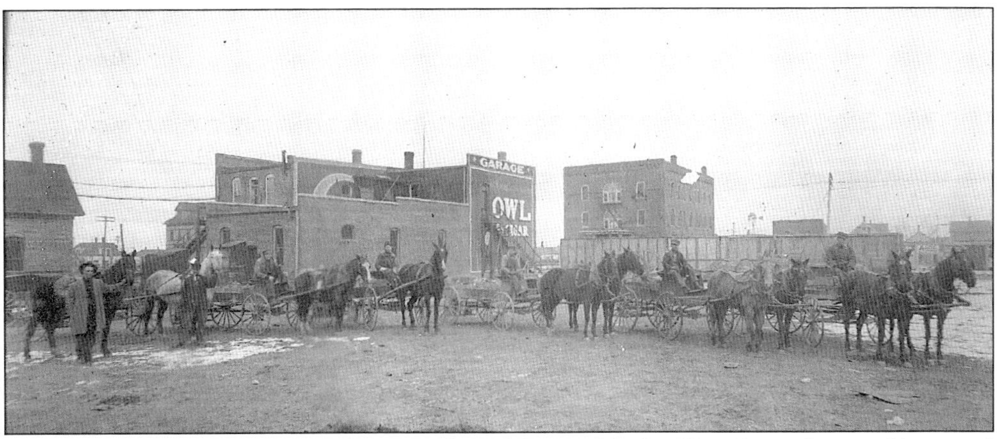

A horse and buggy lineup sits in the west alley of the 400 block of Box Butte. Being a "drayman" was a popular occupation of the day. The Drake is shown to the right of the owl sign.

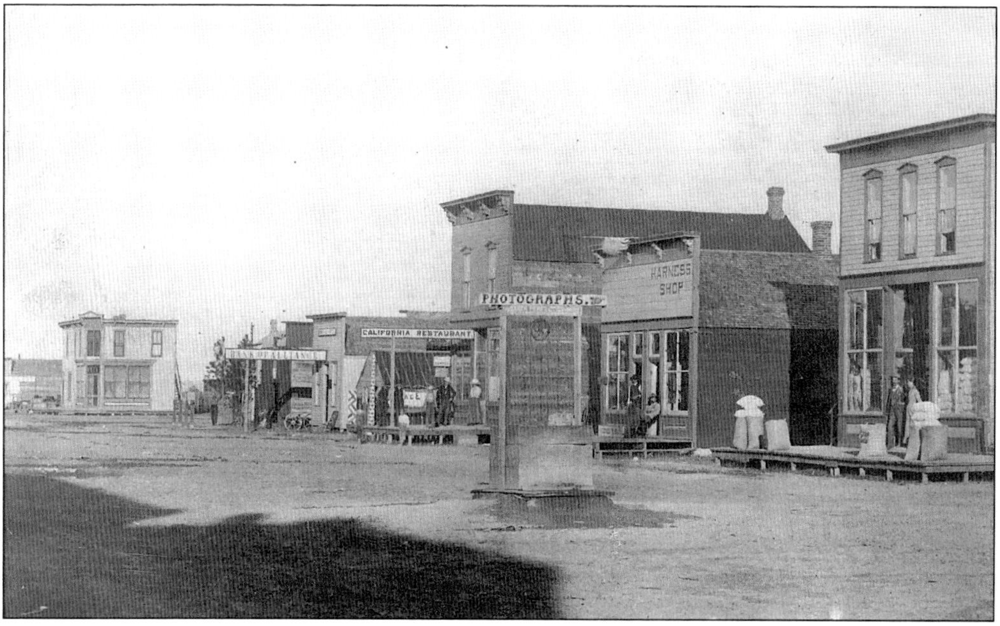

In 1890, this water well sat in the center of Box Butte Avenue and Wyoming Street. The local businesses in the background are the Bank of Alliance, the California Restaurant, Photographs, the Harness Shop, and Mercantile.

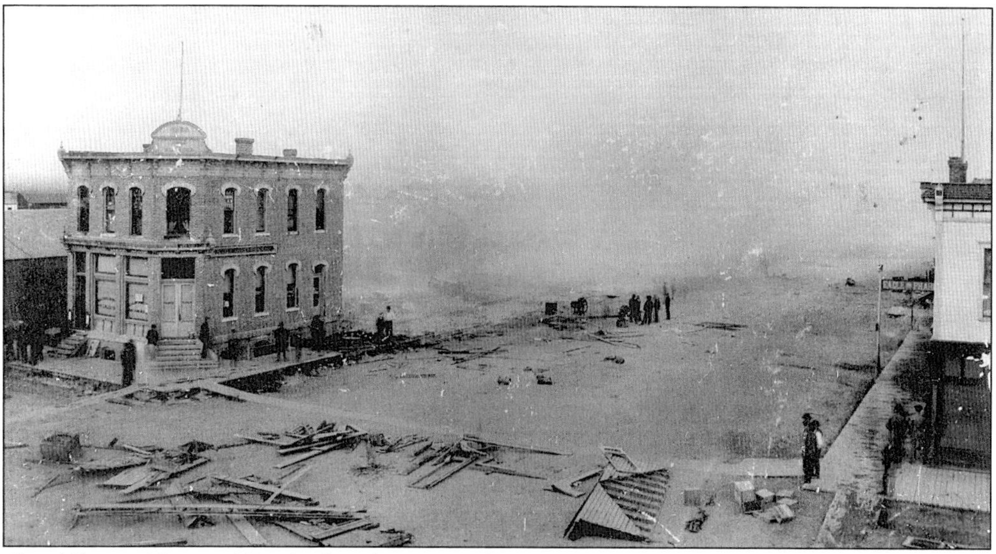

The Alliance National Bank, then known as the Bank of Alliance, remained after a disastrous fire. Major fires plagued Alliance until most major buildings were rebuilt from brick.

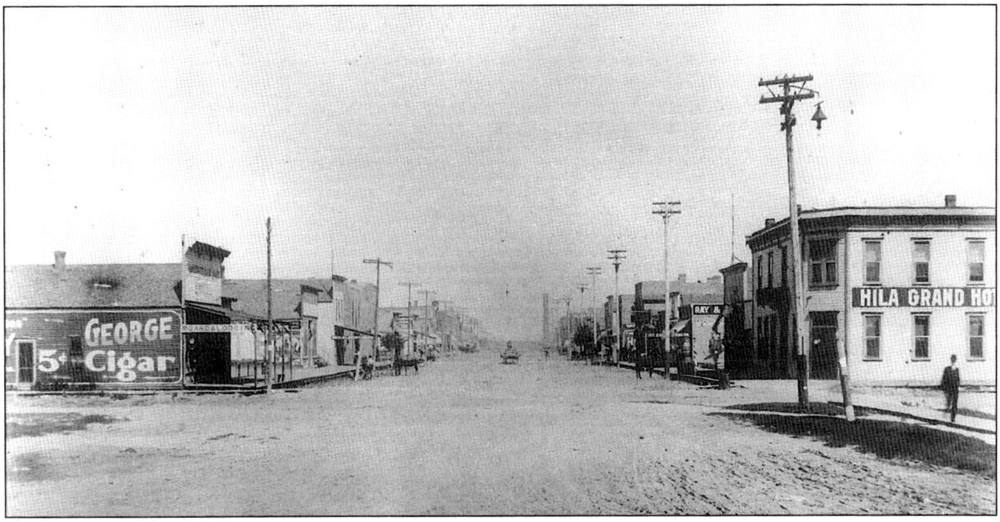

First and Box Butte housed the hotels due to its close proximity to the depot. Here we have Board and Lodging on the left and the Hila Grand Hotel, which was later the Alliance Hotel Annex. Both were welcome sites to the weary traveler on the many trains heading east and west through Alliance's early years.

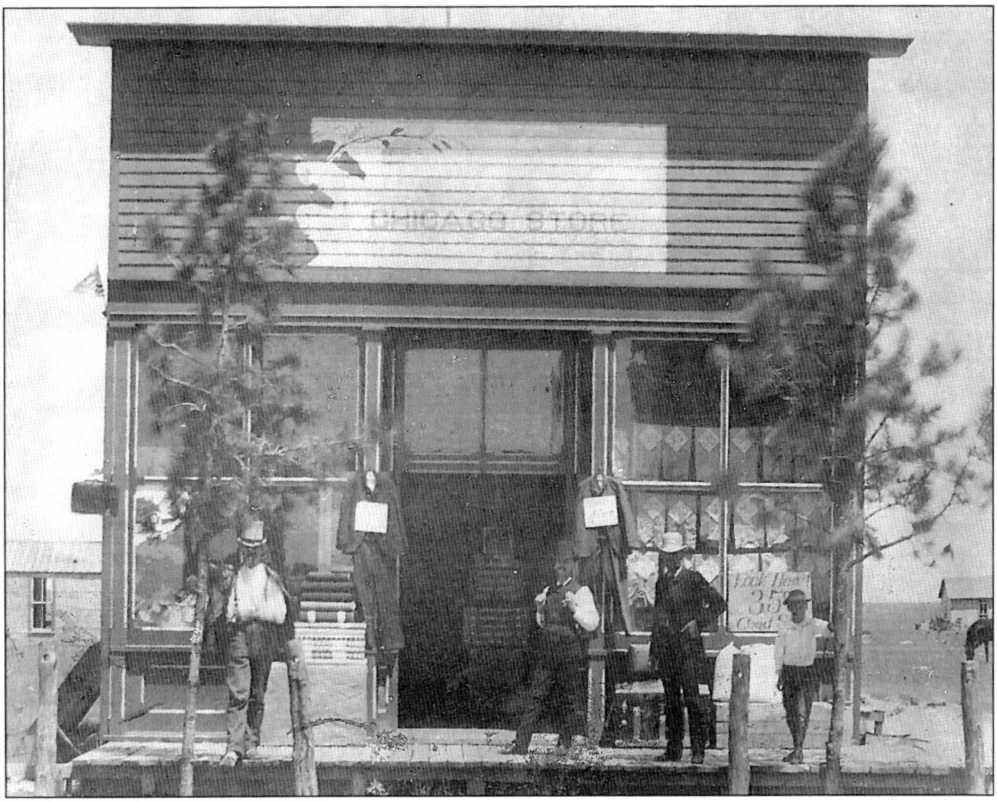

This is the Chicago Store, one of the earliest established businesses in Alliance. It was a general store, which meant that you could find a little of everything in it. Notice the suits hanging on each side of the front door. This photo was probably used in their advertisements.

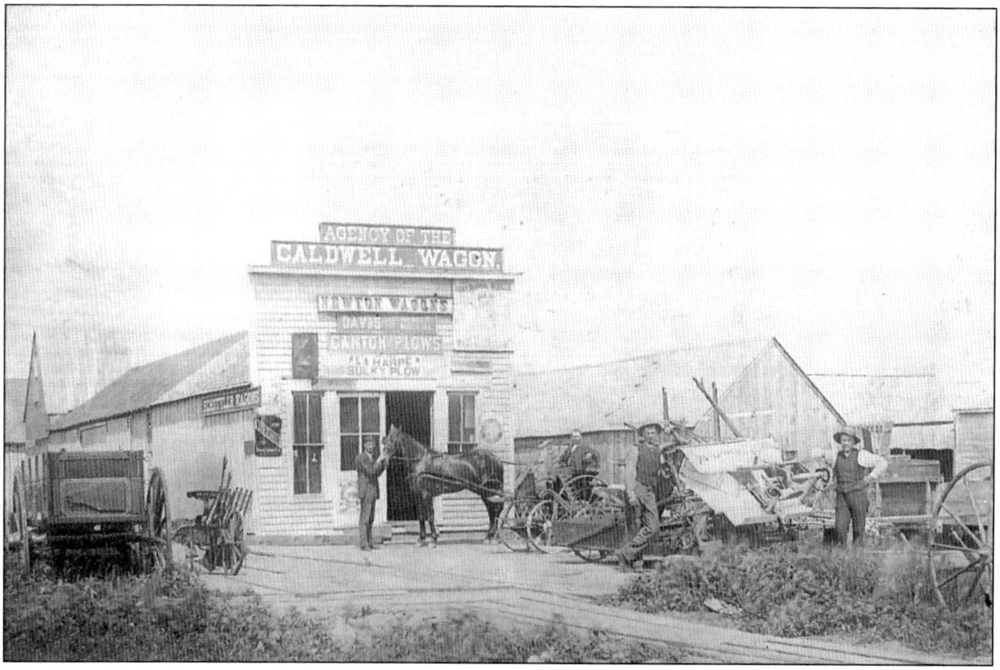

J.R. Van Boskirk is standing beside his favorite horse "Woods" at his implement business office in Alliance, c. 1890. The signs on the building proclaim "Agency of Caldwell Wagon, Newton Wagon, Davis Sewing Machine, Canton Plows, L. A. Harpe Sulke Plows, and Shuttler Wagons."

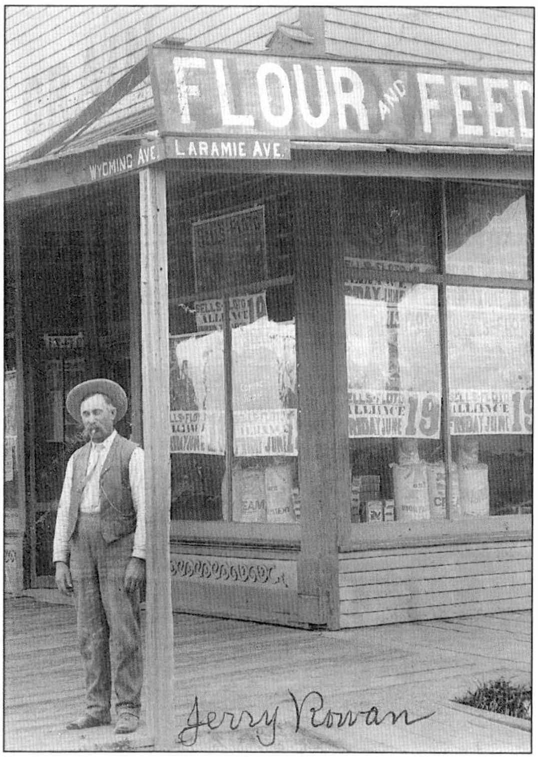

Jerry Rowan's Feed Store at Wyoming (Third) and Laramie, is now the site of Kiefler and Moller Accountants. The man in front is Jerry Rowan.

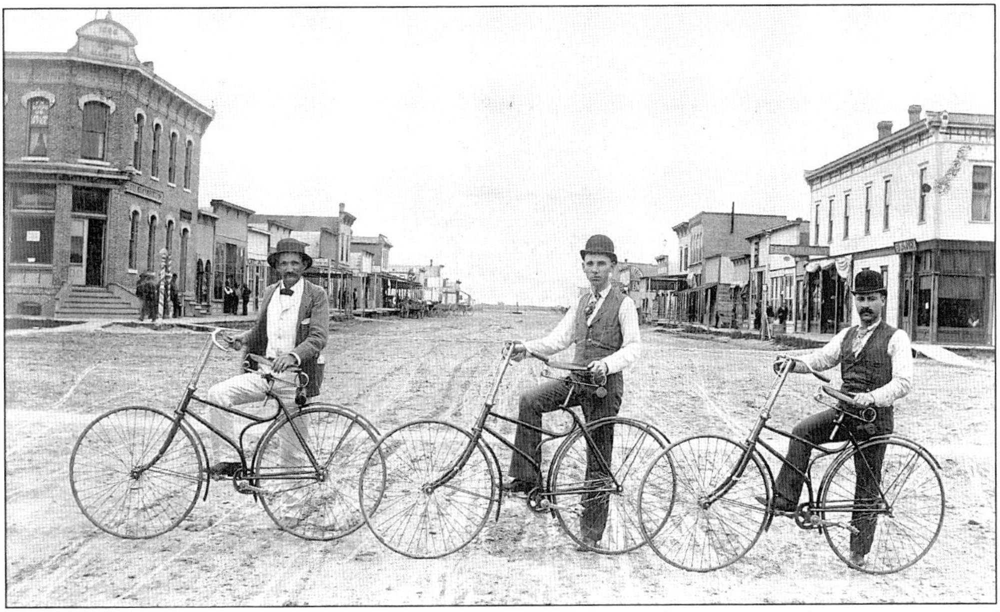

These three young gents show the popularity of bicycles as they pose at the intersection of Wyoming and Box Butte Avenue. Wyoming later was renamed Third Street. The gents are, from left to right: Jimmie Lucas, Frank Sands, and Lou Shawver.

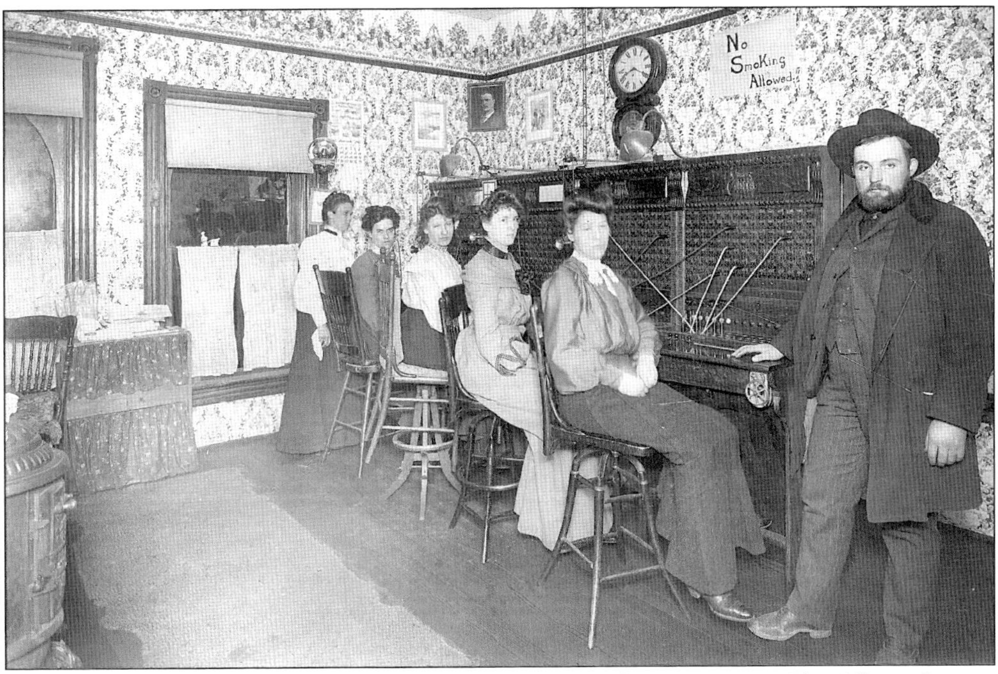

The first telephone exchange brought communication to Alliance in 1899. The Alburn Co. was the first telephone company. On February 19, 1964, Alliance had the distinction of being the first city in the nation to have touch-tone phones. Pictured in this 1905 photo are, from left to right: Bert Carr, Bertha Anderson, Dora Davis, Anna Krayick, and Alyce Ryckman.

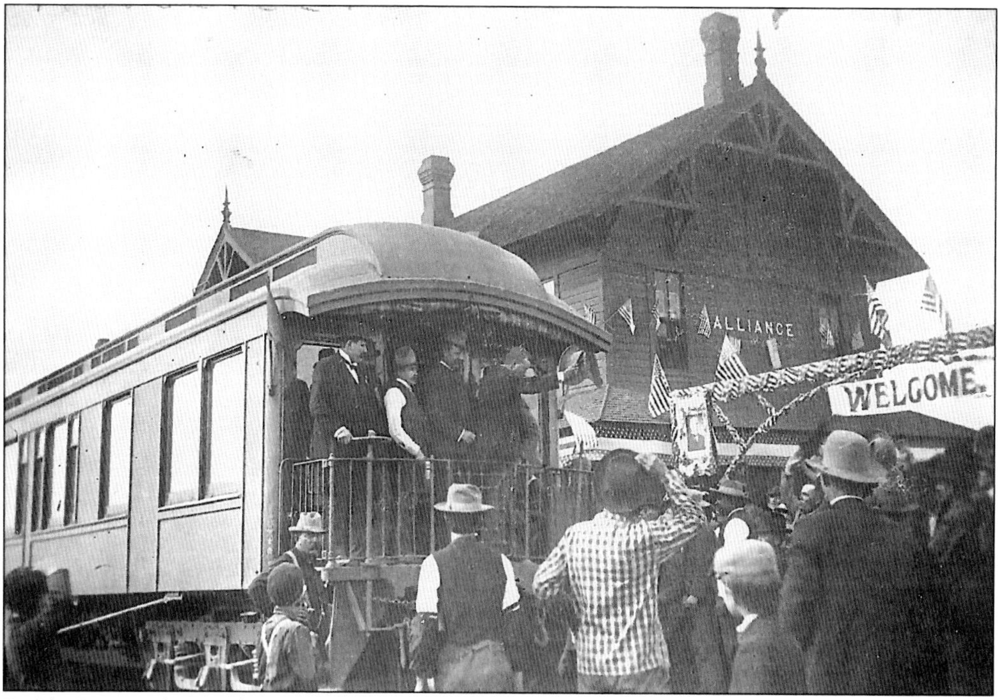

Teddy Roosevelt stands, arm extended and hat in hand, on the rear platform of his special train campaign car at the original Alliance depot on October 2, 1900. The welcome sign and arch with framed pictures of McKinley & Roosevelt were put up by direction of Railroad Division Superintendent Phelan. Alliance's ornate wooden depot burned to the ground on November 27, 1906.

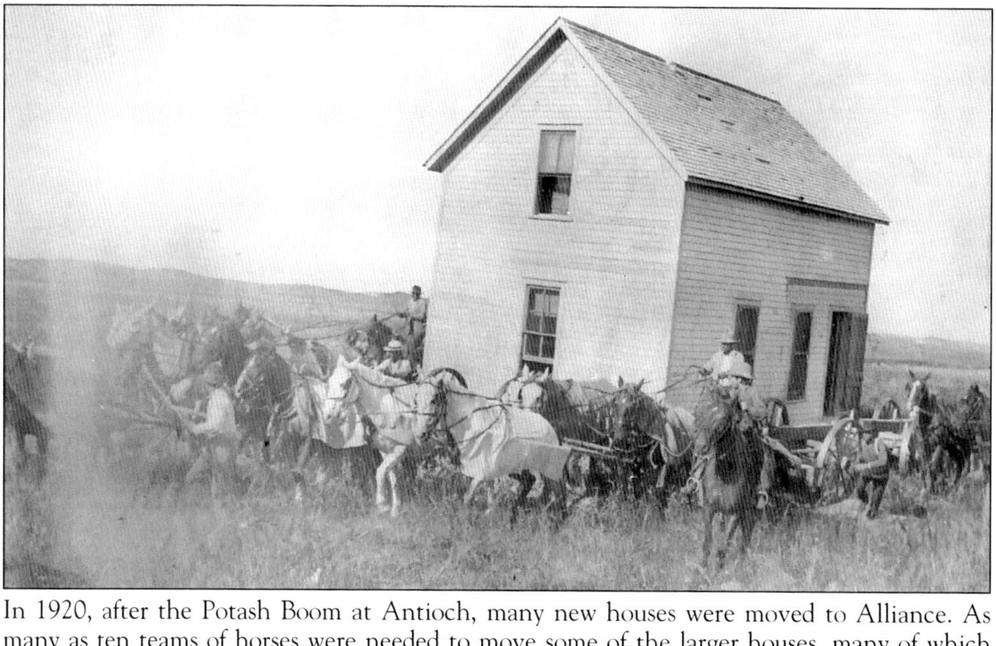

In 1920, after the Potash Boom at Antioch, many new houses were moved to Alliance. As many as ten teams of horses were needed to move some of the larger houses, many of which are still in use today.

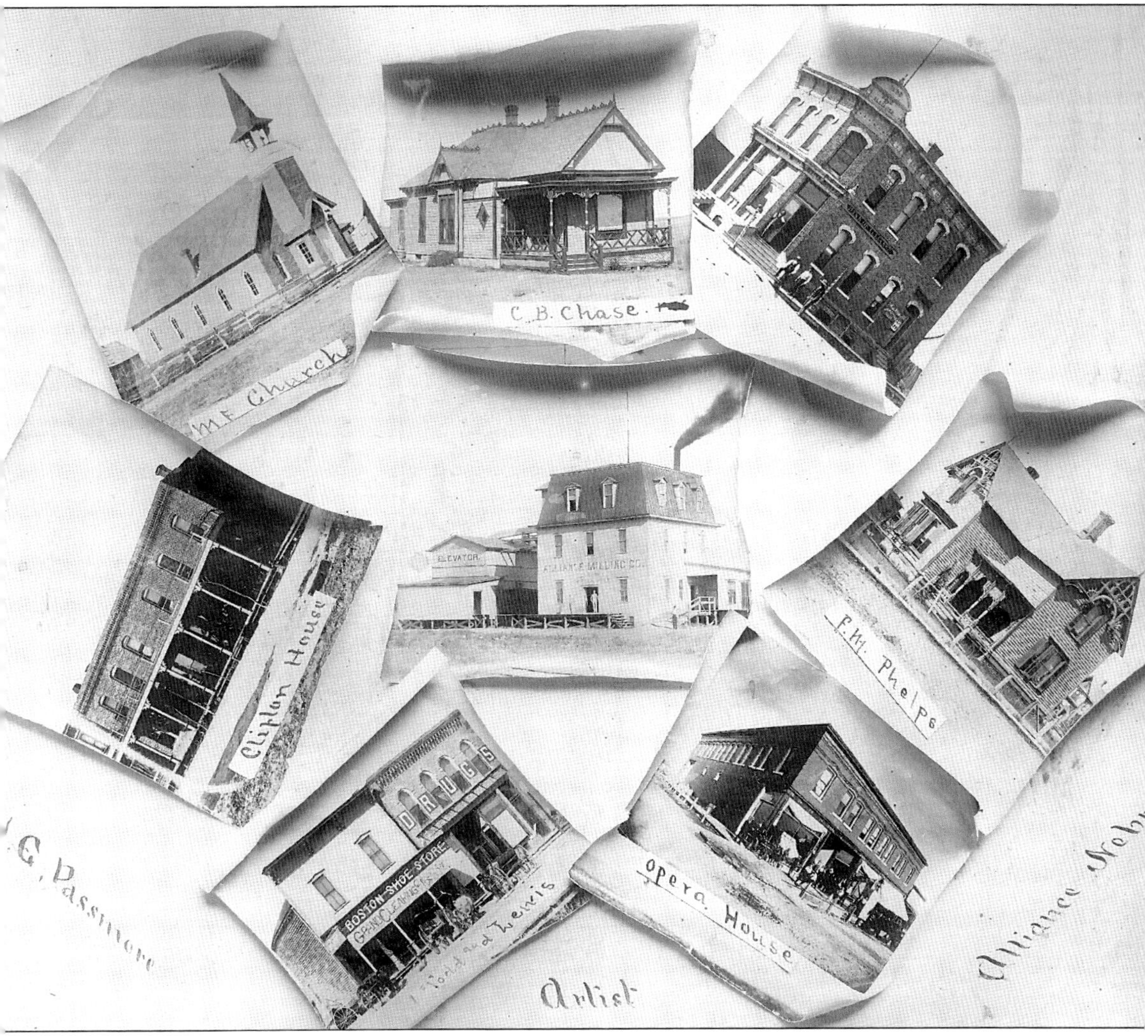

Local photographer W.G. Passmore created this Alliance montage. From left to right are: the first Methodist–Episcopal Church, CB Chase residence, Bank of Alliance, Clifton House Hotel, Alliance Milling Company, FM Phelps residence, The Boston Shoe Shop and Todd & Lewis Drug Store, and the Opera House. These were all built before 1900.

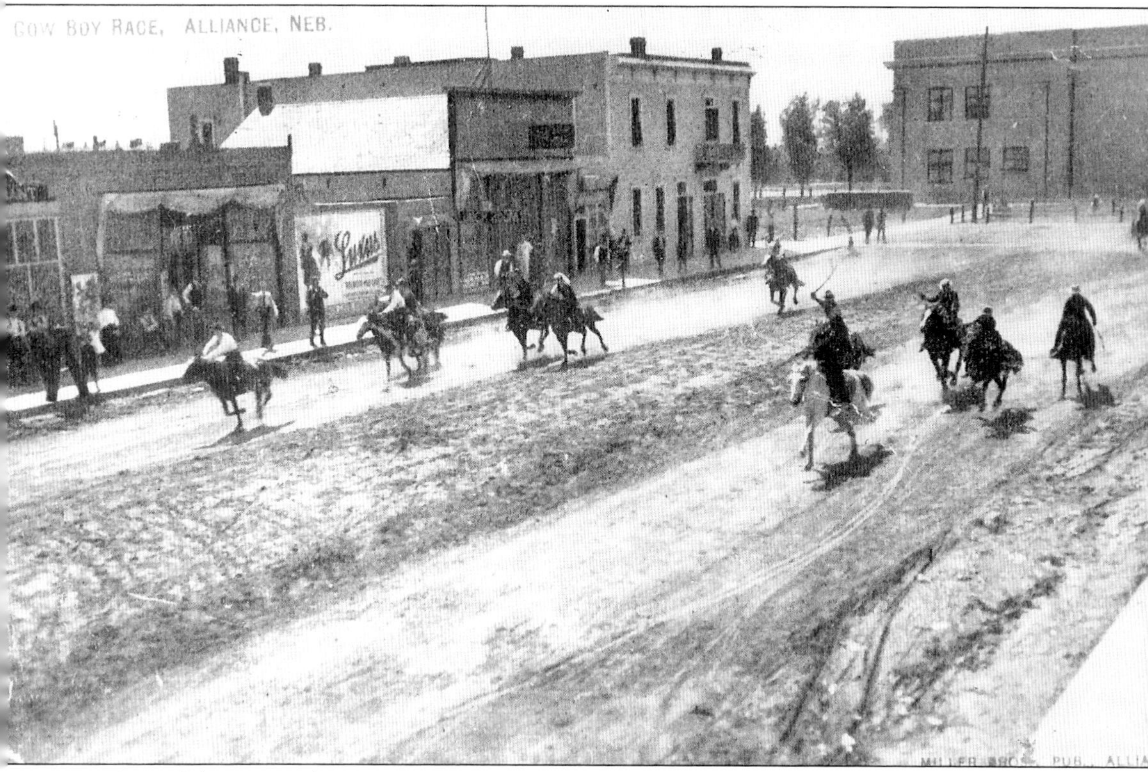

One of the greatest horse races in Alliance took place when the two biggest railroad contractors were rivals. Mike Elmore's "Flora E." had topped the track record at St. Louis earlier that year. The other contractor, Higgins, was running "McGinty." Both had laid a heavy bet, and their men were backing them to the limit. Uncle Zed Goodwin, a big man of almost 300 pounds, was backing "Flora E," and was right out in front of the bleachers to see the finish of the race. It was a close race, but "McGinty" won. As the horses crossed the line, Uncle Zed plunked both hands into his side pockets, yelling "By Golly Jiminy!" Just then his suspenders gave way, and Uncle Zed stood in the pants that nature gave him! The crowd bellowed and roared. Those who knew Uncle Zed say that there is no doubt he laughed with the crowd.

Two

Anchors in a Small Town

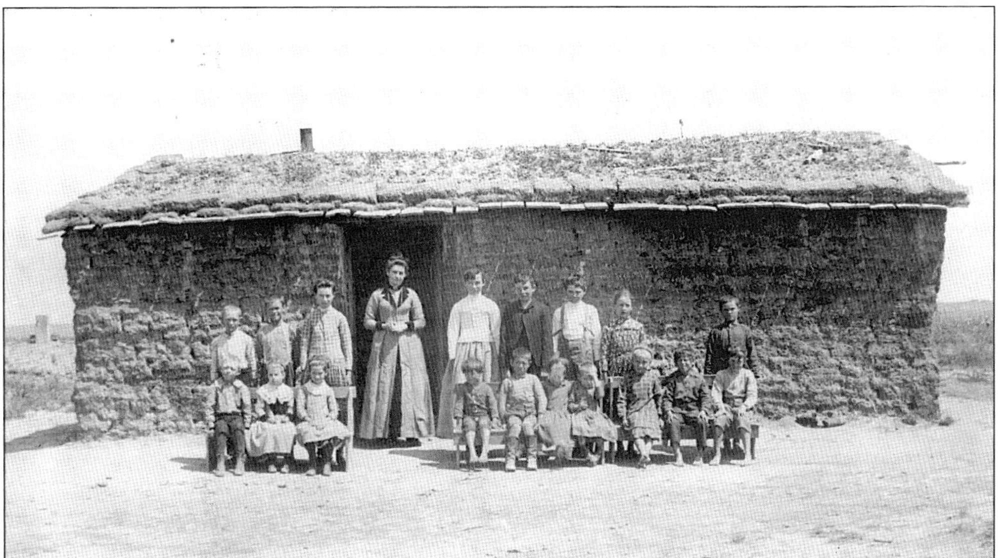

A sod schoolhouse was the start of education in Box Butte County in 1888. The teacher was Charlotte Worley, famed "Potato Queen." Children were from the Pepper, Gildersleeve, Benedict, Silk, Whitney, Johnson, Berger, and Corman families.

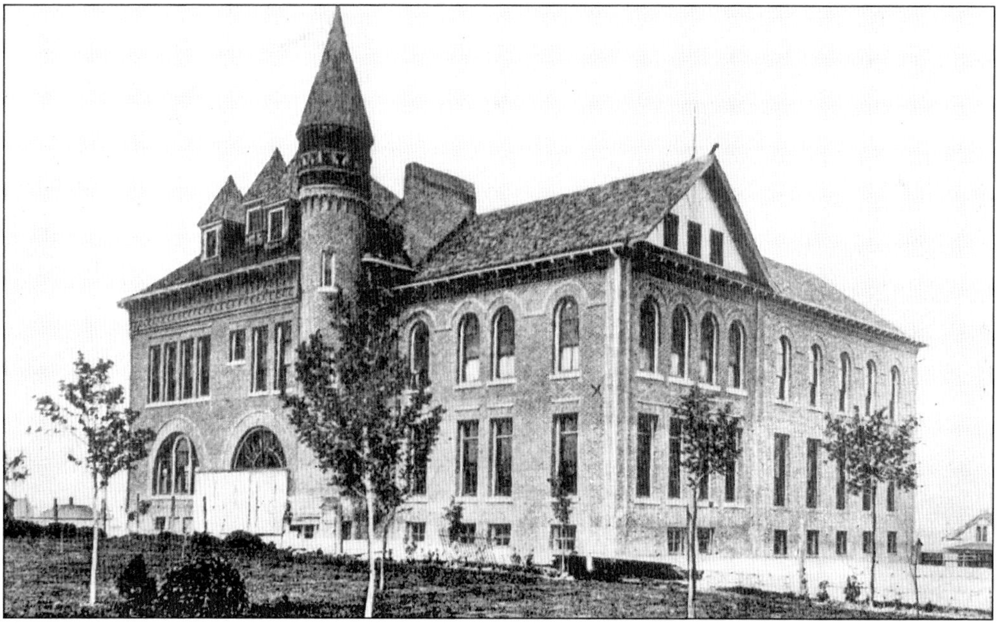

The Central School was built *c.* 1894. In 1912, a fire destroyed the building and all of its records. It was rebuilt at Seventh and Box Butte on the same lot, where it remains today. The first Central School was the only one in town and was home to all grades. In 1896, the first class graduated with six students.

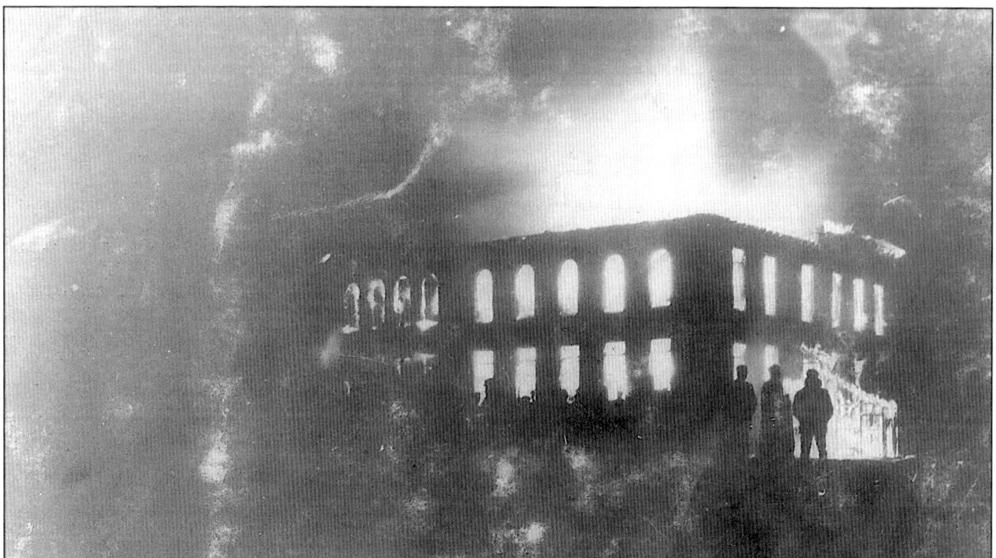

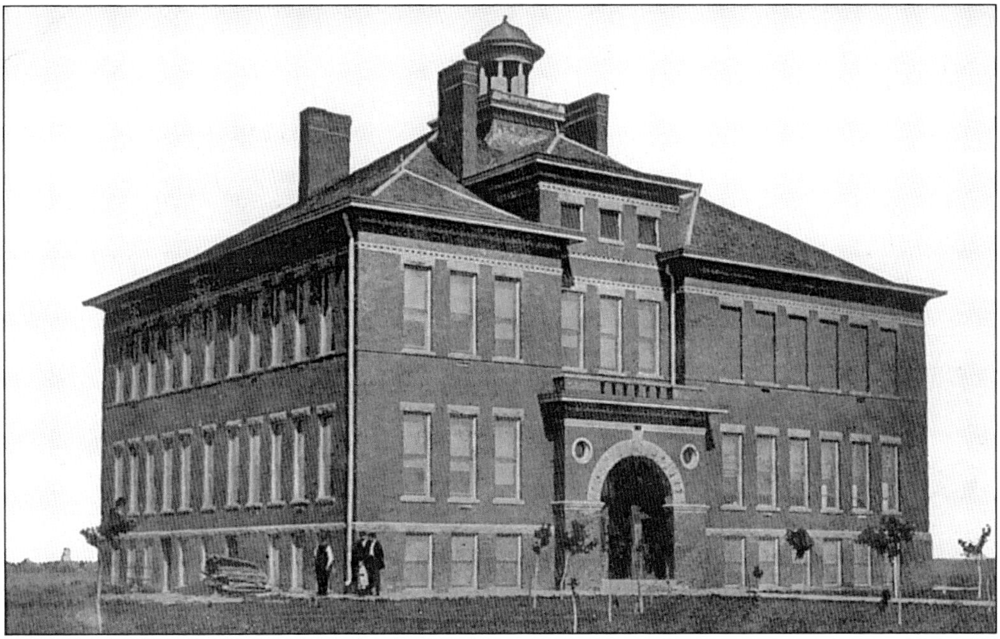

The Alliance High School was built in 1907 at Eleventh & Box Butte for $20,000. In 1920, a $250,000 bond was issued to expand the school to Eleventh and Laramie. This part is still in use as the Alliance Middle School. The schools "traded places" in 1968, when the high school moved to the building at Fourteenth and Laramie. A gym, band room, and classroom wing are the more modern additions.

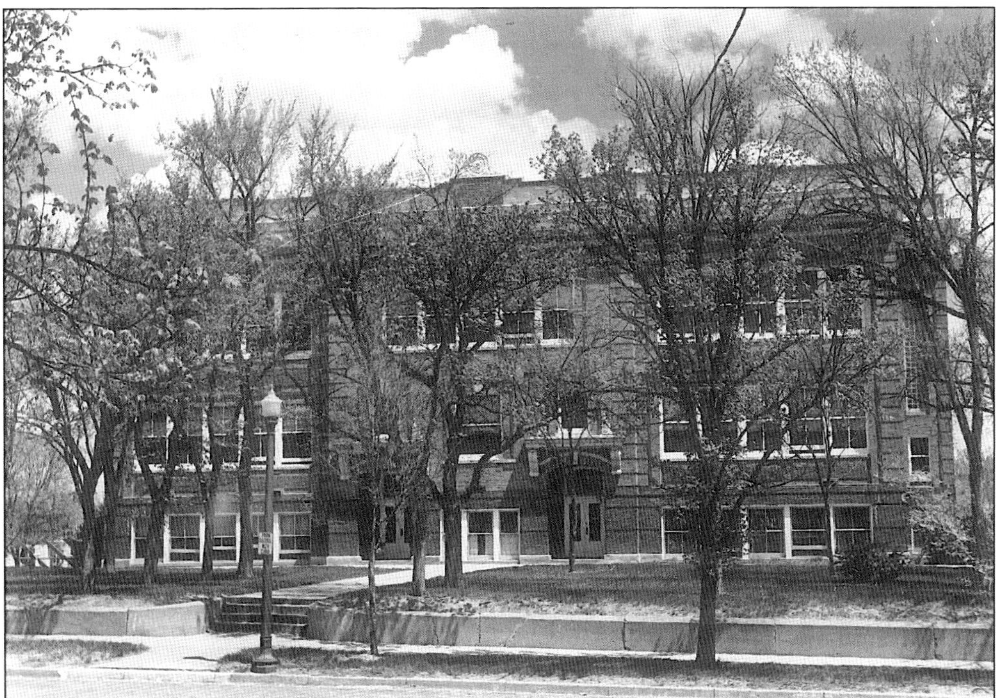

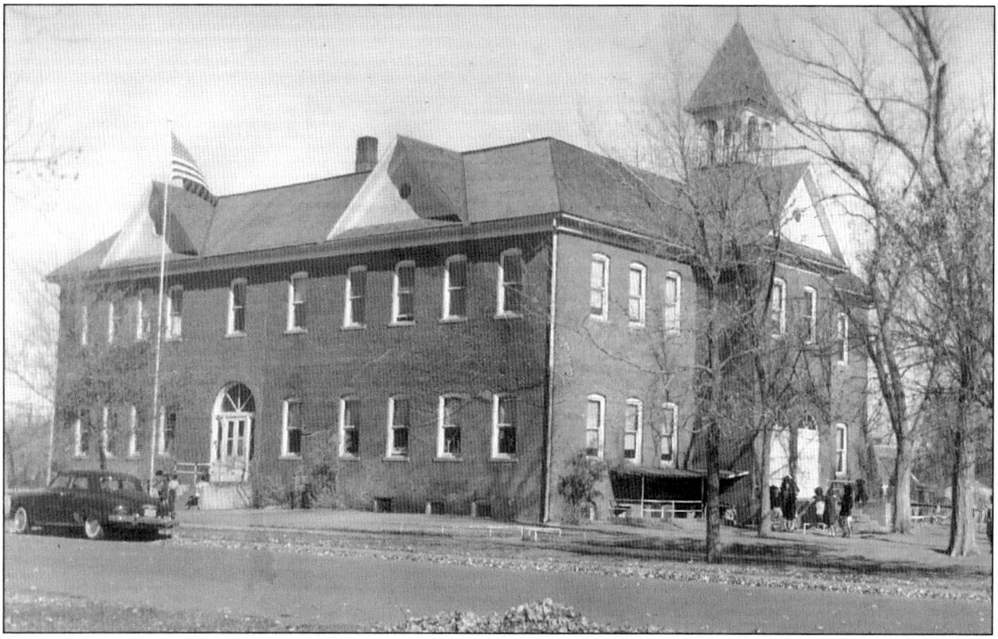

The Emerson School was built in 1904 for $9,000 at Fifth & Emerson, today the site of the Presbyterian Church. In 1949, the school was rebuilt at Seventh & Black Hills and has had two additions.

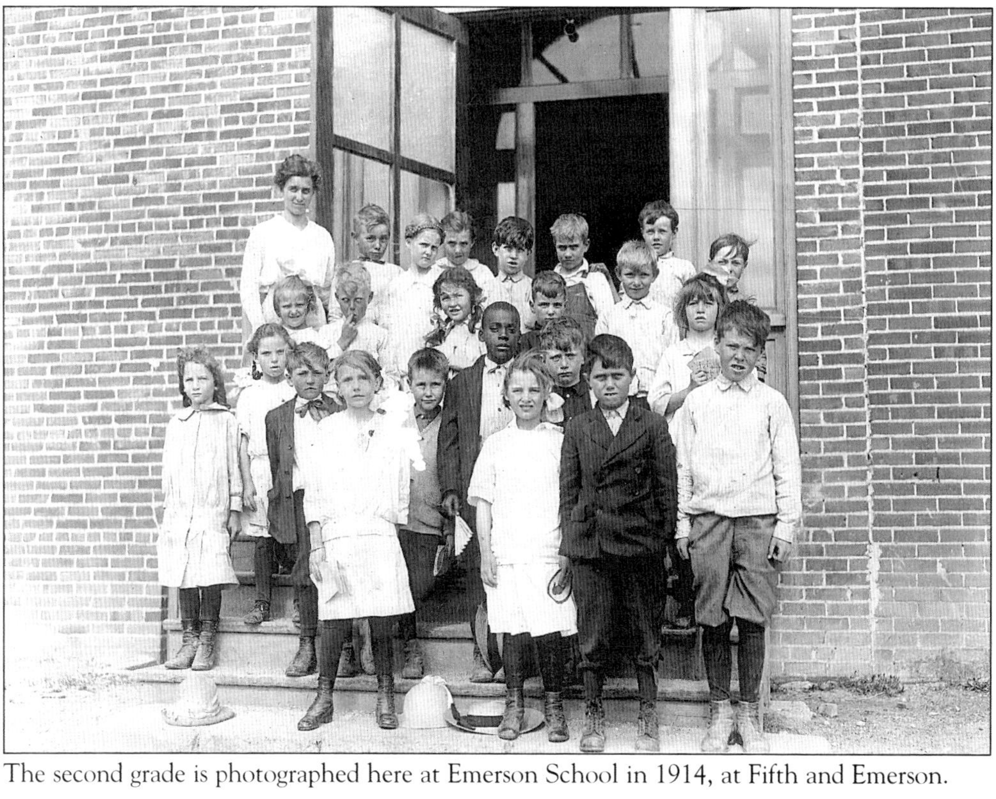

The second grade is photographed here at Emerson School in 1914, at Fifth and Emerson.

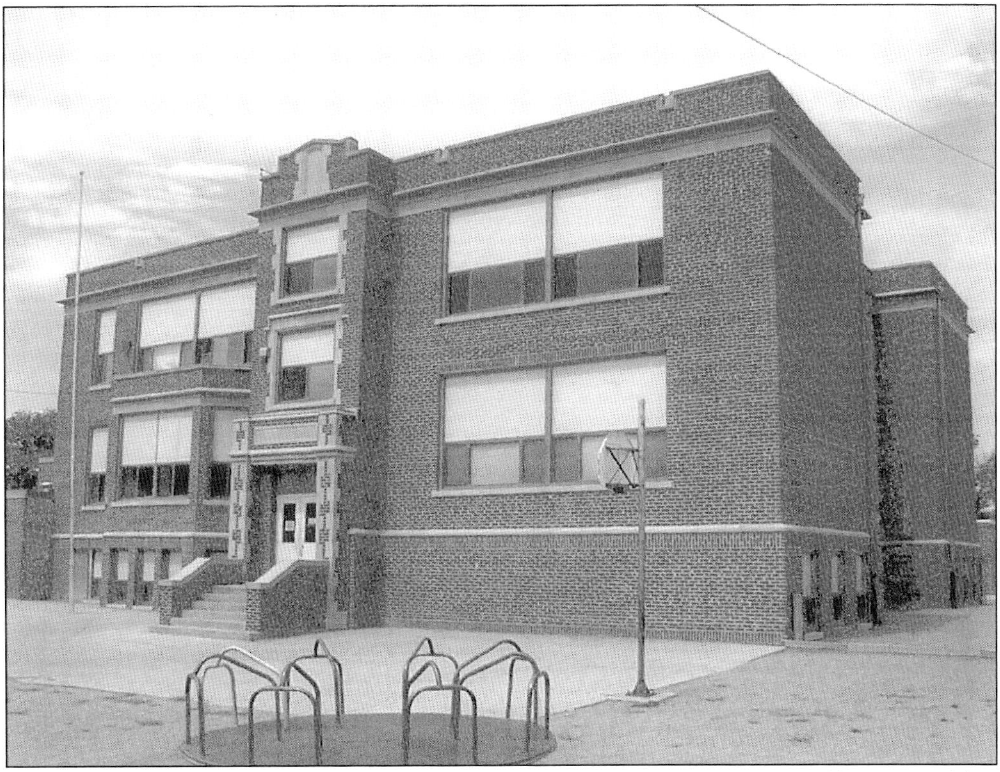

Grandview School was opened in 1923, at Sixth and Grand. The school is still in use and has undergone additions.

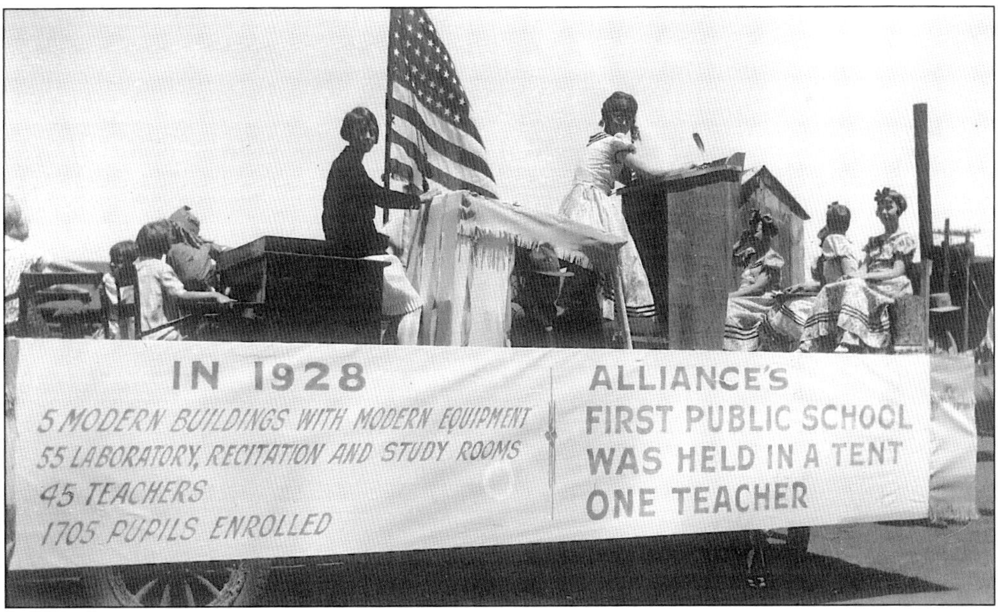

This float in a 1928 parade tells the story of education in Alliance. The first public school was held in a tent with one teacher. In 1928, there were five modern buildings with 55 classrooms, 45 teachers and 1,705 pupils. My, how they had grown!

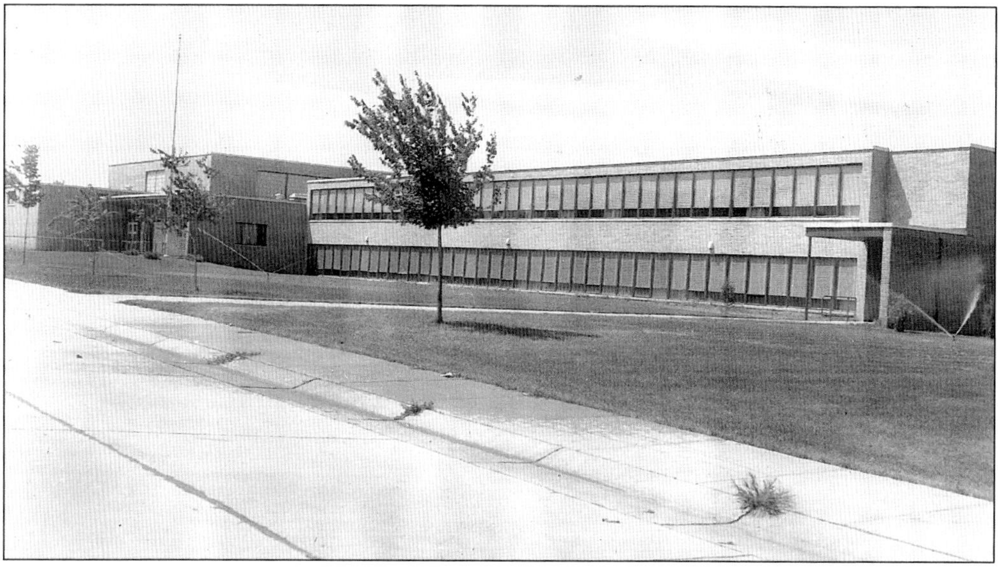

The first junior high was built in 1953, and included a multi-purpose room. In 1961, a quarter-million-dollar bond added a community building. A vocational wing was added in 1967, and in 1968, this building became the high school. Approximately three hundred students attend this school. There is also an active community education program for area adults.

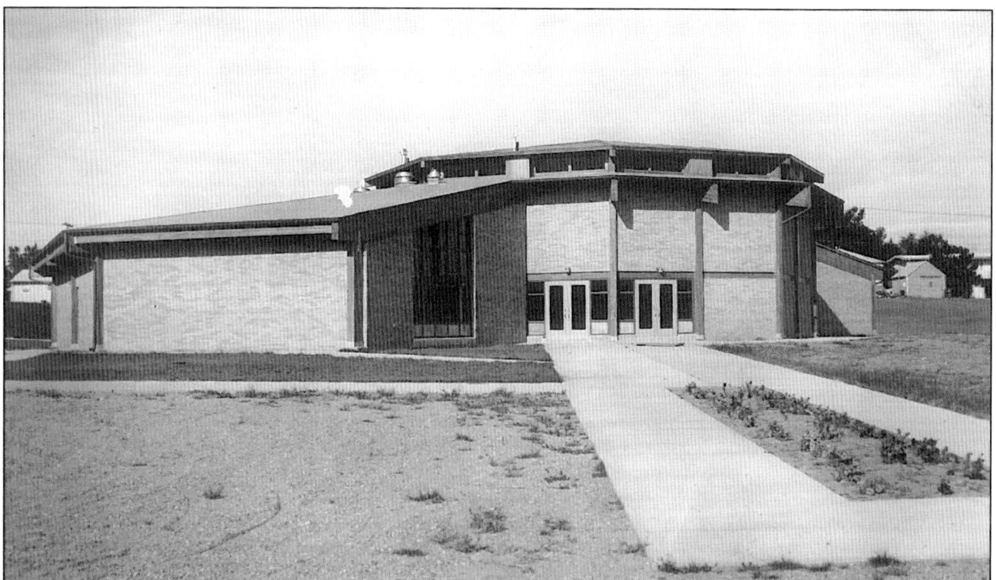

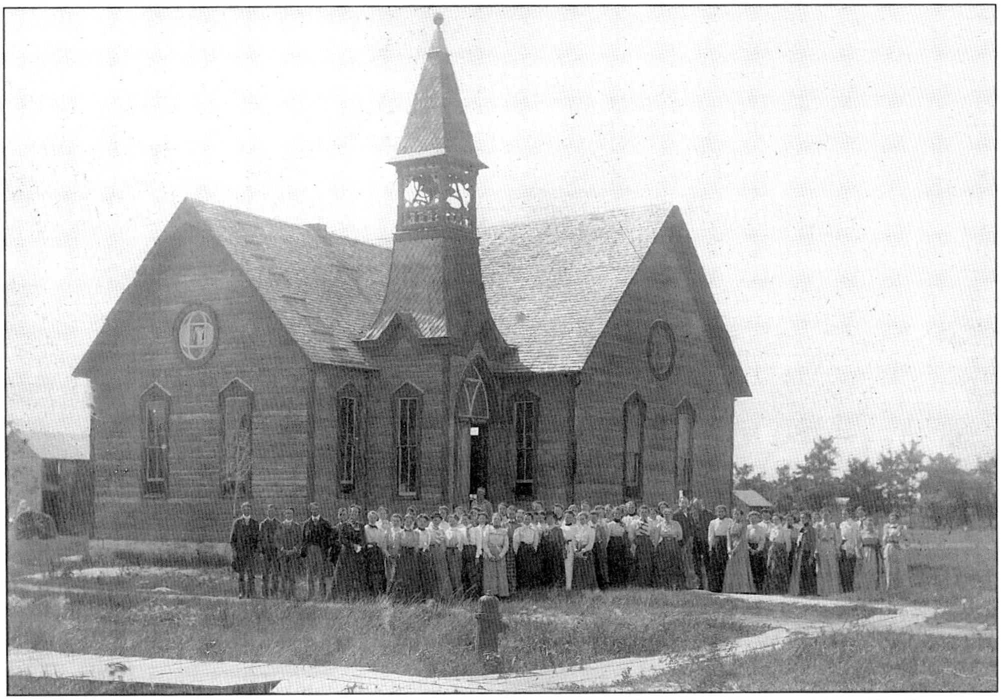

The Alliance Normal School was first held in the Methodist church. In 1912, Chadron was given a charter over Alliance because of the seven saloons here. Later it became Chadron State College. Normal training was all that was required to become a teacher in the early years.

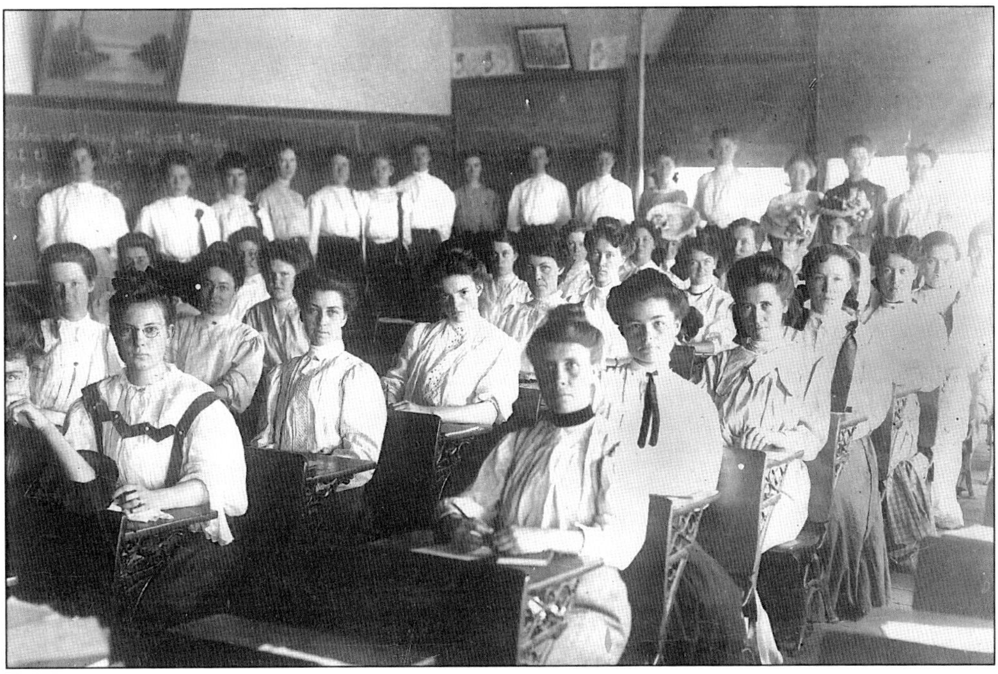

Alliance was home for the Junior Normal from 1903 to 1914. This classroom was held in the old Central School with Susan Frazier as the teacher.

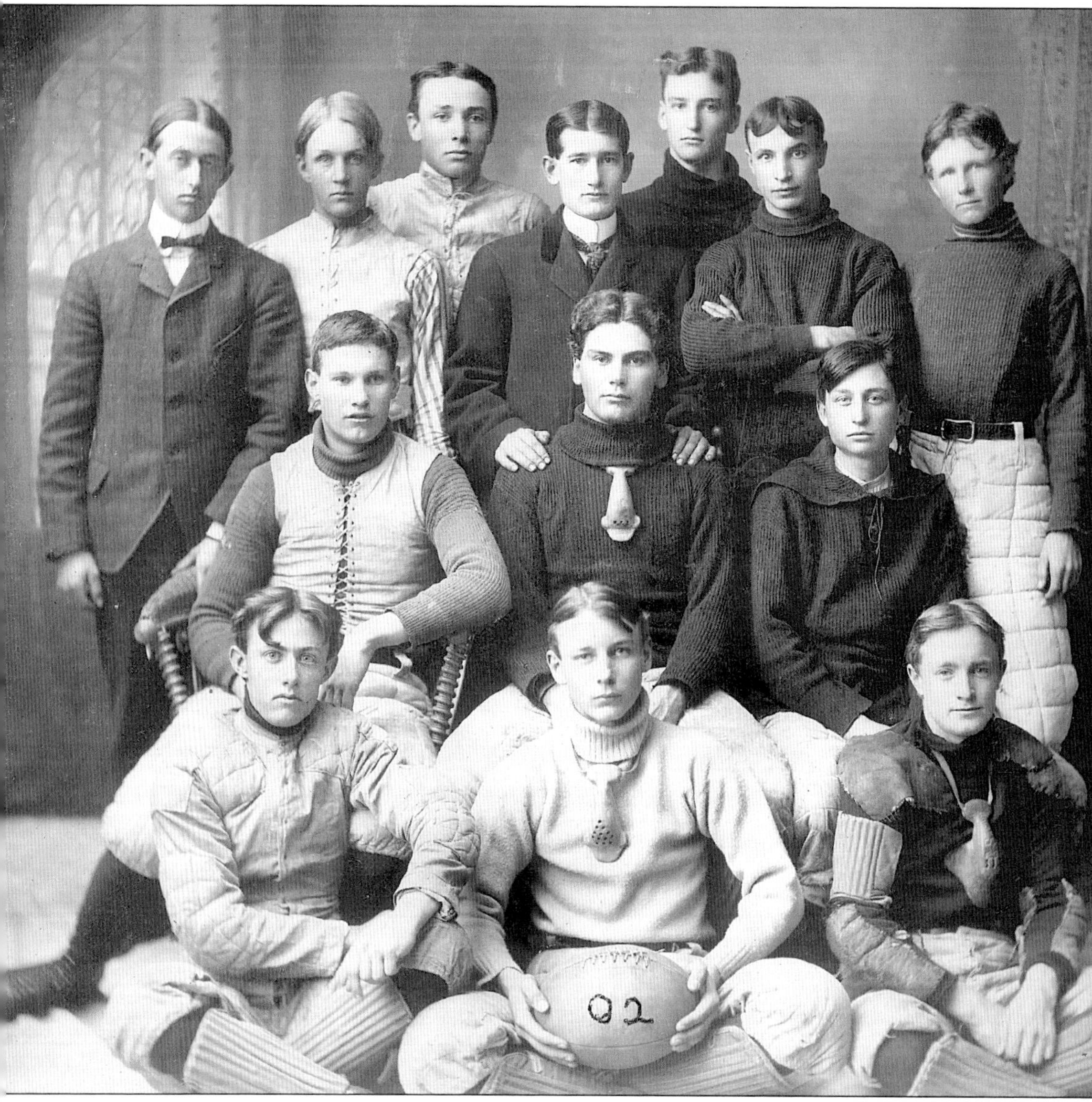

The 1902, the AHS football team consisted of sturdy young men who played with very little protective gear. Note the nose guards. Players were, from left to right: (front row) J.D. Emerick, S. Smyser, and J. O'Conner; (second row) C. Spacht, E. Englehorn, and J. Von Boskirk; (back row) P. Parkin, H. Jameson, L. Cantwell, T. Campbell, Coach B. Ufford, R. Worley, and R. Rodgers.

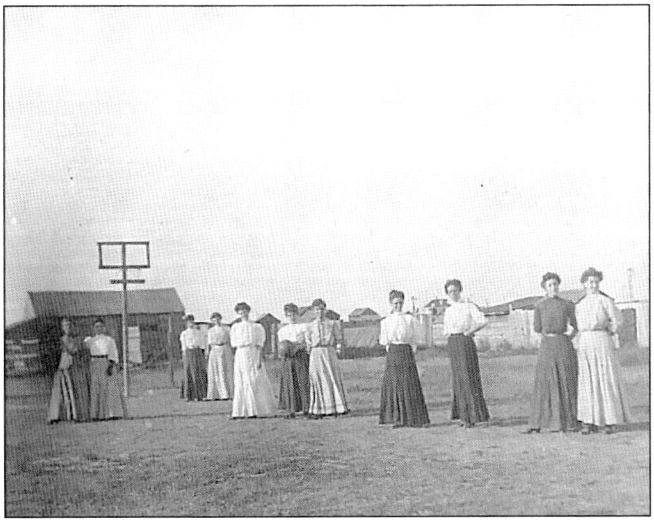
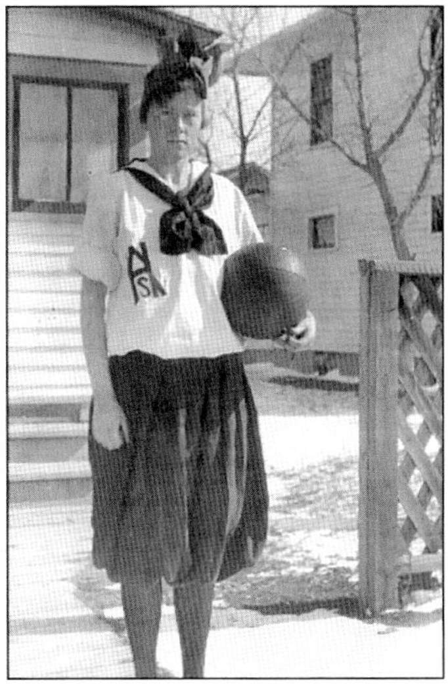

Women's sports flourished in the early years. This early basketball team included Mrs. A.J. Cole and Bertie Gregg Redfro. The unidentified player from the 1920s shows off her bloomer uniform.

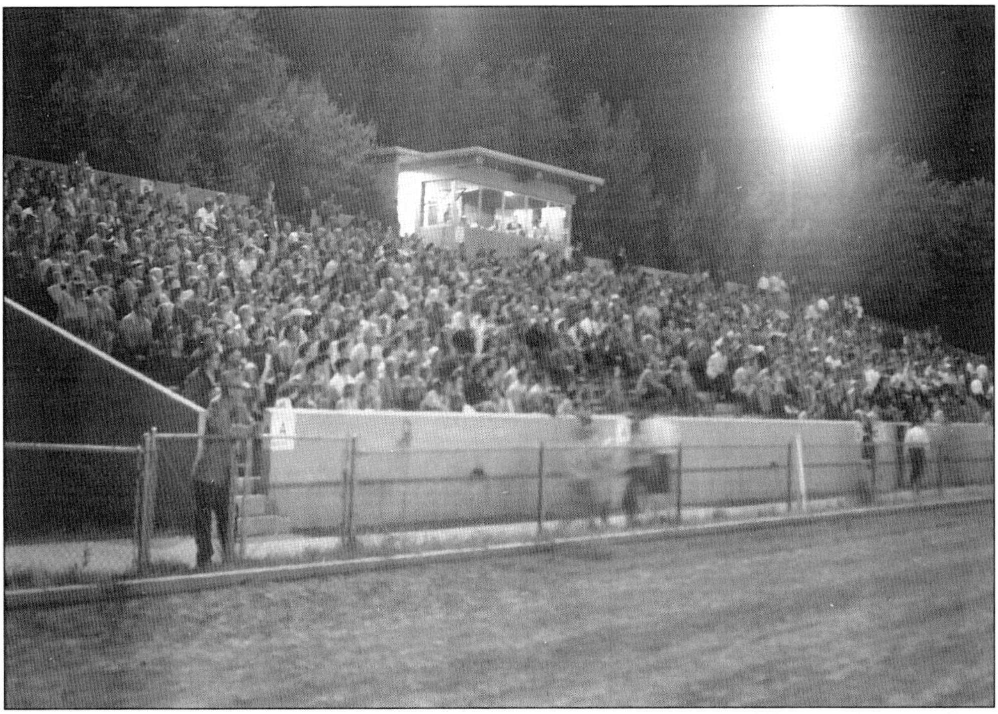

On cool Friday nights, many Alliance residents find themselves at Bulldog Stadium to cheer on the Bulldogs.

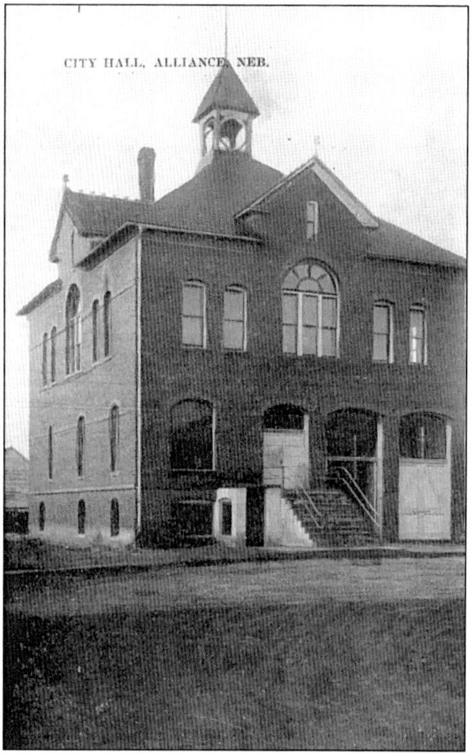

The first city hall was located at 115 East Third Street and had city offices, meeting rooms, and an armory-fire barn on the ground level.

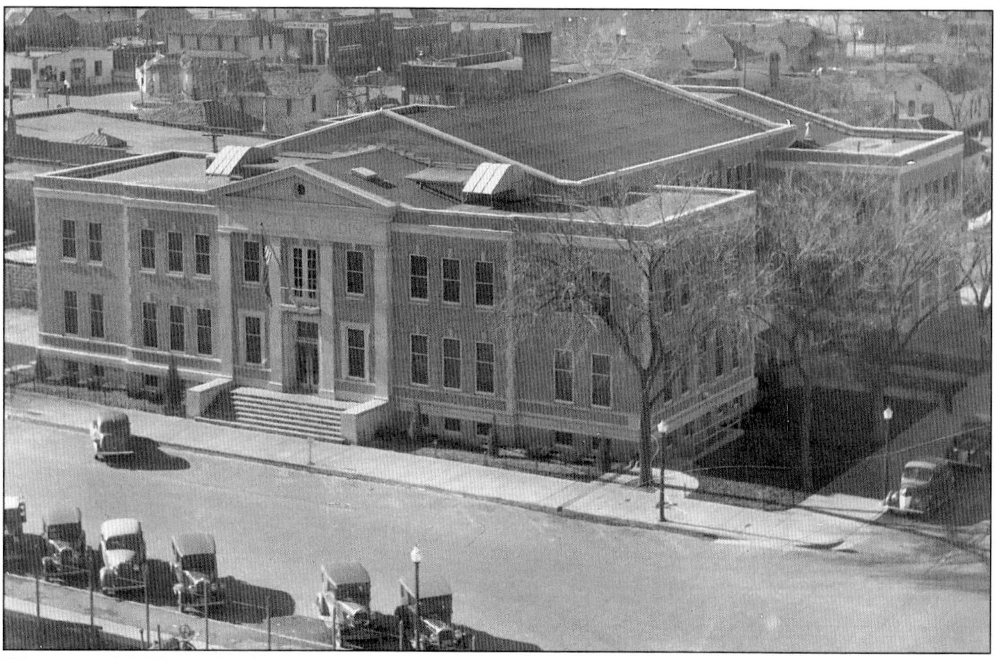

The year 1936 brought the WPA construction of a new city hall. Offices, an auditorium, police department, city jail, and fire department filled out this modern building. The fire department moved next door in 1981 to a new addition, and the building and zoning department and the fire chief moved into the old fire hall.

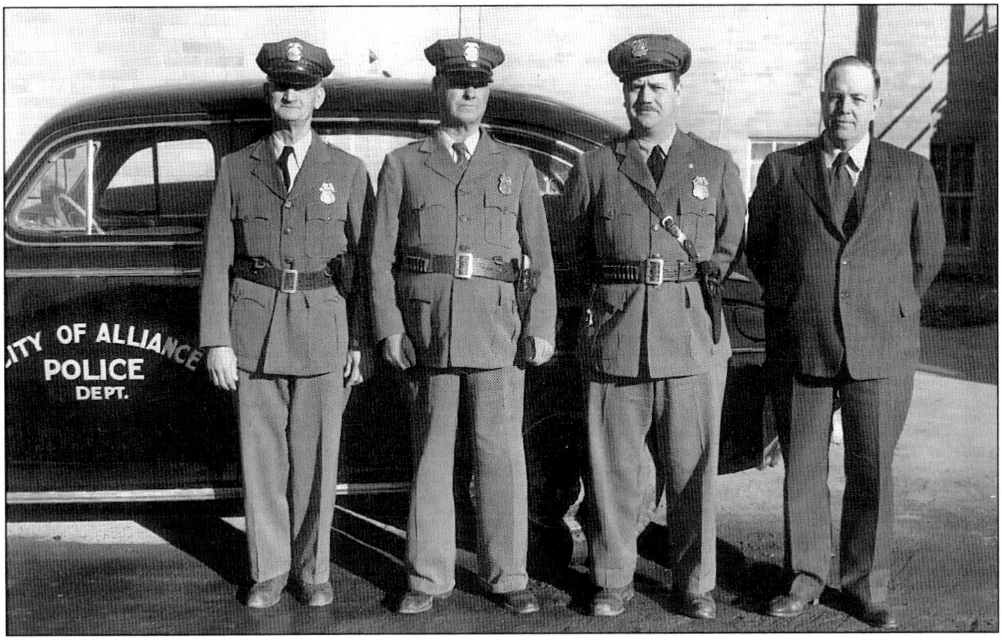

The early police force protected Alliance without any form of communication except the local blinking street light at Third and Box Butte. This has progressed into a regional law enforcement center that has every modern communication from high tech radios to lap top computers. From left to right: Leonard Pilkington, Isaac Barrett, Doug Thomas, and Harold Wingstad.

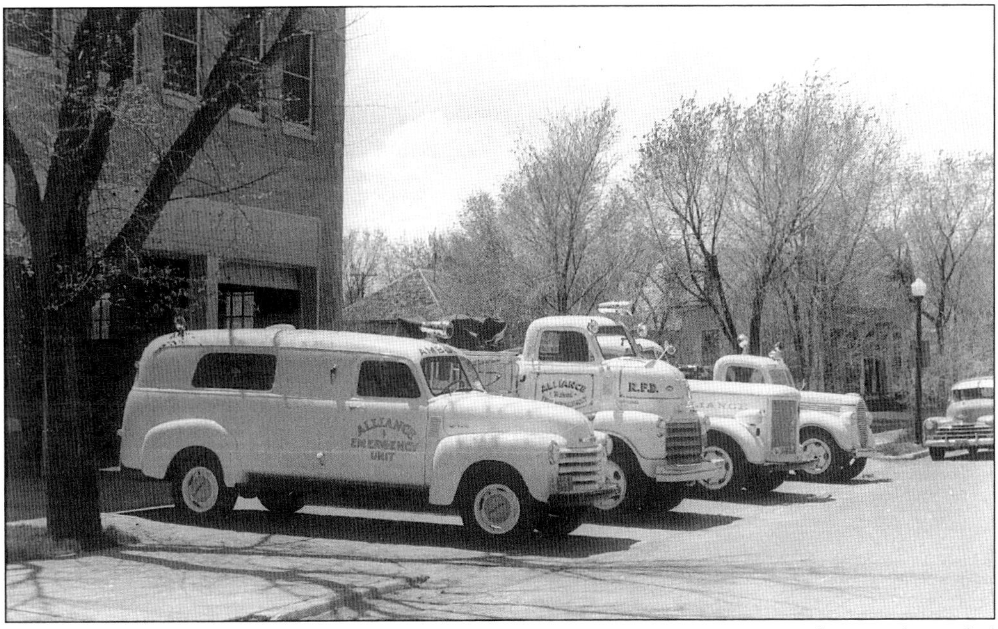

The Alliance Volunteer Fire Department stands ever ready to serve. Alliance depended solely on limited paid firefighters and a large volunteer force, whose home had always been in the city hall. The current department boasts a ladder truck that reaches 100 feet to fight fires more efficiently.

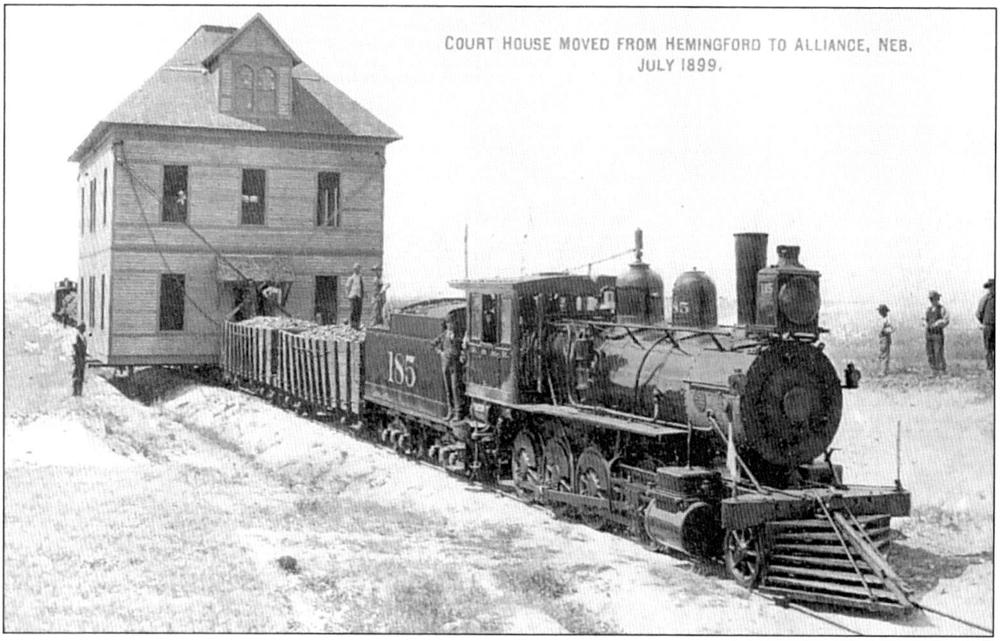

The Box Butte County Courthouse was one of the most famous, or "infamous," places in Alliance history. Built in Hemingford in 1897, it was moved to Alliance by train after a third vote by Box Butte County residents. Not content with being designated the county seat, the Alliance residents wanted the courthouse that went with the designation. The wooden structure, complete with records, was moved 18 miles by train. The move took 45 men five days to accomplish. The event was written up in *Ripley's Believe It or Not*.

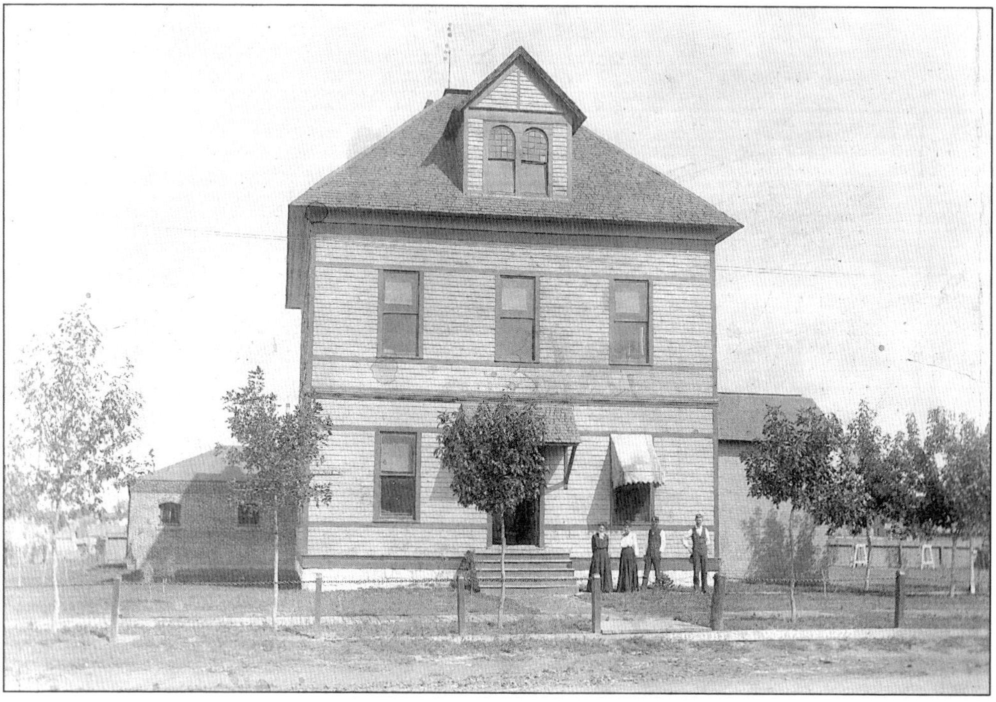

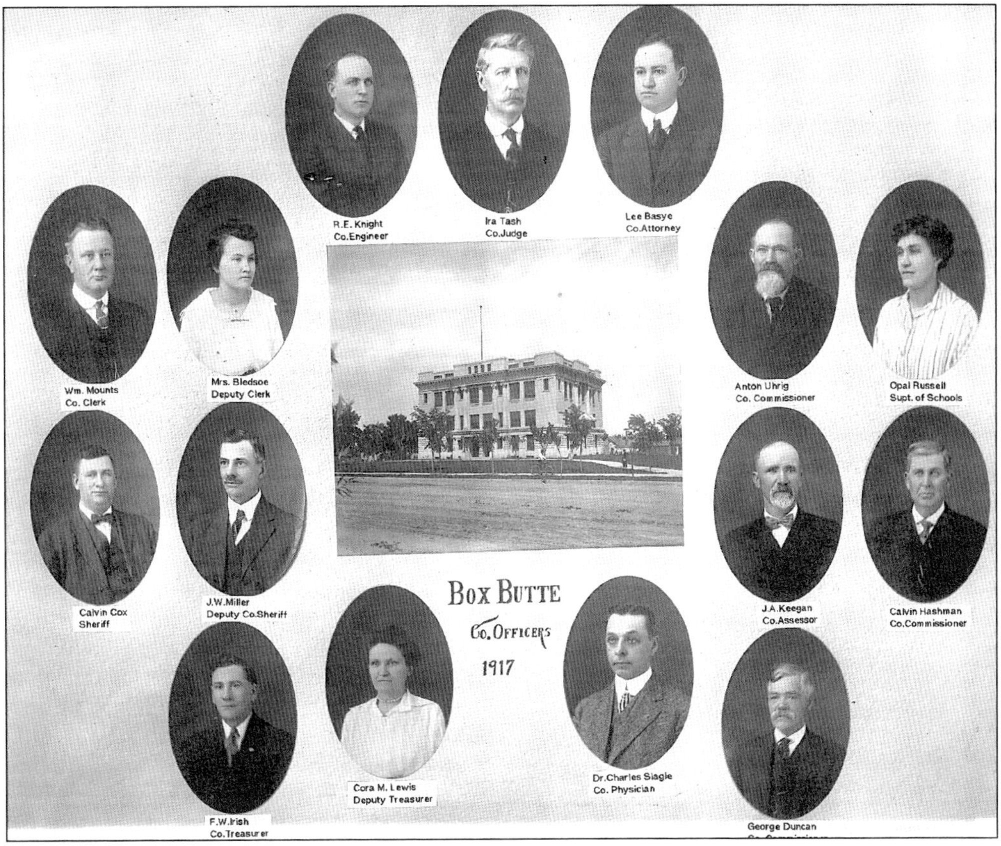

Box Butte Co. Officers pose in 1917.

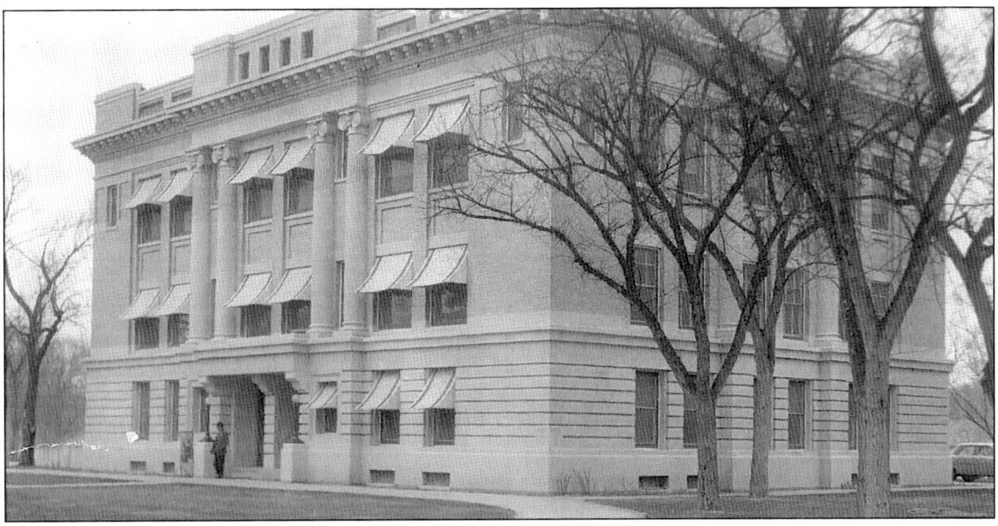

The current Box Butte County Courthouse sits in the same spot as the original one at Fifth and Box Butte Avenues. The brick and masonry structure in a Beaux-Arts style boasts such features as a stained glass skylight, marble wainscoting, wrought iron stairs, and a tile mosaic of the Nebraska state seal on the main lobby floor. It was constructed in 1914, and is the center of Alliance today. It is on the National Historic Register.

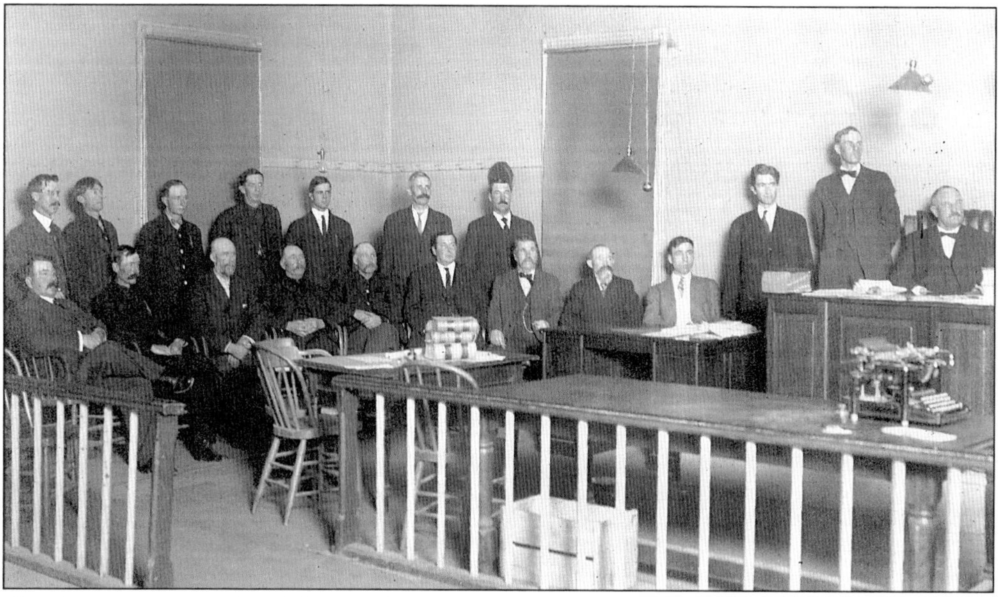

This district court trial in 1899 involved a group of the most prominent men of the time. The jury included, from left to right: L. Boyer, L. Buechinstein (foreman), T. Johnson, F. Seidler, J. Morley, J. Ingersen, T. Lawler, A. Payne, W. Buchner, F. Harris, J. Carmichael, M. Delaney, E. Boyer, unknown. At the desk were Frank Phelps, Clerk of District Court, and Col. J.G. Maher (stenographer). Attorney for the plaintiff was William Mitchell, and for the defense was W.G. Simonson. Judge Westover presided.

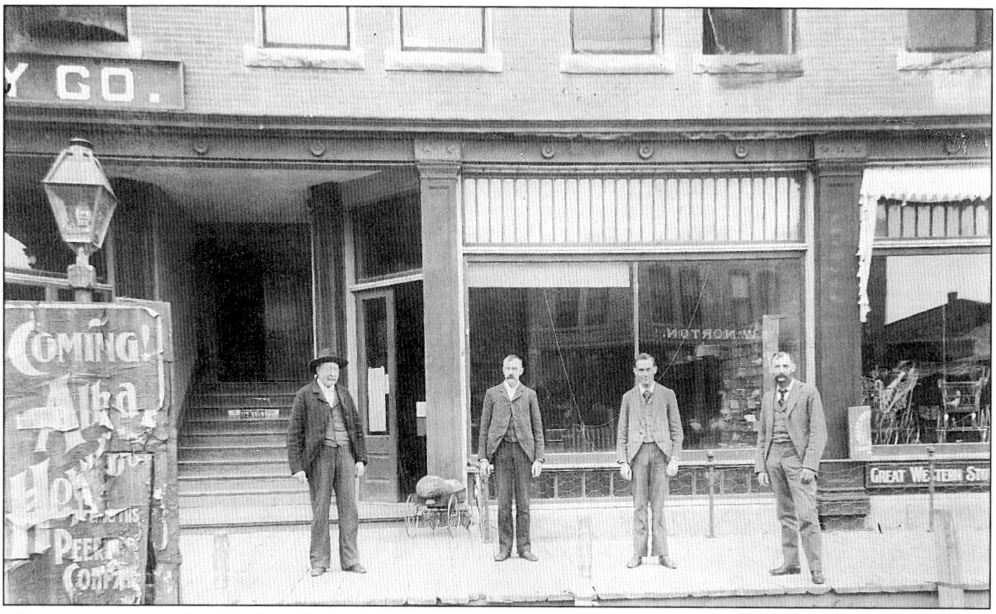

The entrance to the Phelan Opera House was located at 321 Box Butte Avenue. This versatile building also housed many other businesses over the years, including a grocery store, ladies' apparel store, library, hardware store, dentist, and restaurant. It held temporary offices for county officials, as shown here. From left to right are: Mr. A.M. Miller, Co. Treasurer; Mr. F.M. Phelps, Co. Clerk; Mr. A. Muirhead, Assistant Co. Treasurer; and Mr. J.H.H. Hewitt, Co. Judge.

Three

KEEPING THE FAITH

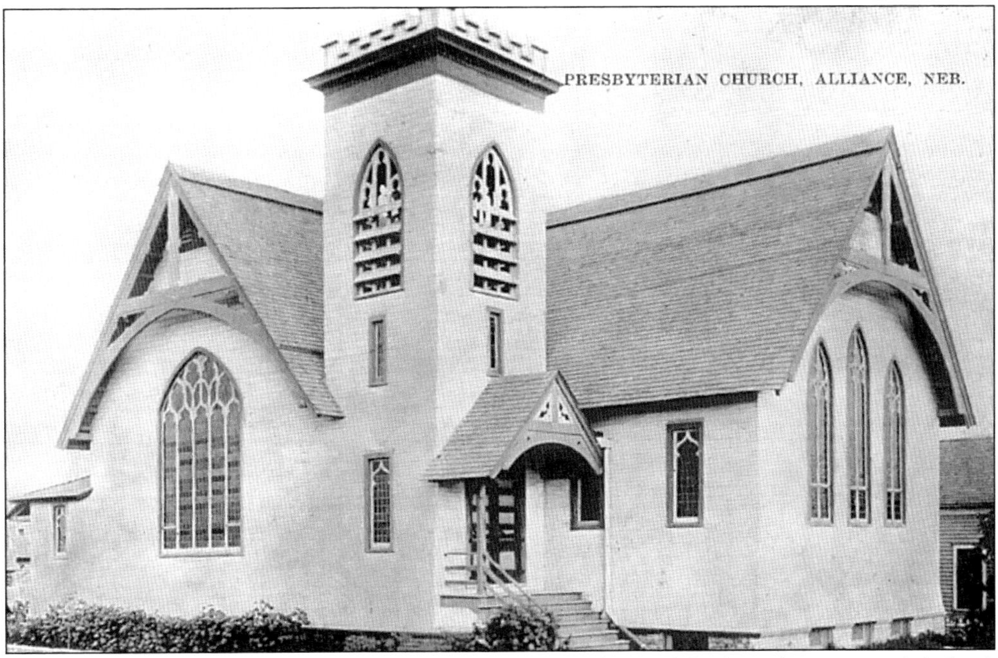

Alliance's first church was the First Presbyterian Church, paid for by subscriptions (pledges) and a loan. The building was built at Seventh and Box Butte in 1904, with Reverend H.P.V. Bogue as minister. The church was moved to its present home at Fifth and Emerson in 1956. The new sanctuary was completed in 1964.

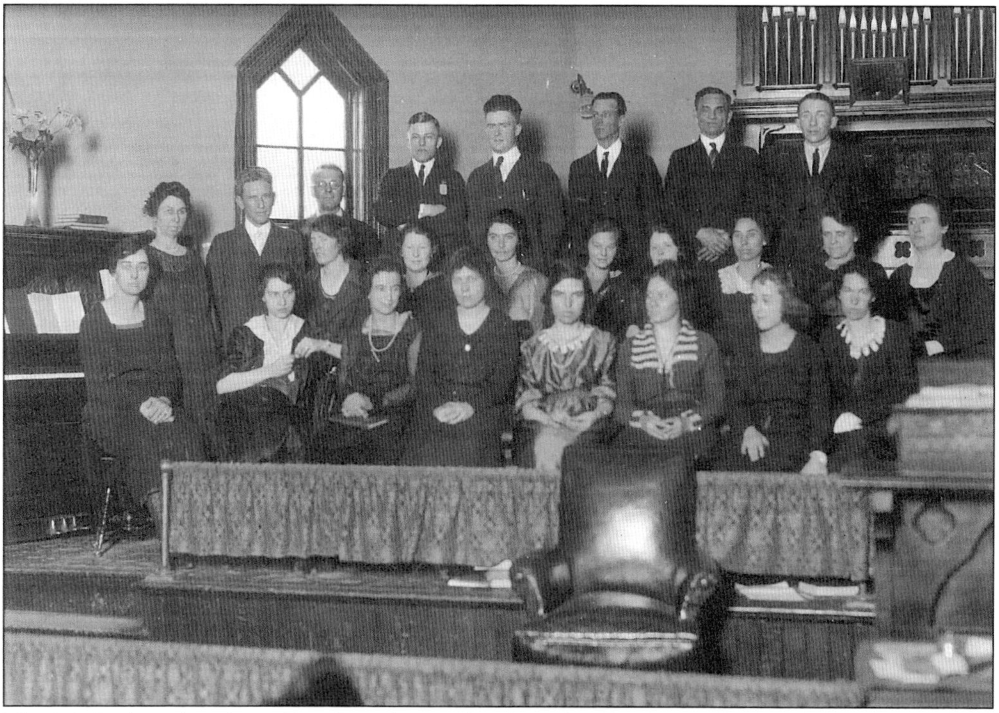

The Methodist church on East Fourth was the first church in Alliance to install a pipe organ (hand-pumped). The choir leader and organist was Inice McCorkle and Dorothy Hershman was pianist.

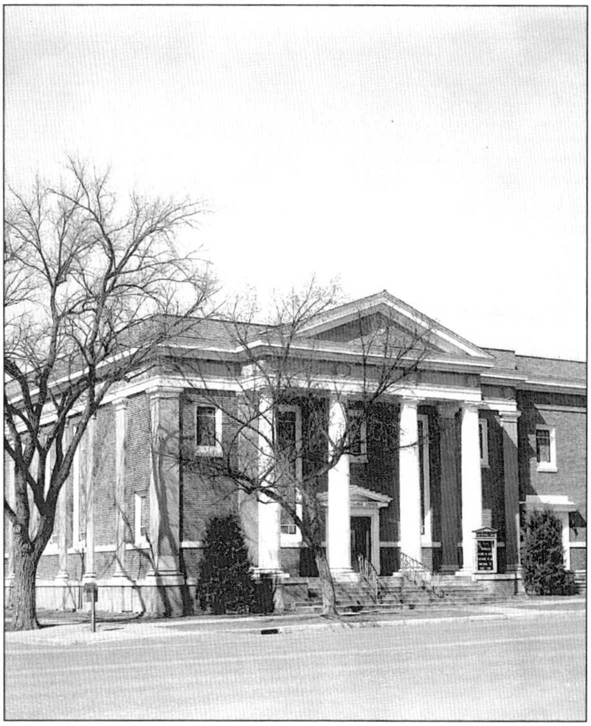

United Methodist Church is presently located at Seventh and Box Butte. Methodists met in a sod house east of Alliance, and later in a dilapidated downtown building. The first church was built in 1889 at Forth and Niobrara, with a value of $2,480. The church on Box Butte was built in 1922, with an educational wing in 1962, and parsonage in 1963.

The present location of the Holy Rosary Catholic Church is at Ninth and Cheyenne. Catholic masses were celebrated in the area as early as May 1886, but it was not until 1894 that the first Catholic parish with a resident pastor was established in the county. The first church building was erected on the corner of Fifth and Niobrara, for the cost of $8,000.

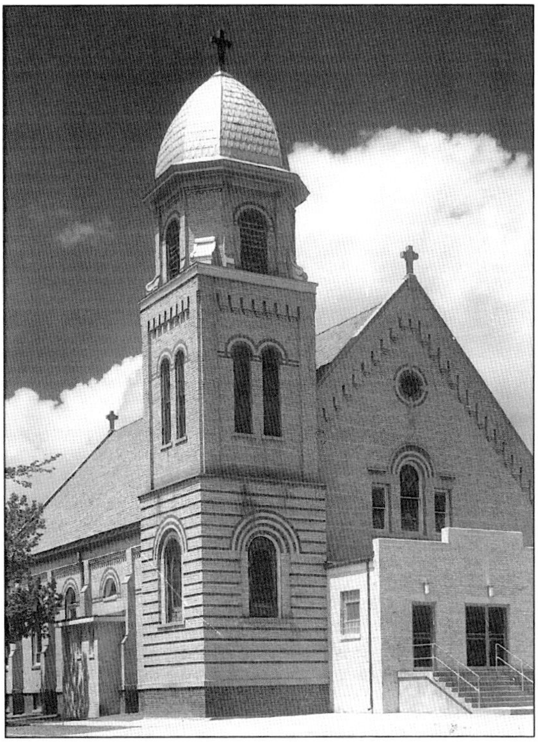

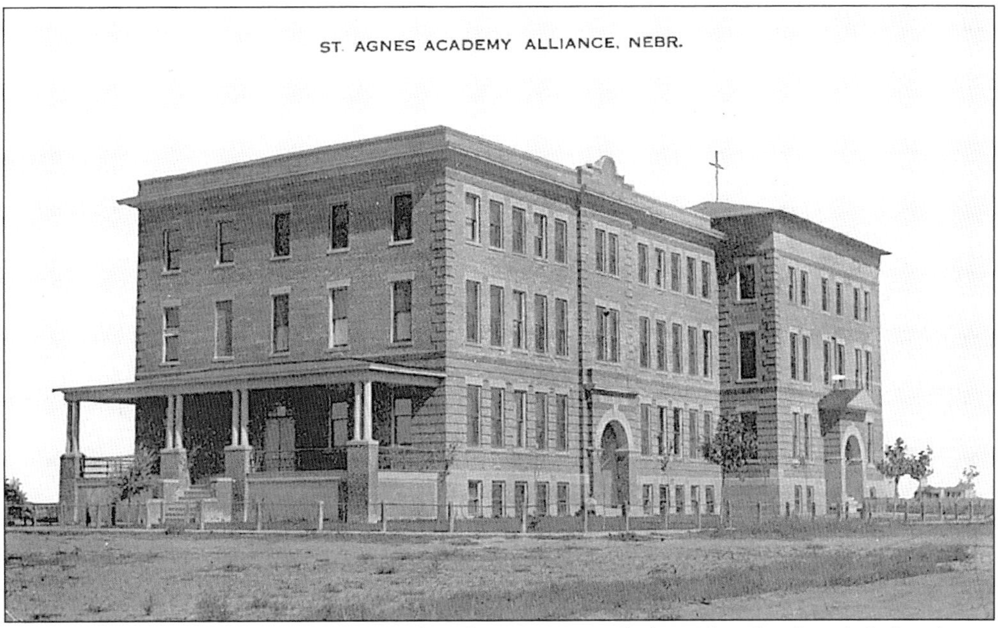

Father William McNamara, Pastor of Holy Rosary Catholic Church, founded St. Agnes Academy. The first building was constructed in 1908. An addition was completed in 1910, and another in 1922. Until 1925, the high school was limited to girls only, and the first graduating class of boys was in 1928. In the fall of 1961, the Academy was limited to day students. Today it includes kindergarten through eighth grade.

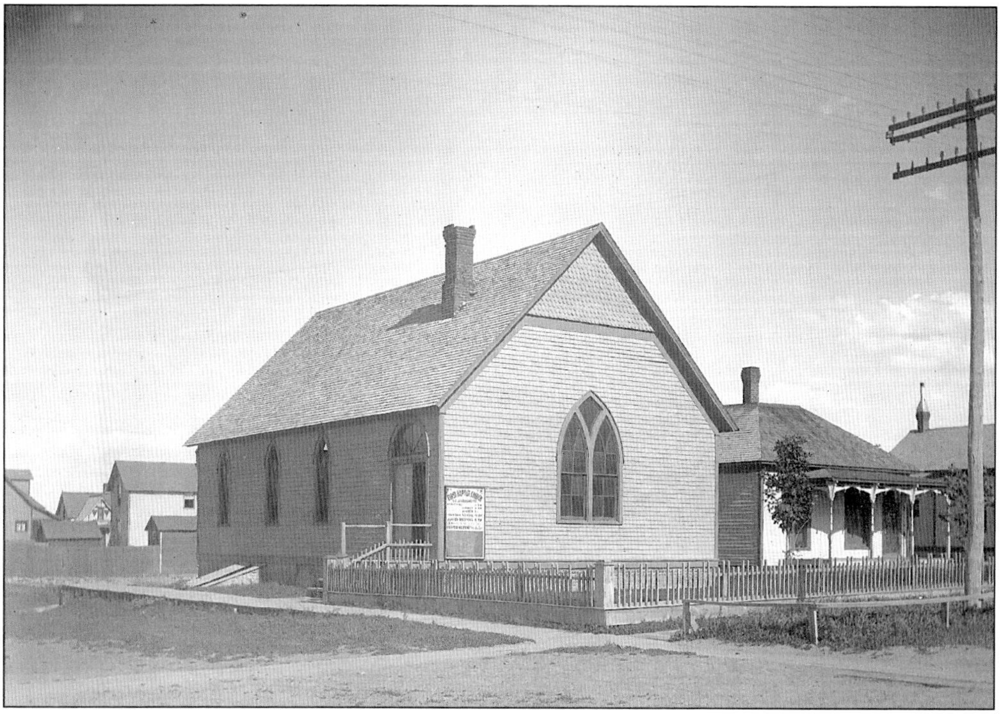

The First Baptist Church of Alliance was organized with 18 members in 1892. In 1896, the congregation built a church building at Seventh and Laramie. In 1897, there were 180 persons enrolled in Sunday school. A new church building was completed in September 1962, at Tenth and Yellowstone.

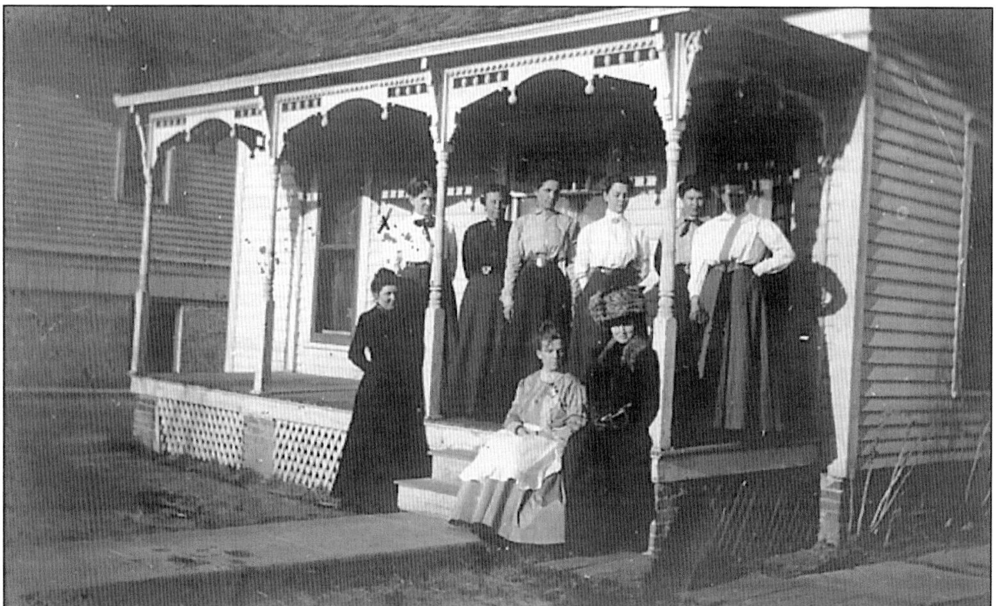

Pictured is a gathering of women at the Baptist parsonage in Alliance. Mrs. Perry is by the post and Mrs. Wolverton is beside her. The pastor's wife is sitting on the steps.

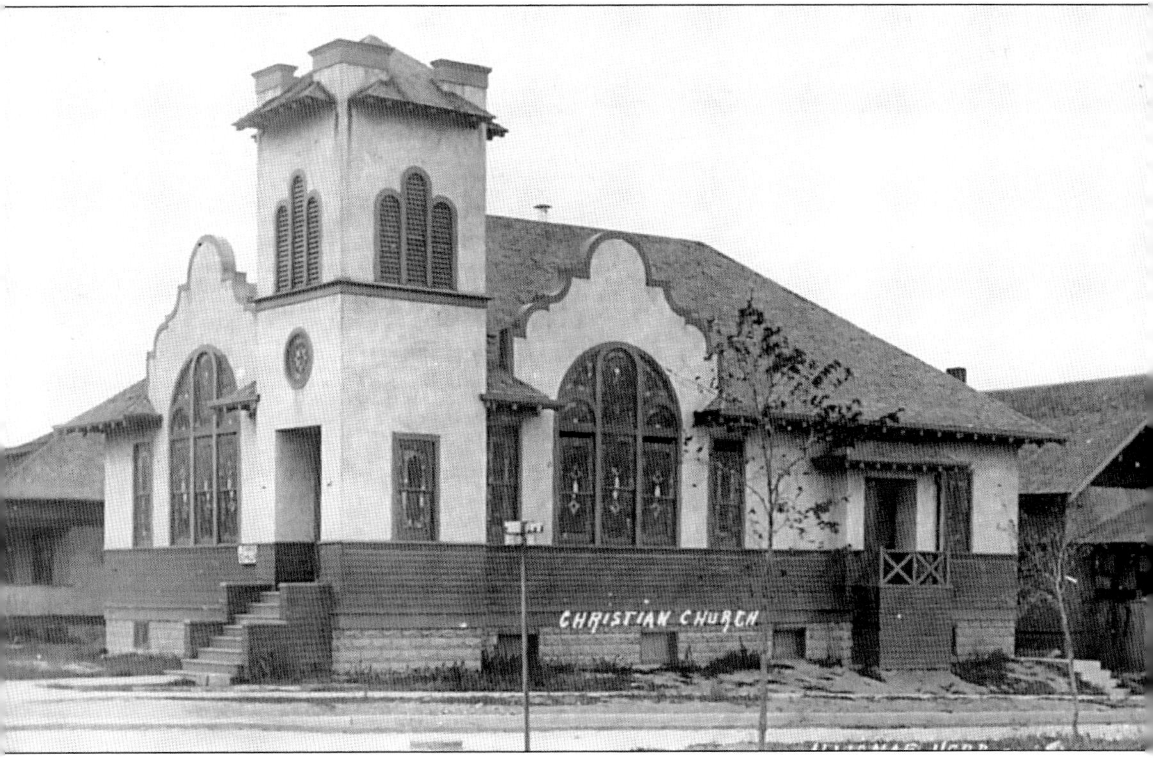

The Christian Church was organized in the early 1890s in a schoolhouse, and later held services in a sod house erected for that purpose 12 miles southwest of Alliance. Repeated efforts to erect a permanent structure did not succeed until 1911. The first property was at Ninth and Box Butte, with expansion in 1957, and a parsonage built in 1962.

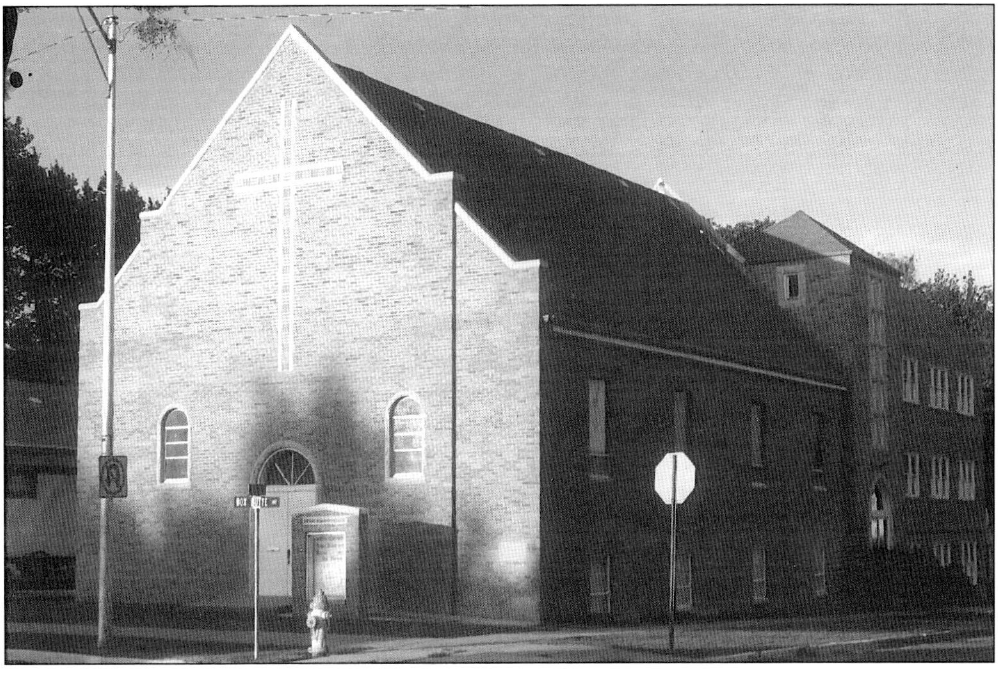

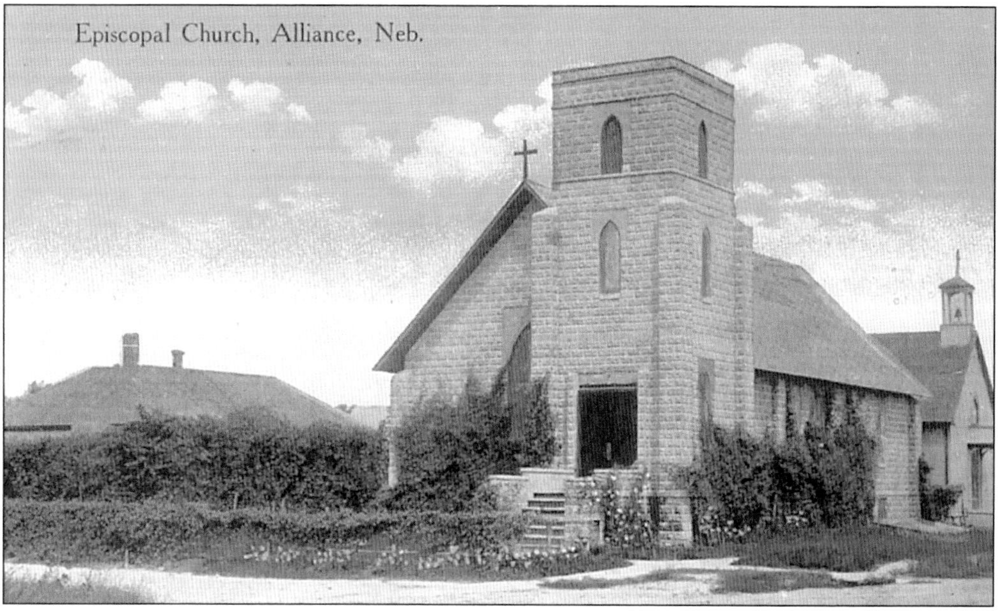

Rev. John M. Bates organized St. Matthew's Episcopal Church society on July 1, 1890. In 1894, a small church was built between Laramie and Cheyenne Avenues. This later became a Sunday school when the cornerstone was laid for a new church adjoining the old one in September 1912. The church was designed by Loch Crane, a student of Frank Lloyd Wright, and was completed in 1969. Alliance City Manager Roberts Laing and council engaged Crane to prepare a "recreation plan," which envisioned a water-theme nearby. Today the church overlooks Laing Lake.

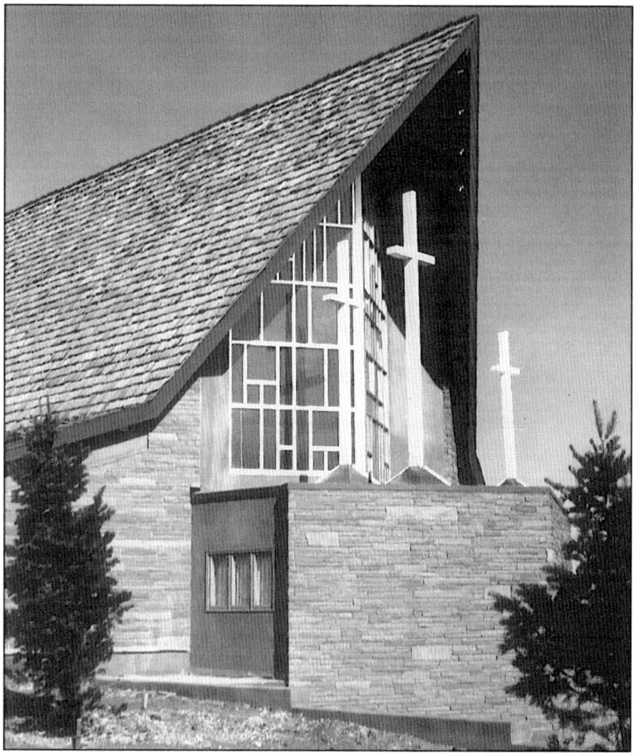

St. John's United Lutheran Church was organized in December 1950, with the cornerstone of the building at Eighth and Black Hills laid in 1951. In 1983, a new building at 2090 Emerson was dedicated.

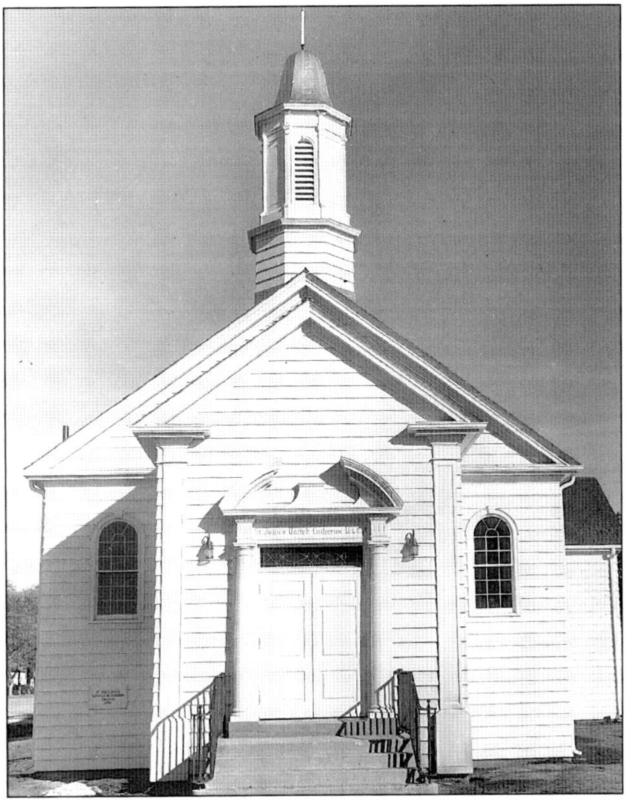

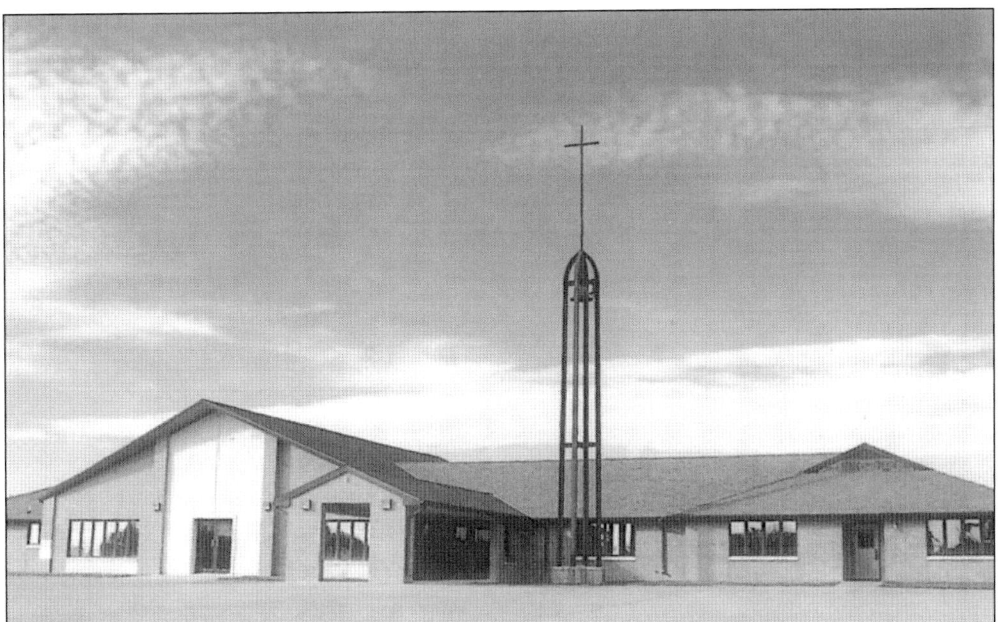

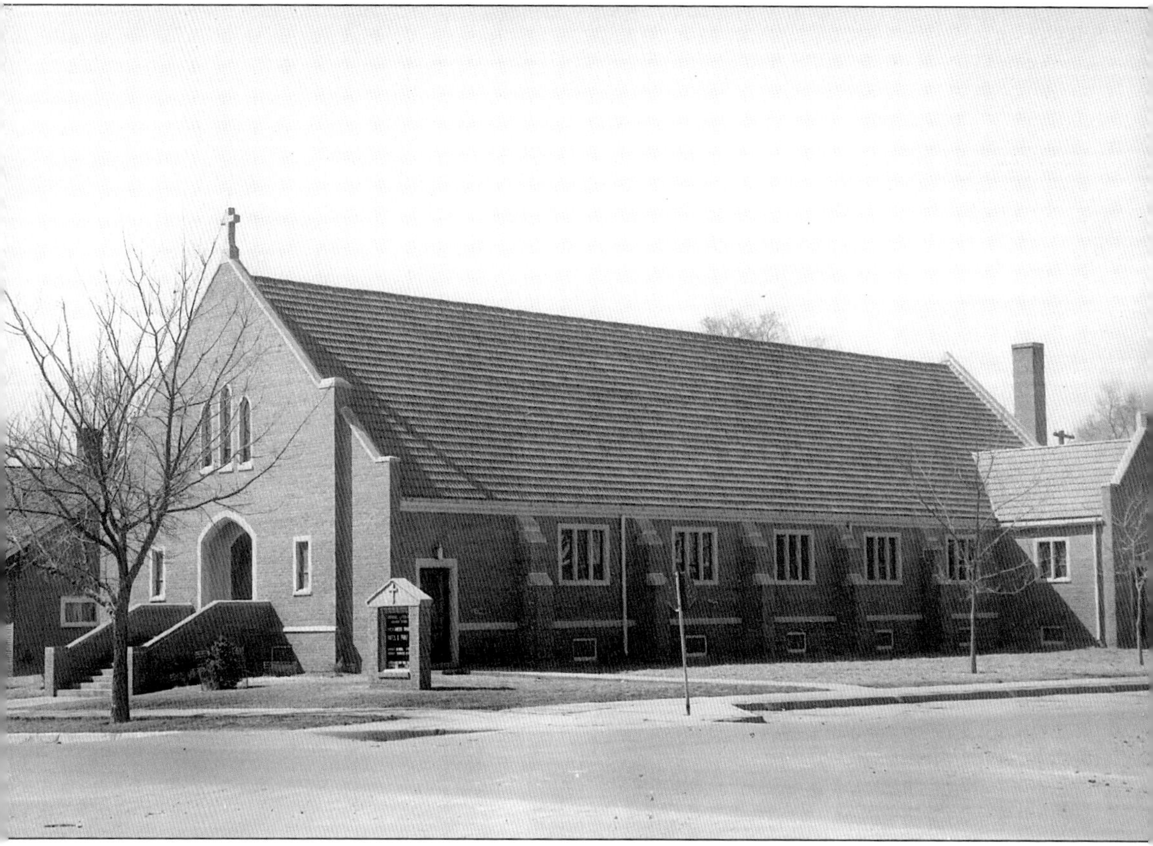

As early as 1892, the Lutheran Church–Missouri Synod conducted worship services in western Nebraska. Immanuel Lutheran Church built its first structure at the corner of Seventh and Yellowstone in 1912, at a cost of $1,638. The church was later moved to Sixth and Niobrara. A new church was built in 1951 at Eleventh and Box Butte, where it stands today.

Four

Notables in Their Time

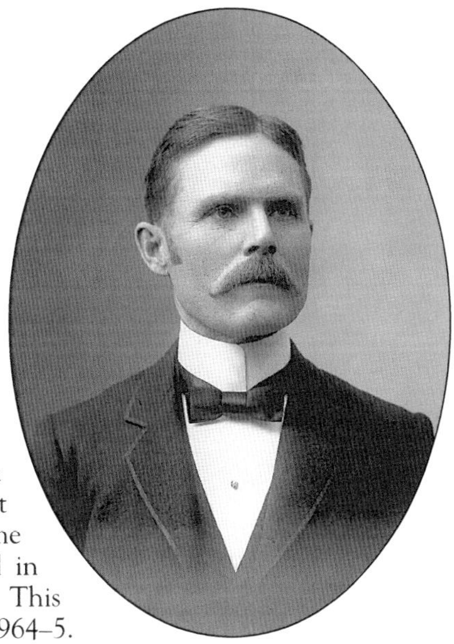

Dr. Frank M. Knight came to Box Butte County in 1886 to practice medicine and engage in real estate, but turned to banking. His first Bank of Alliance, became the Alliance National Bank. He died in 1940, and in his will left a bequest for the building of a museum. This financed the construction of the Knight Museum in 1964–5.

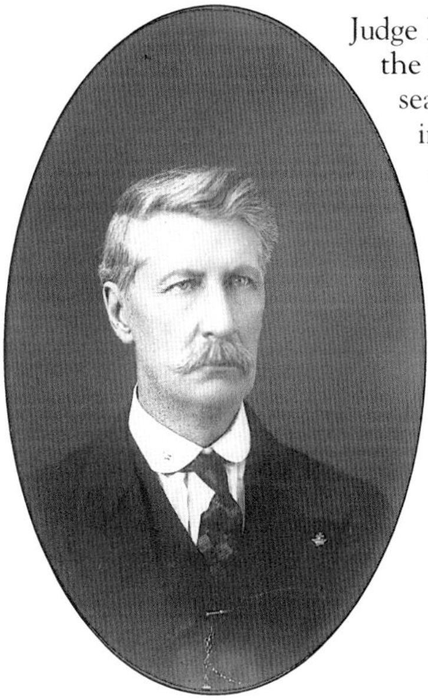

Judge Ira E. Tash and his family had the distinction of being one of the few families that ever lived in all three of Box Butte County's seats. Tash came here in October 1888, and was county clerk in Hemingford for ten years. In 1899, the courthouse moved to Alliance, and the Tash family moved with it. In 1917, he was appointed county judge and then elected to the position until his death in 1935.

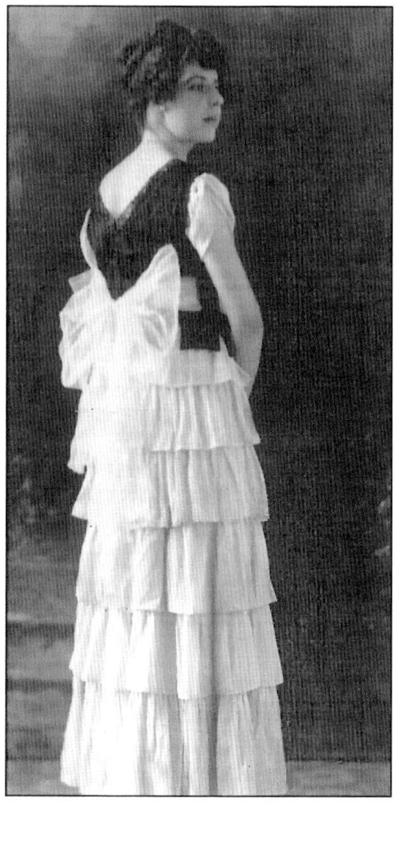

Nell Tash Johnstone, daughter of Ira and Eva, became county clerk under her father in 1925, and then continued her position under P.E. Romig. In 1955, she was appointed police magistrate and justice of the peace. She was also quite active in community activities. She died in 1982.

Rudolphous M. Hampton came west from Ohio in 1885 to homestead near Hemingford. He formed a partnership in a law firm with James Danforth and became a two-career man. In 1889, he and his new wife moved to Alliance, where he became cashier of the American Bank. Hampton was elected mayor of Alliance for the 1890–92 term, then re-elected for 1894–95. He helped organize the Nebraska Stock Growers Association. He also operated a large ranch south of Alliance as well as serving many public enterprises, including the Chamber of Commerce. In 1918, he became president of his bank, now called the First National Bank, then the largest in Alliance.

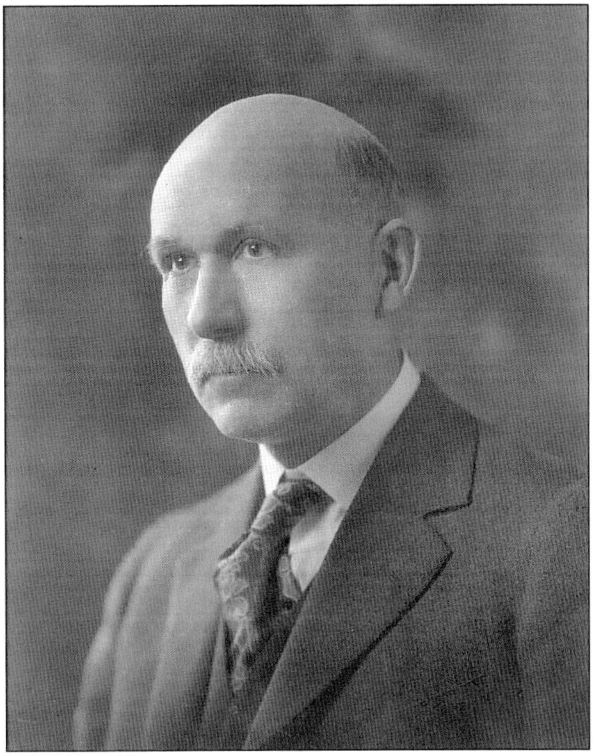

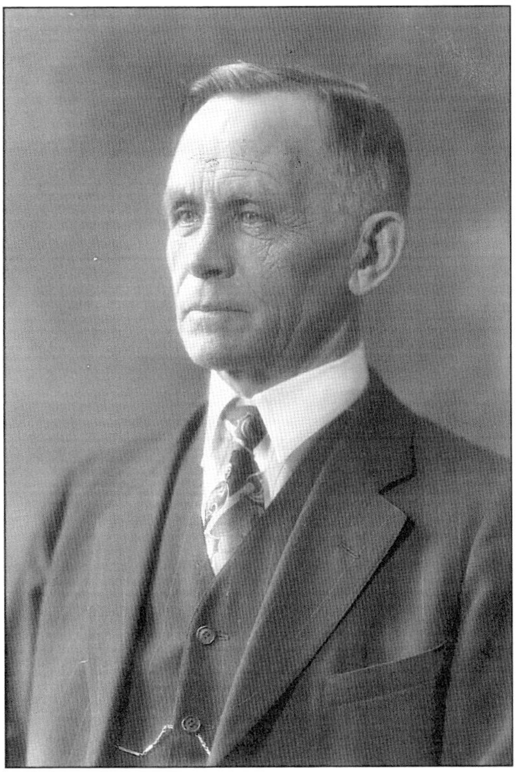

At the age of 22, F.E. Holstein came from Sweden and began a business selling and repairing Black Hills Gold jewelry, located at Fourth and Box Butte. In 1894, he added a drug line and built a new two story building at 316 Box Butte Avenue. At this same time, he increased his jewelry business, as he became the Burlington Railroad's watch inspector.

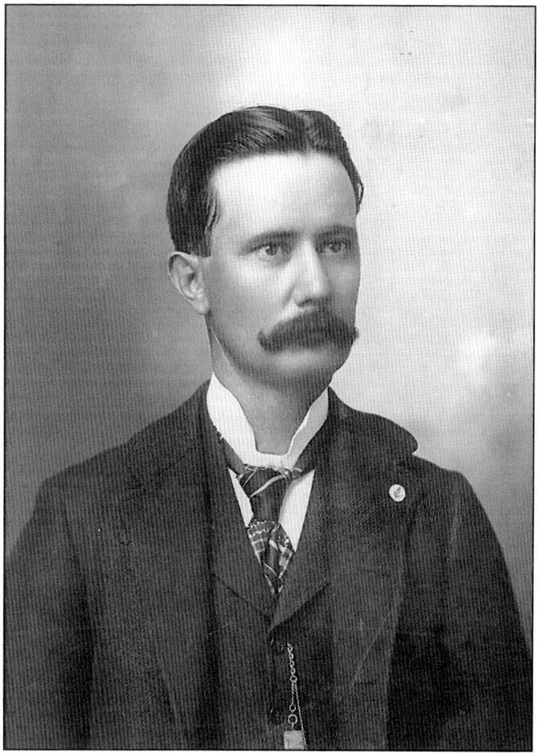

W.C. Mounts came to Box Butte County in 1887. He served as county clerk, clerk of the district court, and as deputy sheriff. Diaries written by Mr. Mounts often mentioned the pleasant carriage rides with his family to visit their former home in Hemingford, where he kept cattle and horses.

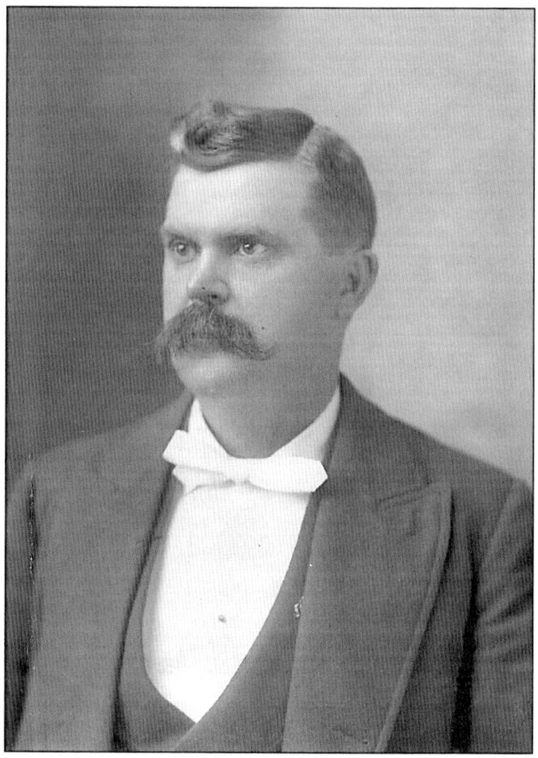

F.M. (Frank) Broome (1864–1953) arrived in Nonpareil in 1886 to work with Gene Heath on *The Grip* newspaper. In 1888, he founded *The Boomer* at Grand Lake, and in 1890 he moved Heath's newspaper to Alliance, renaming it the *The Pioneer Grip*. In 1893, he was appointed receiver of the U.S. Land Office. In 1895–6, he was mayor of Alliance. He was a prolific writer whose articles continue to be sources for historical research. After retirement from the Stock-Growers, he wrote "Frank Broome Says" for the *Times-Herald* newspaper.

John Amos Mallery was born in Newfoundland. He made his way west as a passenger conductor with the railroad and continued to work in this capacity after his marriage. In 1896, he opened a grocery store at 324 Box Butte, which operated for many years.

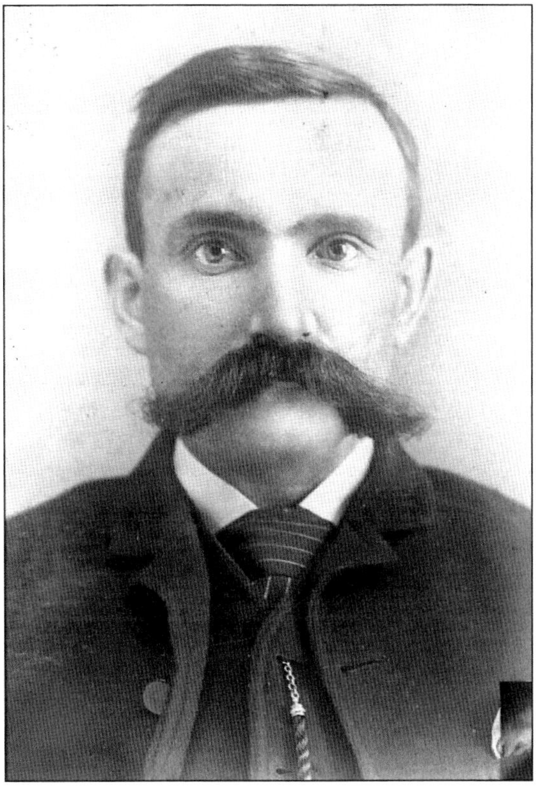

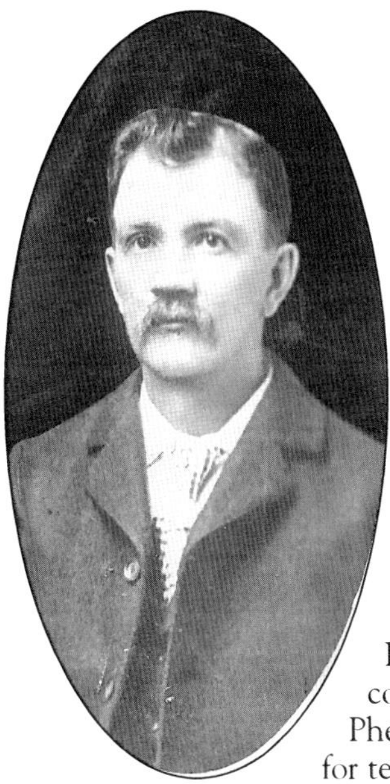

F.M. Phelps (1861–1959) was the first station agent for the Burlington Railroad until 1893, when he began the Box Butte Banking Company. The bank failed in 1896, and he became county clerk in Hemingford. When the courthouse was moved, Mr. Phelps transported all the county records to the Phelan Opera House for temporary storage until the move was made in July of that year.

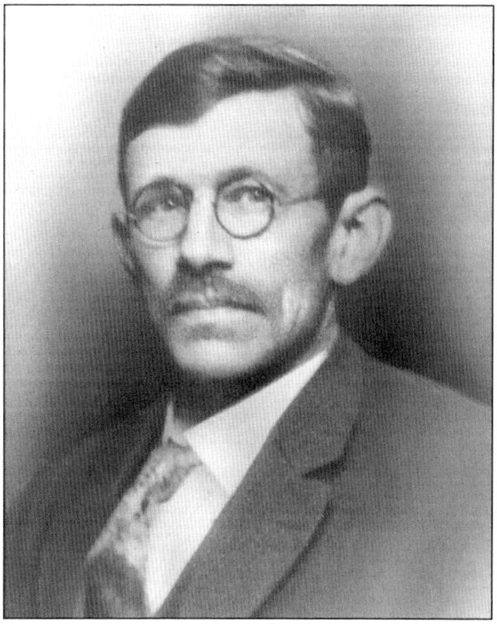

Chenia A. Newberry (1868–1932) rode the rails west from Ravenna in 1888, with his tinner's tool kit. His first shop on Box Butte Avenue burned in 1893, so he rebuilt in brick across the street. Over the years he became a leader not only in business, but in education, city government, banking, and the church. His family still carries on his commitment to Alliance.

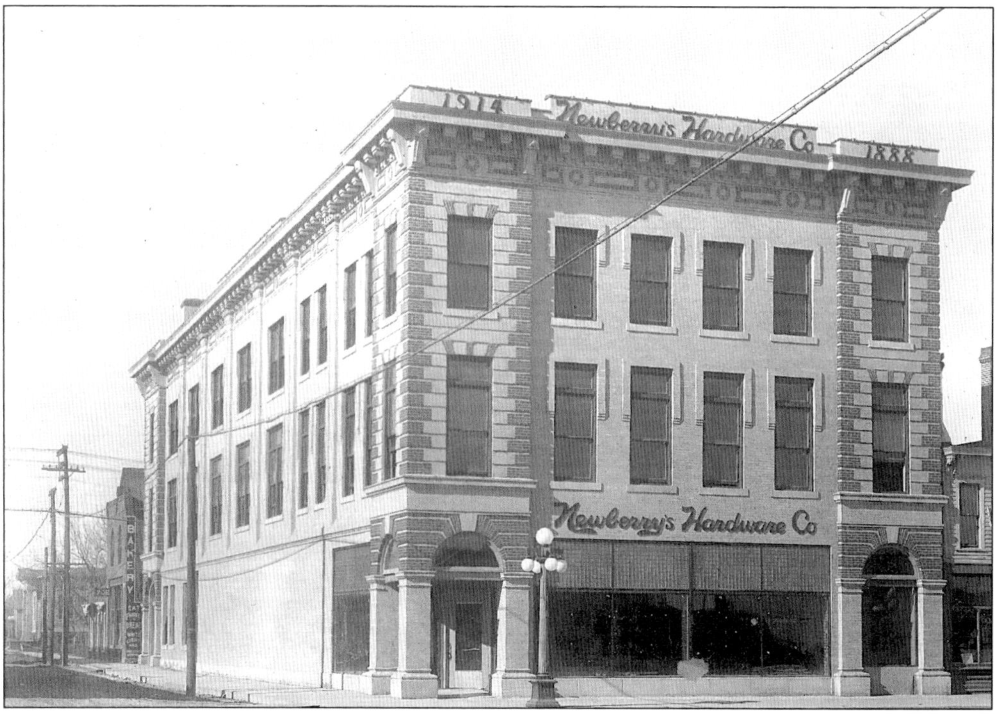

Newberry's was started by Chenia Newberry in 1893, and moved into their three new buildings in 1914. It became the one-stop-shop in Alliance. Dry goods, housewares, saddles and tack, farm implements, and custom-made tinware were just a few of the things available there. It is one of Alliance's oldest businesses that is still in the same family. Grandson Bernard Girard Jr. runs Bernie's in the Newberry Warehouse building at 315 Laramie. He carries much of the same merchandise carried by his grandfather.

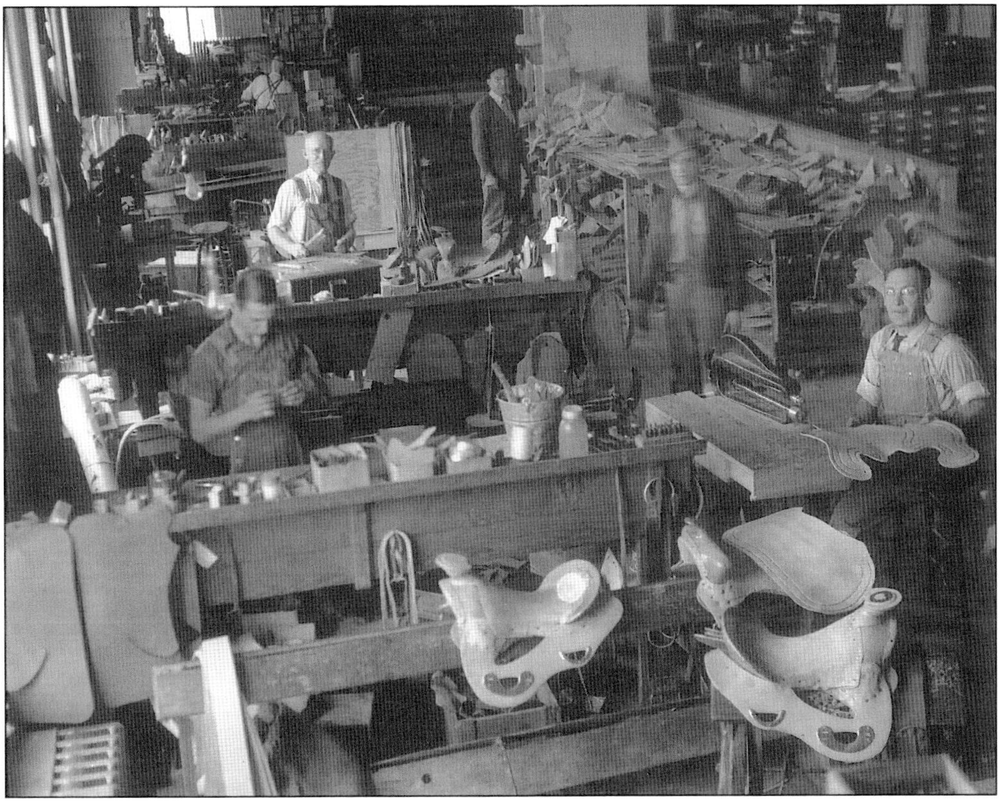

Newberry Saddle Shop is a legend in the Panhandle area. Newberry saddles are still very much sought after by collectors. This photo shows , from front to back: Harry Hanson, J. Pahlow, Al Yackadich, John Noak, Bernie Girard, and Mr. Stemper in the stages of constructing a saddle.

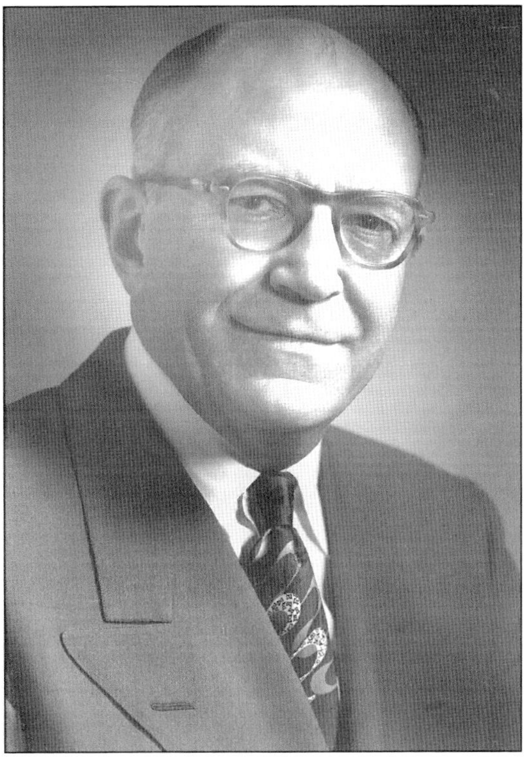

Francis B. Girard, "Bernie," (1898–1981) went to work for Newberry's Hardware in 1925, when he married Helen Newberry. He developed the saddlery and the western wear department, which was a wholesale and retail operation. Bernie became the head of the Newberry store, and many new departments were added. He retired in 1968.

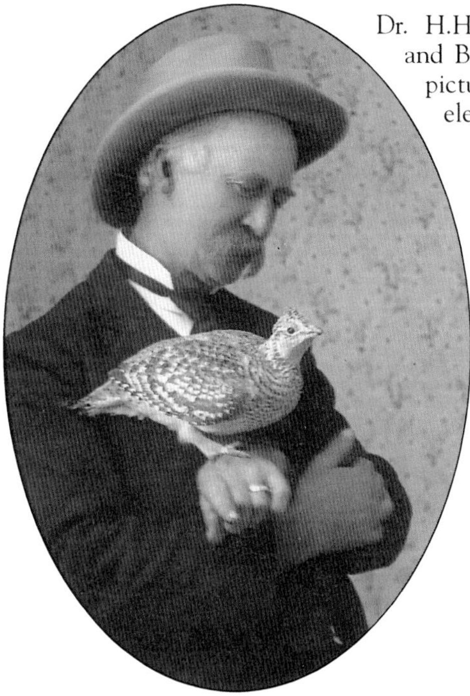

Dr. H.H. Bellwood, senior member of Drs. Bellwood and Bellwood, B&M Railroad surgeons at Alliance, is pictured here with his pet prairie chicken. He was elected mayor of Alliance in 1896, at the age of 40.

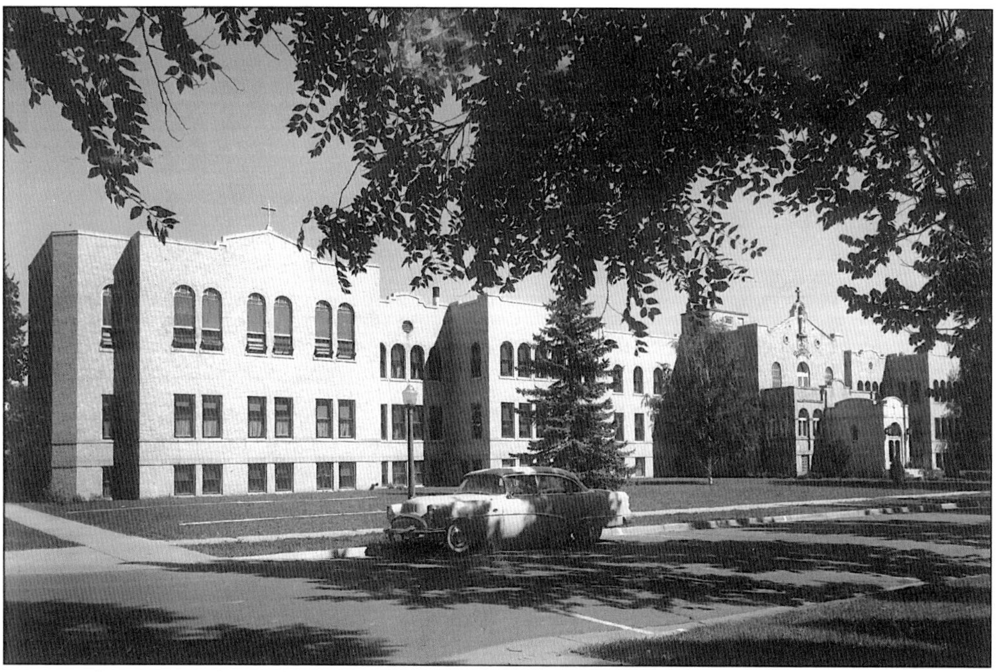

St. Joseph's Hospital, at Eleventh and Toluca, was built in 1910 by the Sisters of Mercy of Omaha in 1916, then operated by the Sisters of St. Francis, of St. Agnes Academy. The hospital began with a 23-bed capacity in its first year of operation. Numerous additions and renovations took place over the years. Peak patient admission was achieved after WW II with an annual admission rate close to three thousand. In November 1, 1976, St. Joseph's Hospital officially closed its doors as a general hospital.

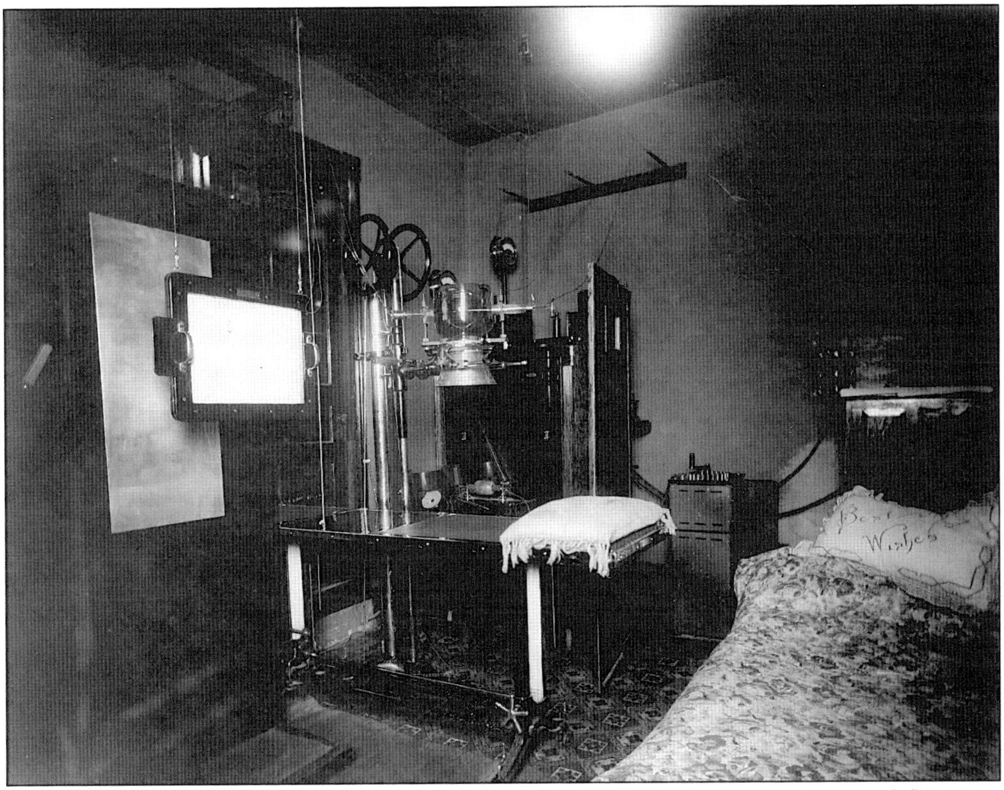

The Slagle Clinic x-ray room located in the Times-Herald building on the second floor was started by Dr. Slagle and moved to 524 Box Butte in 1947. When the doctors retired, the building was given to the city for a public library. It is now owned by the county and serves as offices. There is a health clinic now using the basement, so the building has come full circle.

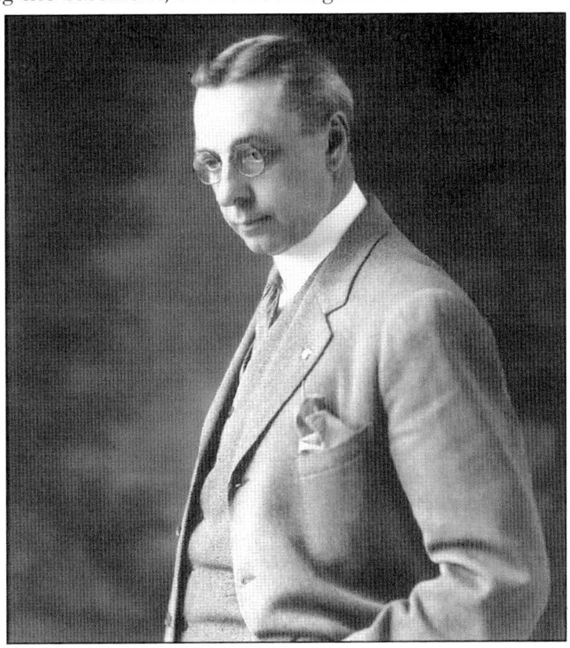

Dr. Charles E. Slagle was born in Oregon, Illinois, July 10, 1870. He entered the University of Michigan, and graduated from the school of dentistry in 1896. During his practice, he also taught dentistry. Meanwhile, he studied medicine and received a degree of M.D. in 1903. Dr. and Mrs. Slagle came to Alliance in 1906 and joined Dr. Bellwood. He was instrumental in the founding of St. Joseph's Hospital, was an instructor in nurse's training, was the railroad surgeon, and was also a Mason. He built the Slagle Clinic at 524 Box Butte. Later he donated this building to his former associates in the clinic. Dr. Slagle died in October 1956.

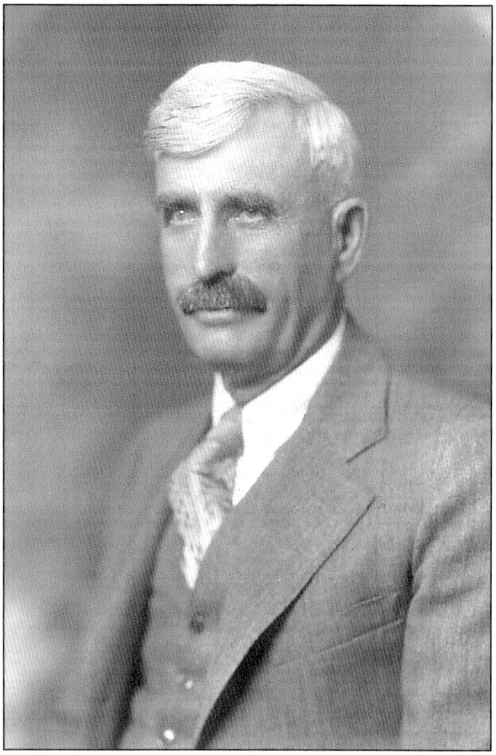

Leo Schill (1864–1961) came to Alliance from Ontario, Canada, to help build the railroad from Alliance to Hemingford. After the railroad was finished, he moved into a sod house 35 miles northeast of Alliance. He married Loula Blair, and to this union eight children were born. In 1913, he bought a farm about 2 miles south of Alliance. Thus became the famous "Schill Dairy" delivering milk and cream by horse and wagon first and later by truck. L.J. Schill had the first electric milking machine in the county and milked 60 cows. He was awarded the Master Farmer award in 1939 for his progressive methods in farming.

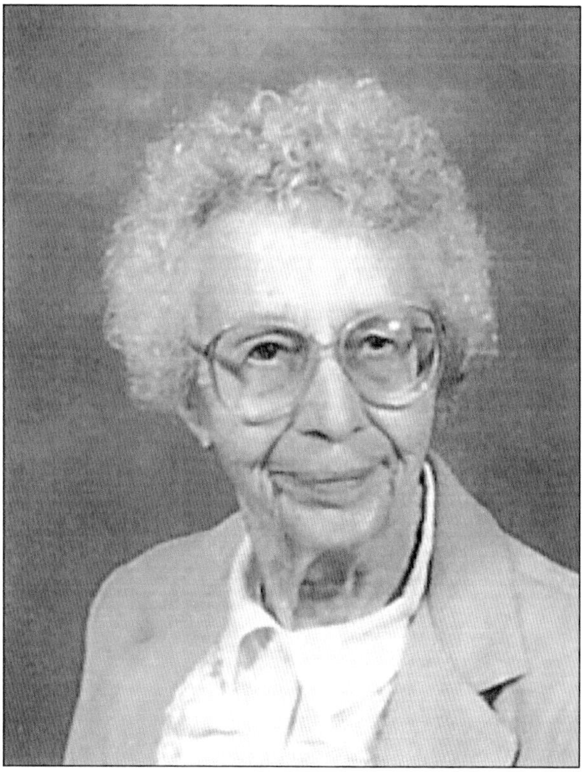

Miss Katherine Schill (1900–99) described herself as "an active old lady." That was an understatement! She graduated in 1916 and taught school for over 47 years. She was a Laubach literacy tutor for many years. As a charter member in many local clubs, her presence was always as asset. Something of great importance to Katherine was her lifelong membership in the Presbyterian Church.

Miss Susan Frazier came to Box Butte County in 1889. Her first school, District 45, 6 miles northwest of Alliance, was a 12-by-14-foot bachelor's board shack, sodded up on the outside to two one-sash windows. In 1912, she was called to the Nebraska State Teachers College in Chadron. She did not retire until she had served 50 years in the educational field. She died in Alliance in 1960.

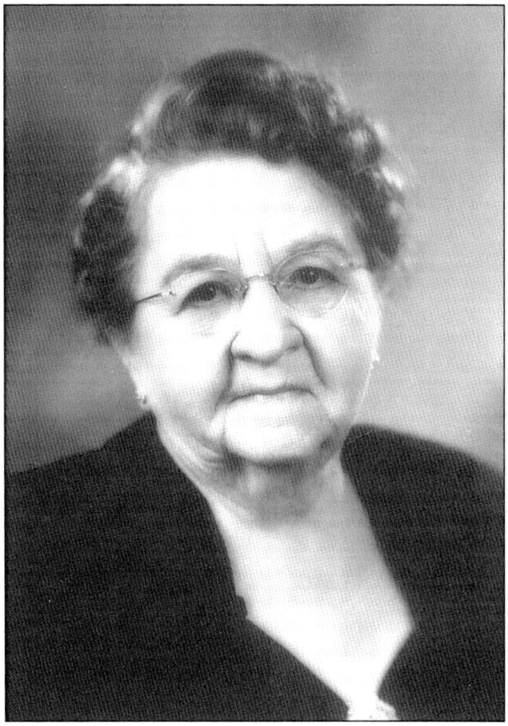

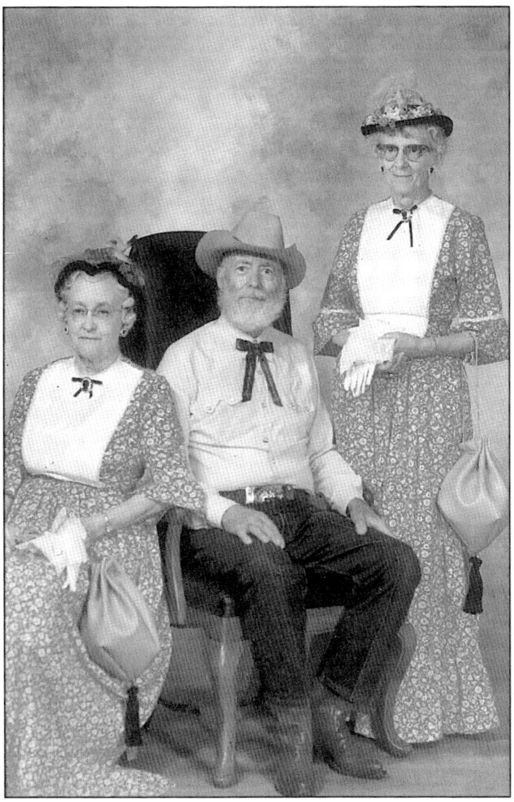

The "Burkholders Three" included Opal (1891–1986), Grace (1894–1999), and Leslie (1900–1977). The family moved to Alliance in the fall of 1906 so the children could attend school. Opal became a teacher in Box Butte County and taught for 23 years. After retiring, she kept the house while Grace and Leslie taught. Leslie started teaching in 1917, and after retiring from public schools, did part-time teaching at St. Agnes Academy until May of 1977. Grace started teaching school in 1910. After retiring from the public schools, she taught for ten years at St. Agnes Academy. The three Burkholders taught a total of 140 years, and many Alliance children benefited from their knowledge.

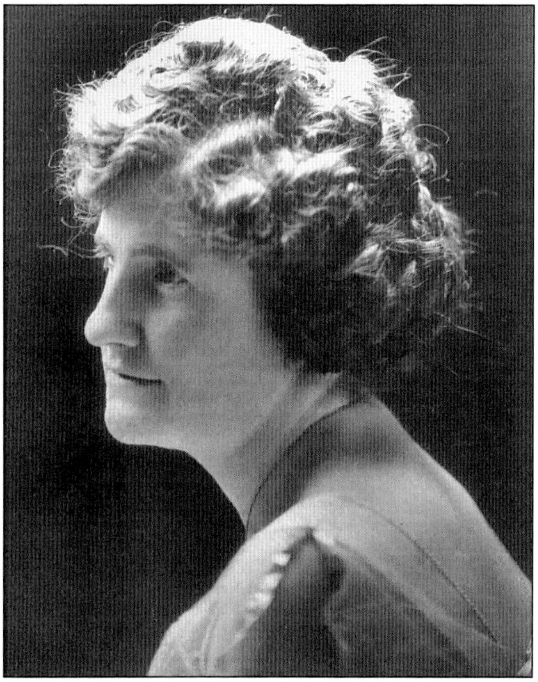

Miss Mabel Worley was the daughter of Lewis and Anna Worley. She was an amateur photographer most of her life. She attended the University of Nebraska as a music major but also worked for Alva Townsend of the Townsend Studios as an apprentice photographer. She came back to Alliance and worked for Mr. Grebe, and in 1919 bought the Grebe Photography Studio (located where the present Alliance Times Herald now stands). In 1928, she had a new studio built next to the Lowry and Henry garage. She was stricken with neuritis and died in October 1930.

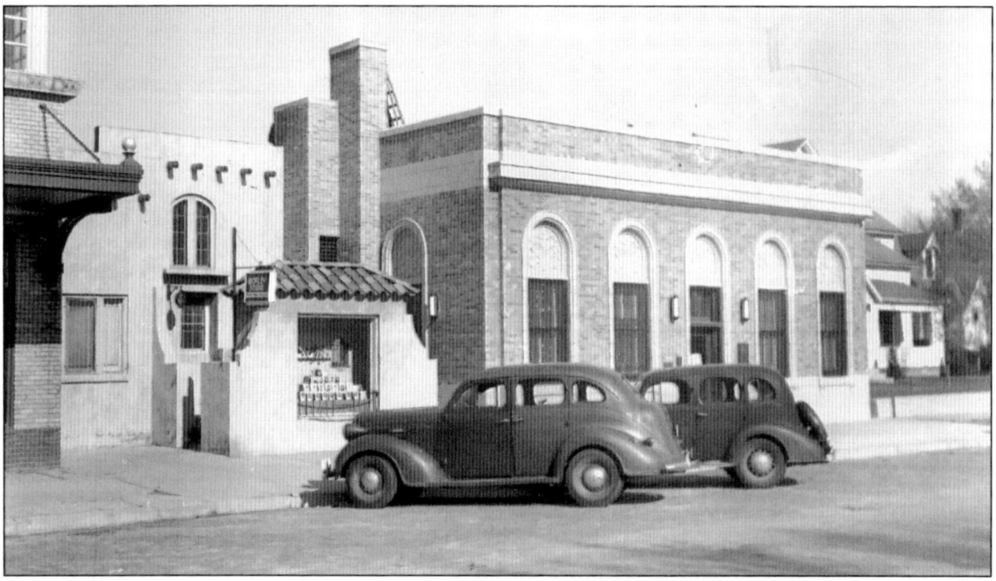

In January 1928, on the lot occupied by the firm of Tuttle and Tash, The Worley Photography Studio was built in a Spanish style of pink stucco, with a patio and brightly colored awnings in blue and orange. It contained a huge fireplace at one end of the entrance room and had 16-foot ceilings. Mabel Worley was the owner and a member of the Photographers of America. She owned the studio until her sudden death in 1930. At that time her sister, Izola Worley, took over the business and hired her nephew, Glen Worley, as photographer in 1931. Glen purchased the studio in 1932 and made Worley Studio the most well known photography studio in western Nebraska. Glen was a master photographer and worked until his death in 1998. His son, Duane Worley, took over the studio and operated it until his retirement in 2000.

Glen Worley, son of Ralph and Edith Worley, was the master photographer of Worley Studio from 1931 until his death in 1998. He was widely known for both portrait and scenic photography. He photographed several generations of many area families. One of his most well known portraits was that of a local man named Hayes Chandler, which won the "National Master Photographers Award" in Chicago, IL. The picture became famous for miles around and was reproduced for many private collections. He also produced a photo of combines in a wheat field that was hung in the U.S. Embassy in India. Glen managed Worley's Studio until his death in 1998.

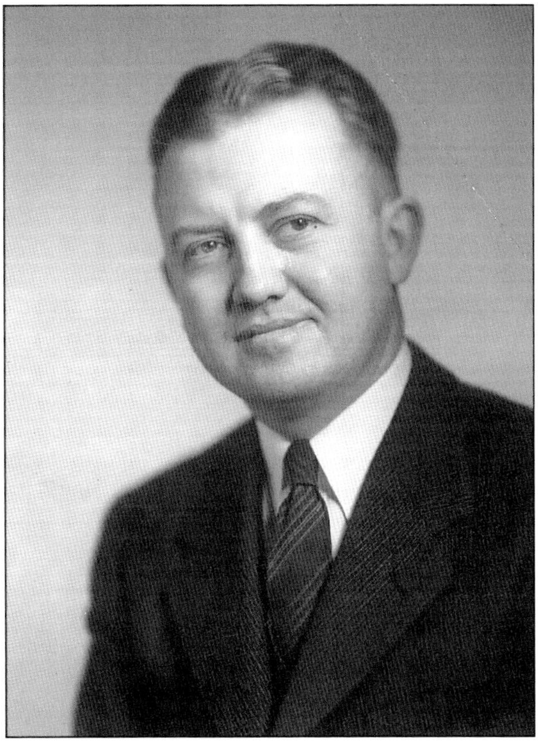

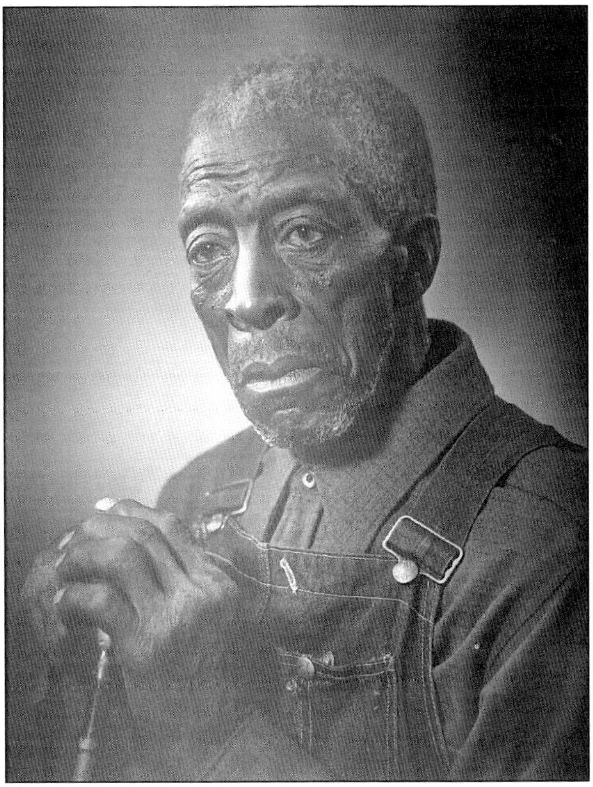

Hayes Chandler Sr. was a most beloved man of Alliance, especially of children, due to his willingness to let them hitch a ride on the back of his wagon as he made trash pickup and gardening rounds. In 1963, he was presented the Chamber of Commerce Outstanding Citizenship Award. The son of parents who had been slaves, he farmed in the Hemingford area from 1915 to 1935, then moved to Alliance where he found hundreds of customers for his services. He and wife, Florence, raised a son and three daughters and five orphaned children of their daughter, Myrtle.

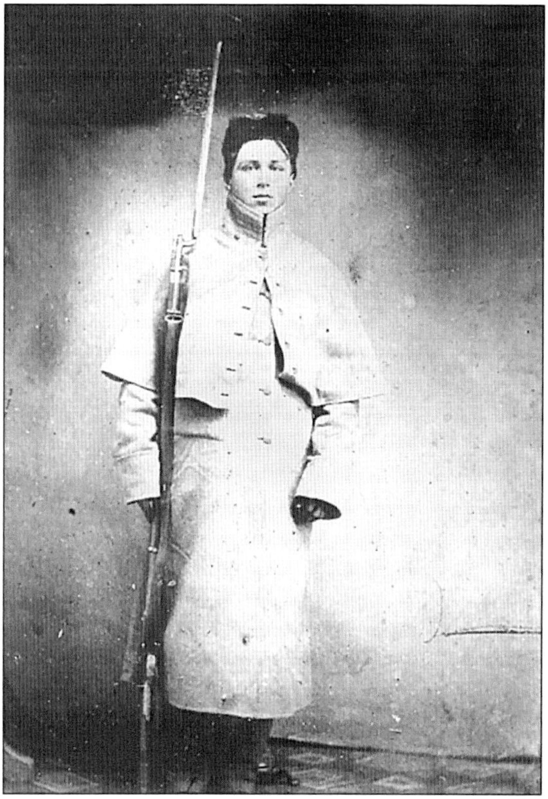

Al Wiker (1847–1931) was a veteran of the Civil War. He joined the army in 1862 at the age of 16 on the side of the Union. Mr. Wiker, looking for excitement, became a cowboy and a scout in the southwest. He then came to Box Butte County and became the county sheriff from 1905–1909. He and his wife ran a boarding house at 624 Box Butte Avenue in his later years.

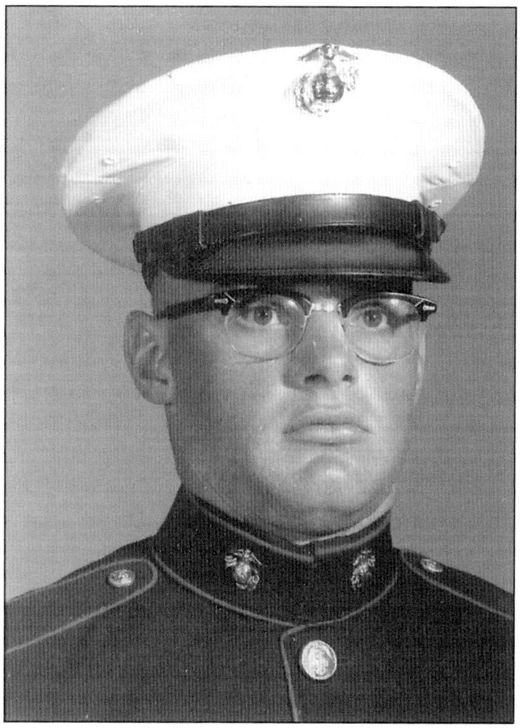

Marine PFC Ronald Coker, a 1965 Alliance High School graduate, earned the Congressional Medal of Honor near the infamous DMZ in the spring of 1969. He has been the only one of hundreds who have served from Box Butte County to be awarded this honor. He is buried in a rural cemetery called Fairview, 14 miles northeast of Alliance. His name is one of the thousands engraved on the "wall" in Washington, D.C. He is not forgotten.

Paul Williams Thompson was born in Alliance to Silas W. and June Williams Thompson. He graduated in the class of 1924 and entered West Point in 1925, and graduated thirteenth in the Class of 1929. He was the first person to attend West Point from Alliance.

As D-Day approached, Thompson was appointed to command the Sixth Engineer Special Brigade, which spearheaded the Normandy assault. He was awarded the Distinguished Service Cross.

After his retirement from the Army, General Thompson joined the Reader's Digest Association as director of the company's European operations. He was the consummate military and corporate leader. He died in February 1996 at the age of 89.

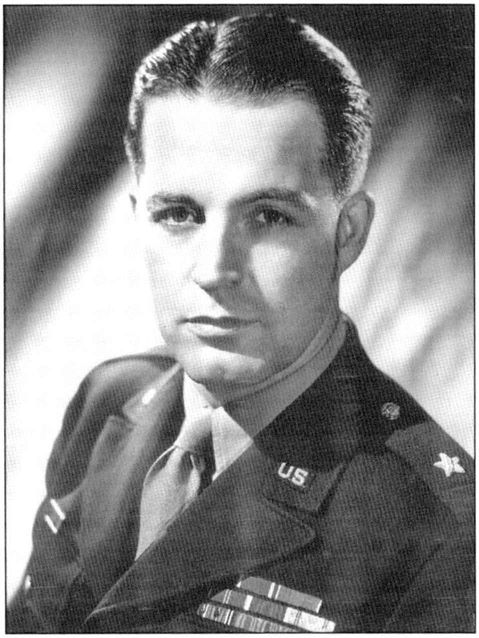

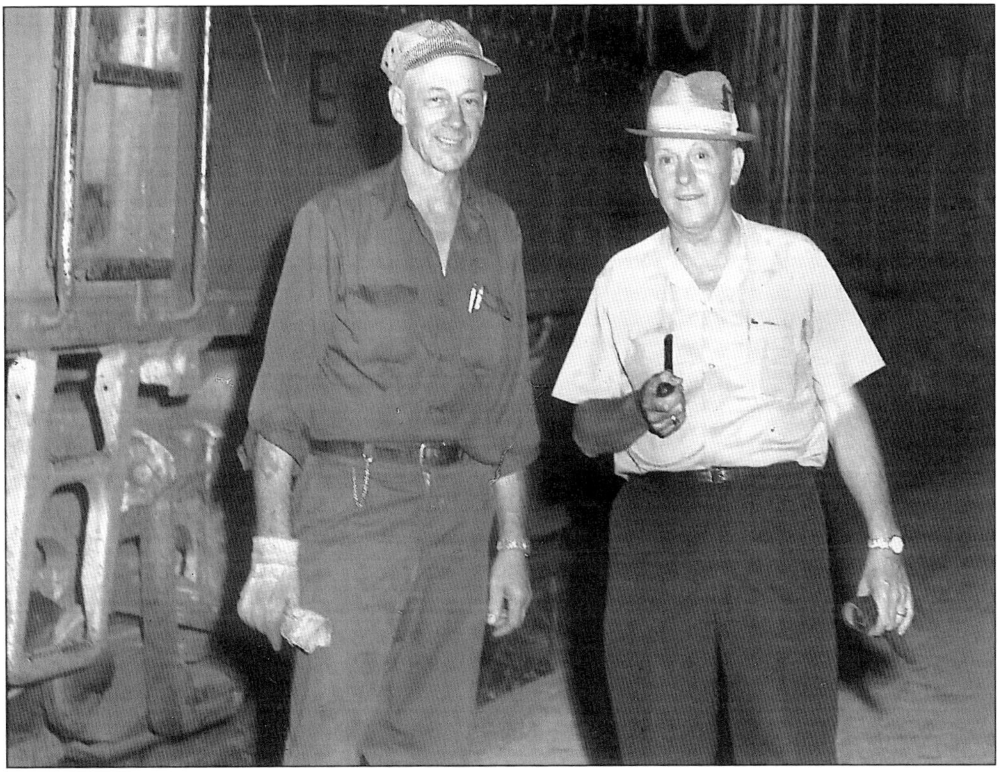

"Man With A Cause" J.O. Butcher (1908–1992), a CB&Q railroad engineer, stands with a fellow railroader Fred Mackey. After retirement, Butcher "took on the city council" advocating change in their method of appropriating utility profits, deferring electrical maintenance, and ceasing to generate power at the municipal power plant.

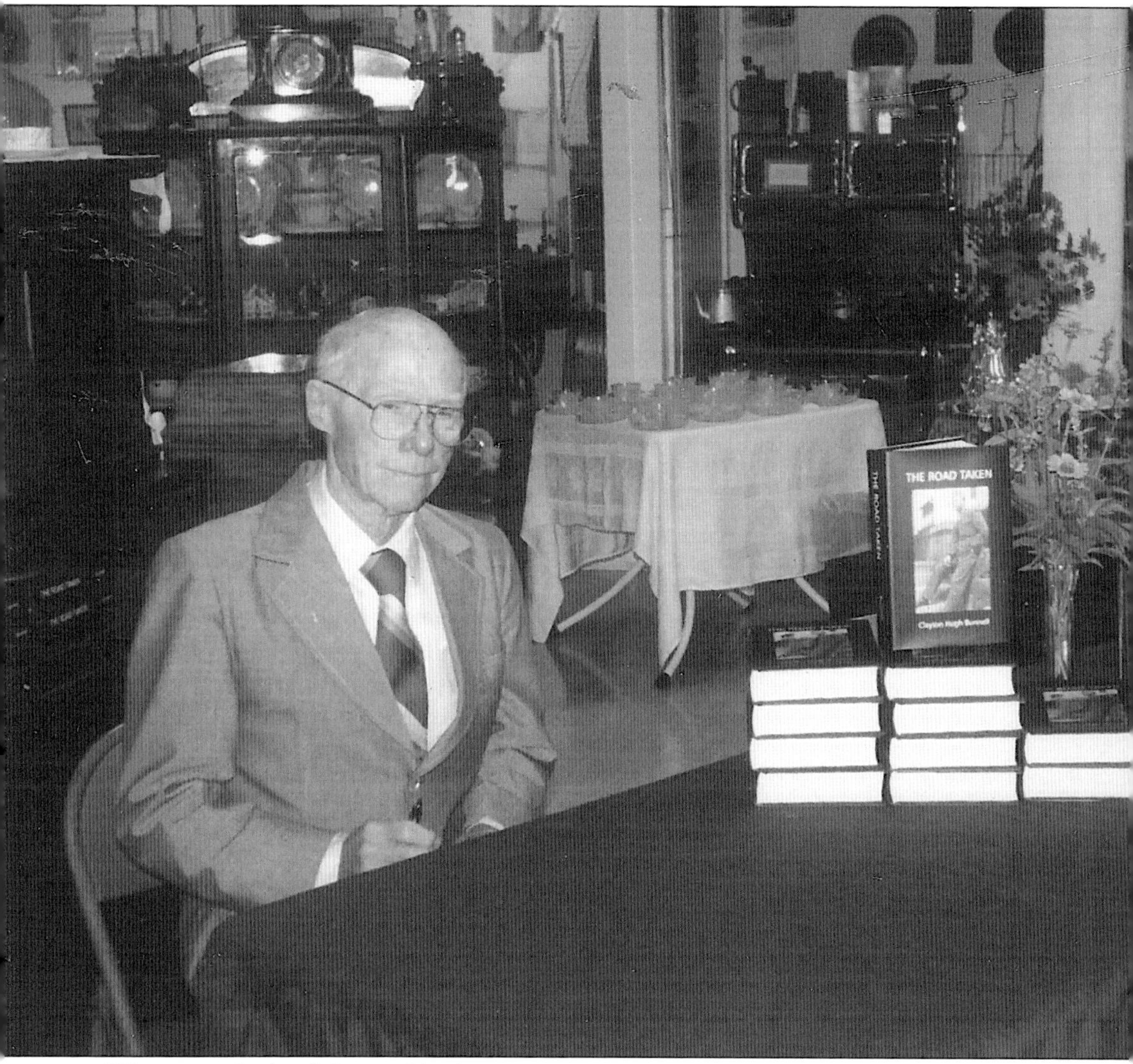

When you think of the world of newspapers, one man comes to mind—C. Hugh Bunnell (1916–2000). Hugh came to Alliance after his WW II service and started working for Ben Sallows. He moved up to editor of the *Alliance Time Herald* and his career spanned over 50 years. Hugh also served as the unofficial historian of Alliance. He is greatly missed by the community.

Five

Planes, Trains, and Automobiles

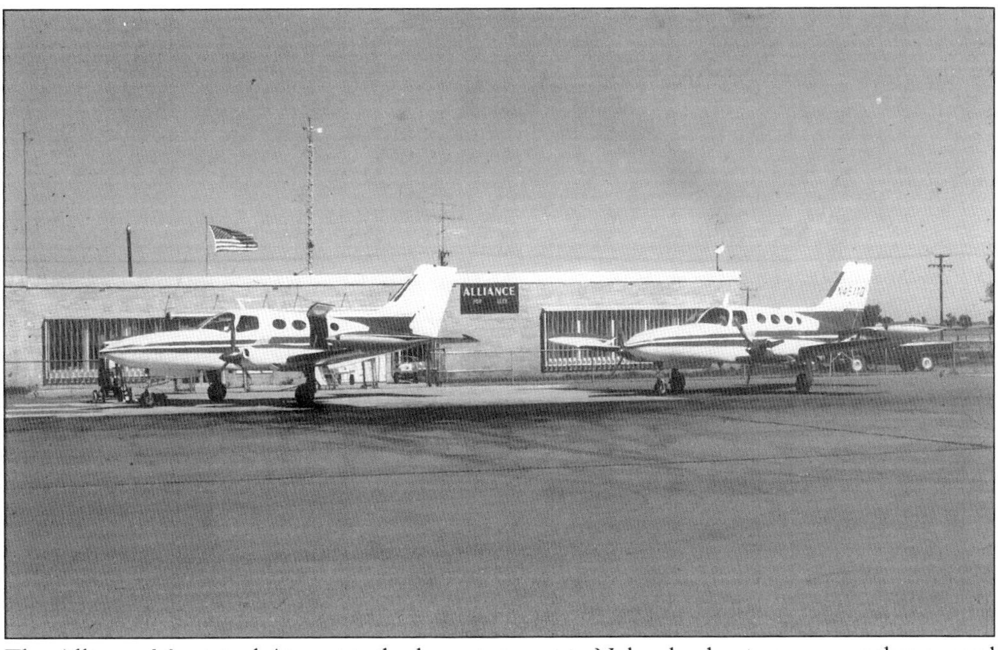

The Alliance Municipal Airport is the largest airport in Nebraska, having runways that exceed 9,000 feet! The airport was inherited from the U.S. Air Force after the closure of the air base. The terminal was built to house airline services and offices. Various restaurants have been there at one time or another.

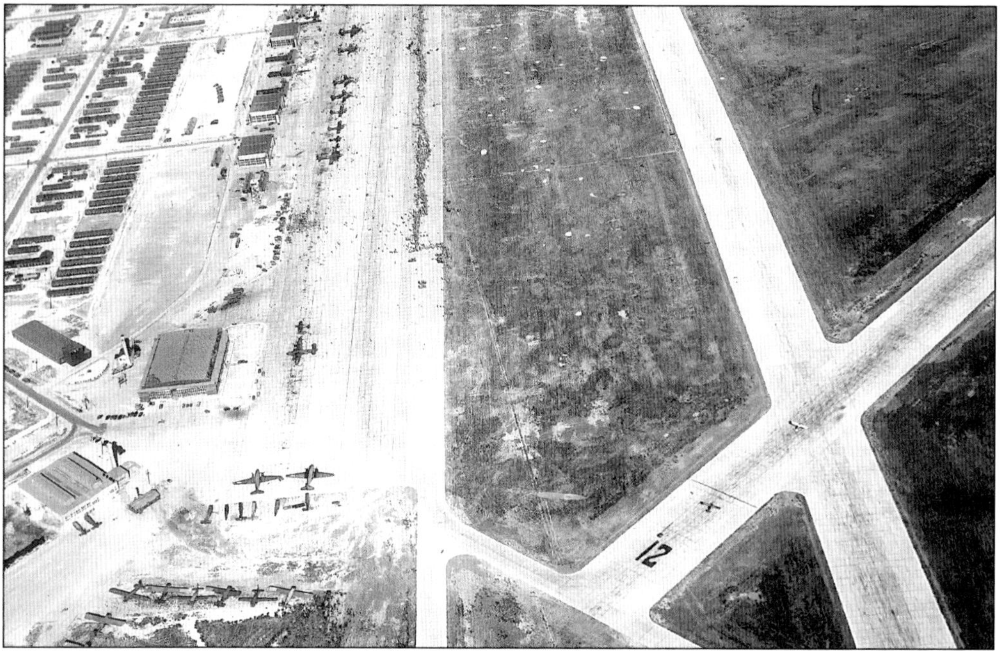

The second largest event, after the coming of the railroad, was the decision to locate the U.S. Army Airbase here in 1942. Patriotism was at a fever pitch after Pearl Harbor, and Alliance became a boomtown over night. This aerial view shows the runways, hangers, command centers, and barracks. The cost was $15 million, and covered 5,000 acres including land leased from area ranchers.

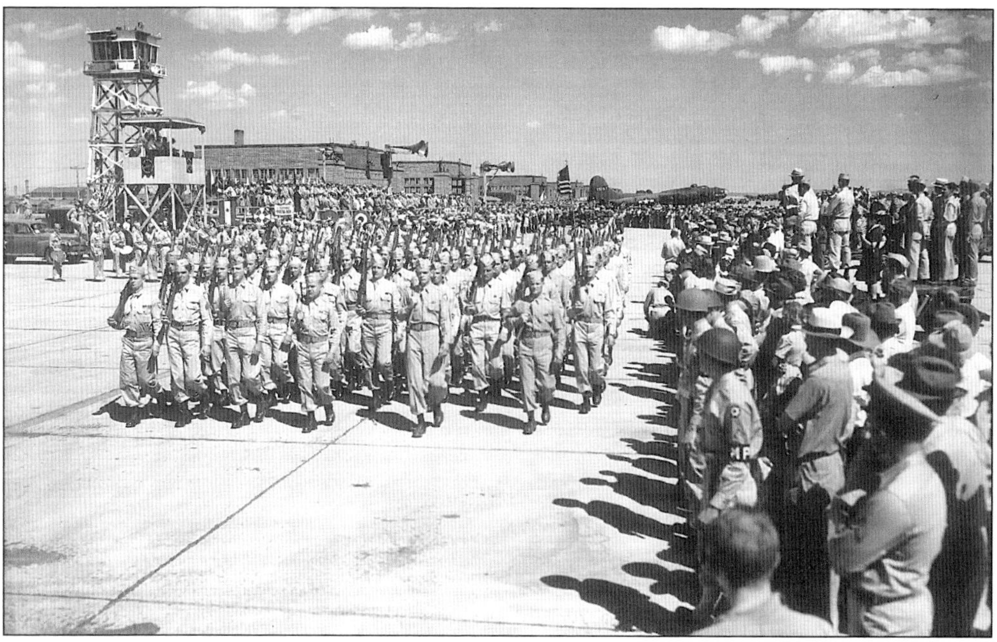

A demonstration of modern airborne warfare was brought to the public, all 66,080 of them, on Sunday, August 22, 1943. This was the largest crowd to ever assemble in the Panhandle. The paratroopers passing in review were part of the forces that landed on D-Day.

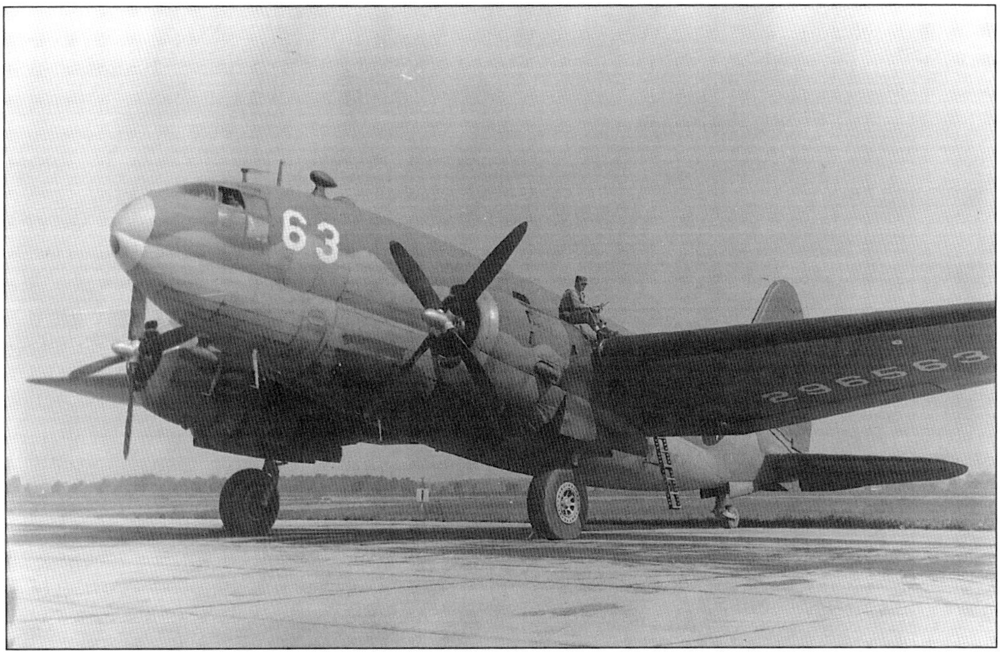

Planes like this C-46 were seen in the skies on a daily basis. Over 15,000 paratroopers and glider infantrymen filled the base, and parachutes blossomed over the stark sandhills skyline.

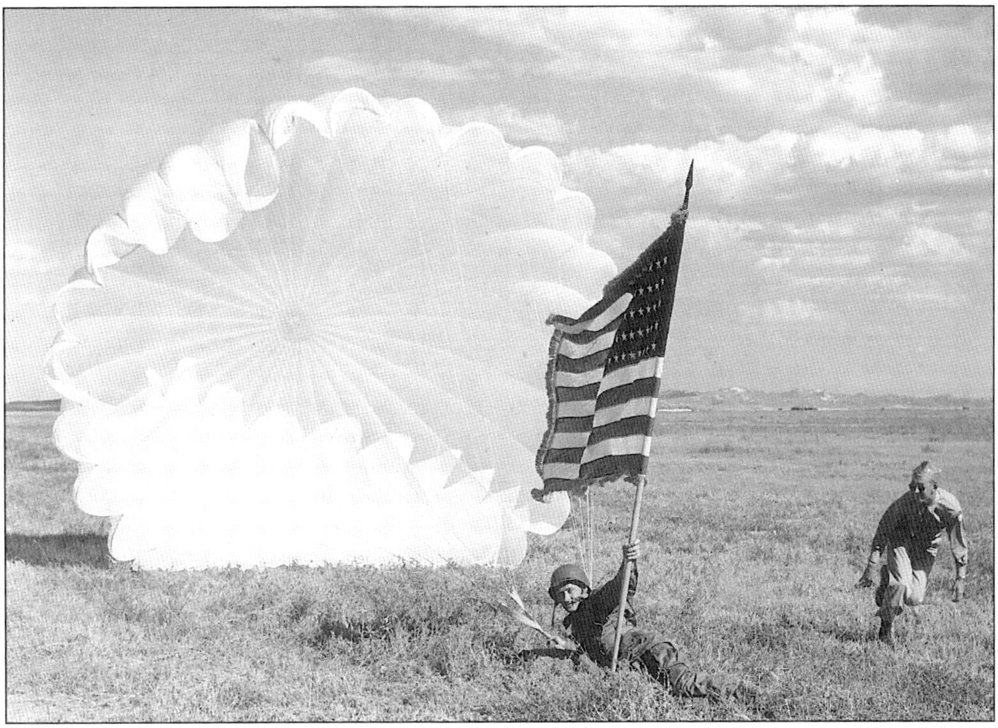

Pictured is one of the many 507th Paratroopers with a successful landing. Many families and civilian workers swelled the Alliance population to more than 10,000 overnight. Temporary housing was built on the east side of the city. "Chimney Town" is still in use as senior housing.

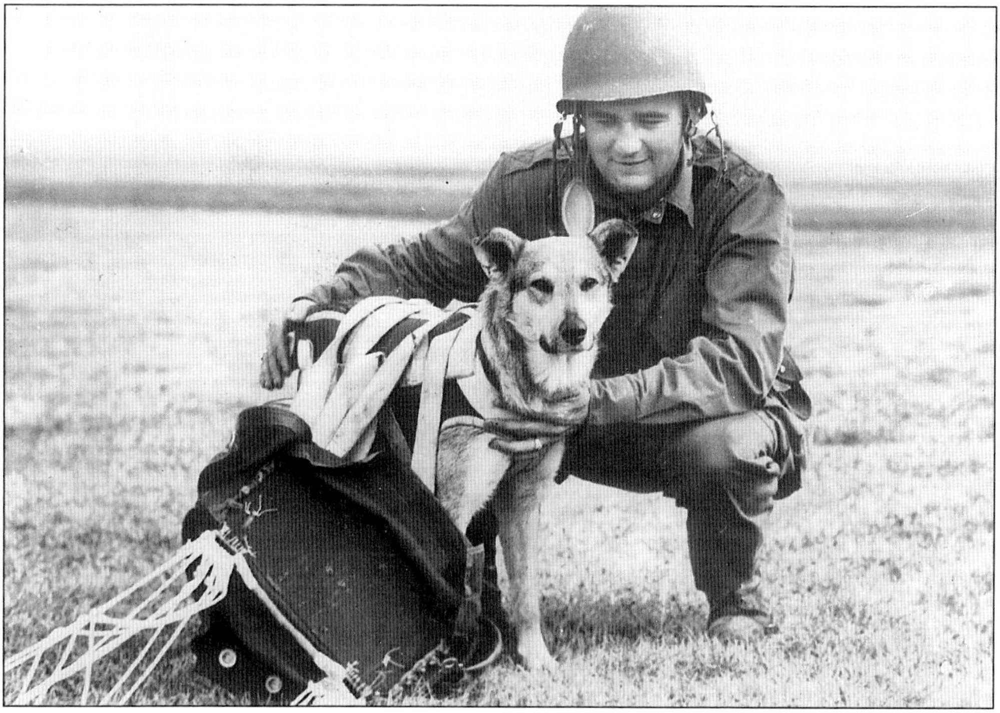

One of the most famous paratroopers on the air base was Geronimo, the mascot of the 507th Paratroopers. Geronimo is shown here with Pvt. Johnny Williams in April 1943.

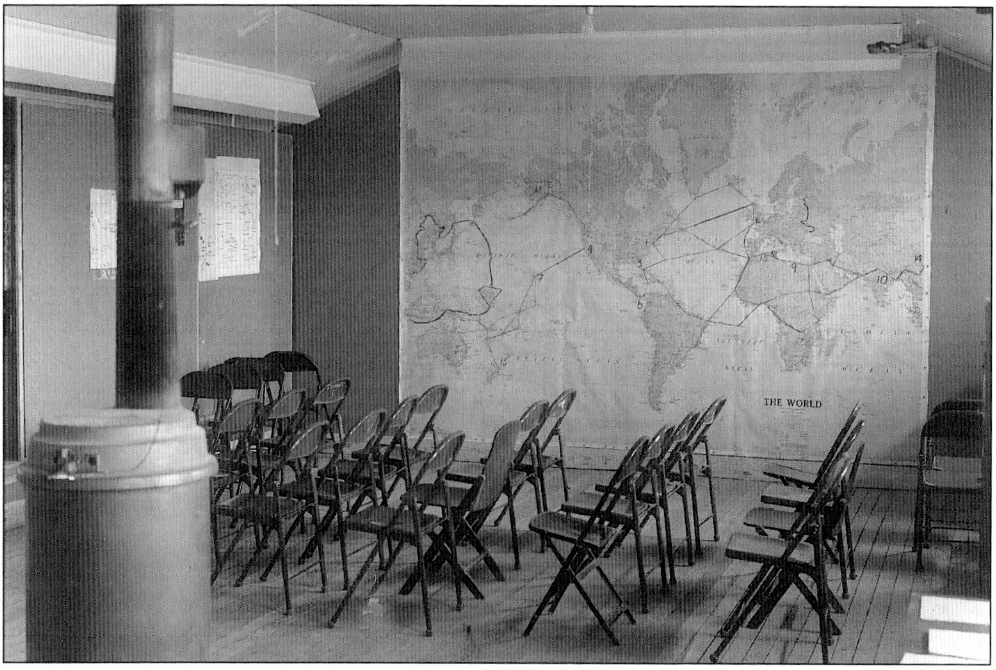

The "Invasion Room" classes were held here to train the paratroopers for their eventual mission to Europe. Also on the base was a library, green house, bowling alley, officers club, bank, and many other services to make the airbase a city within itself.

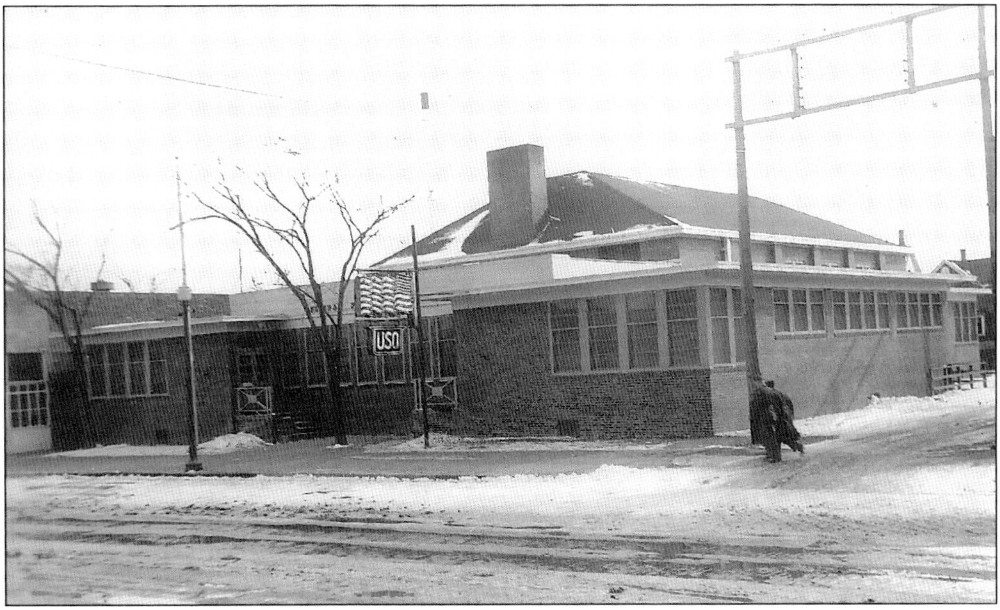

Built in 1942 as a home for the USO affiliated with the airbase, this home was purchased by the American Legion Post 7 in 1946 for $22,500. They had been holding their meetings in the basement of the Alliance Times-Herald building. A dramatic fire in 1976 leveled the Legion, and new headquarters were found in 1977 on West Third Street and Ramblin Road. The old site was rebuilt into two separate restaurants.

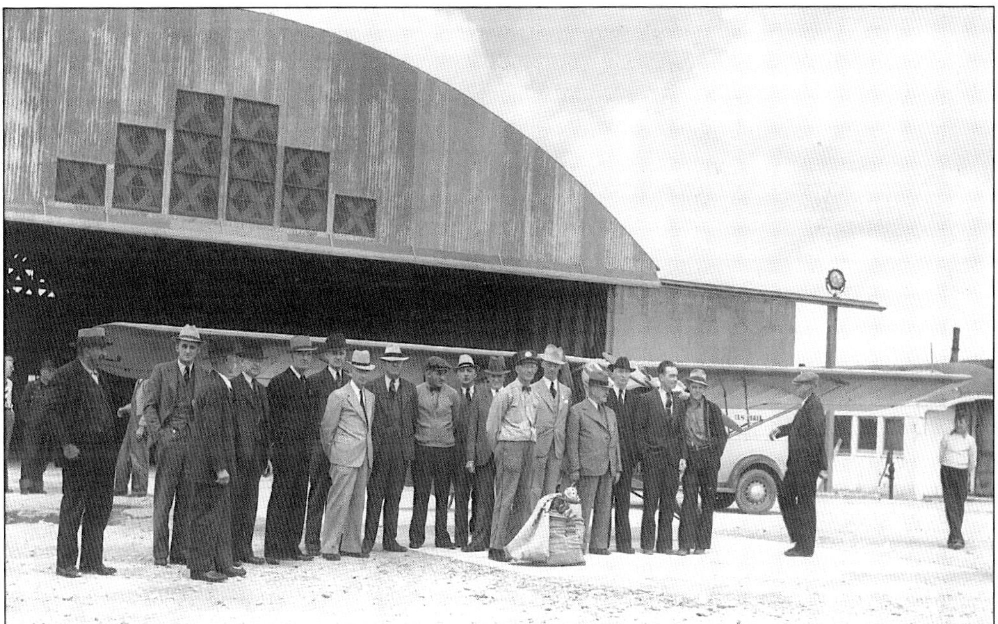

The Alliance Airport at one time linked the golf course, racetrack, and industry. This group of Alliance officials and businessmen await the first U.S. Airmail plane on its trial flight. Foster Wambaugh is in the uniform by the mail sack. Note the airport "water works"—a hand pump on the right.

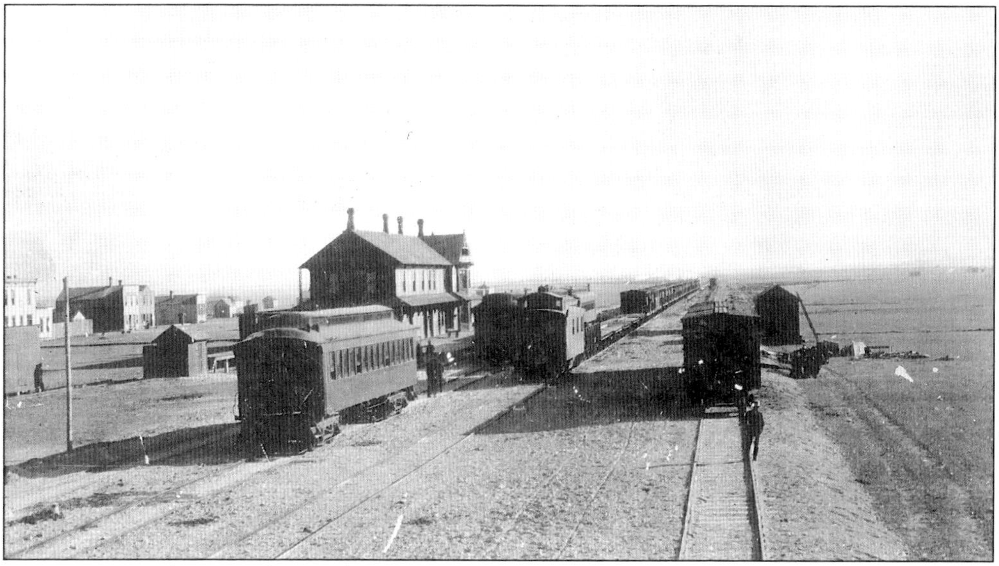

In June 1887, the Lincoln Land Company bought most of a school section. Part of it was designated for railroad right of ways, shops, and round house, with mile posts 366 "west of the Missouri" on the east side, and 367 on the west side. The railroad grade and tracks reached Alliance by January 27, 1888. By 1890, over eight hundred people lived in Alliance. These four tracks have swelled to 41 tracks of various lengths with a yearly average of 75 trains a day.

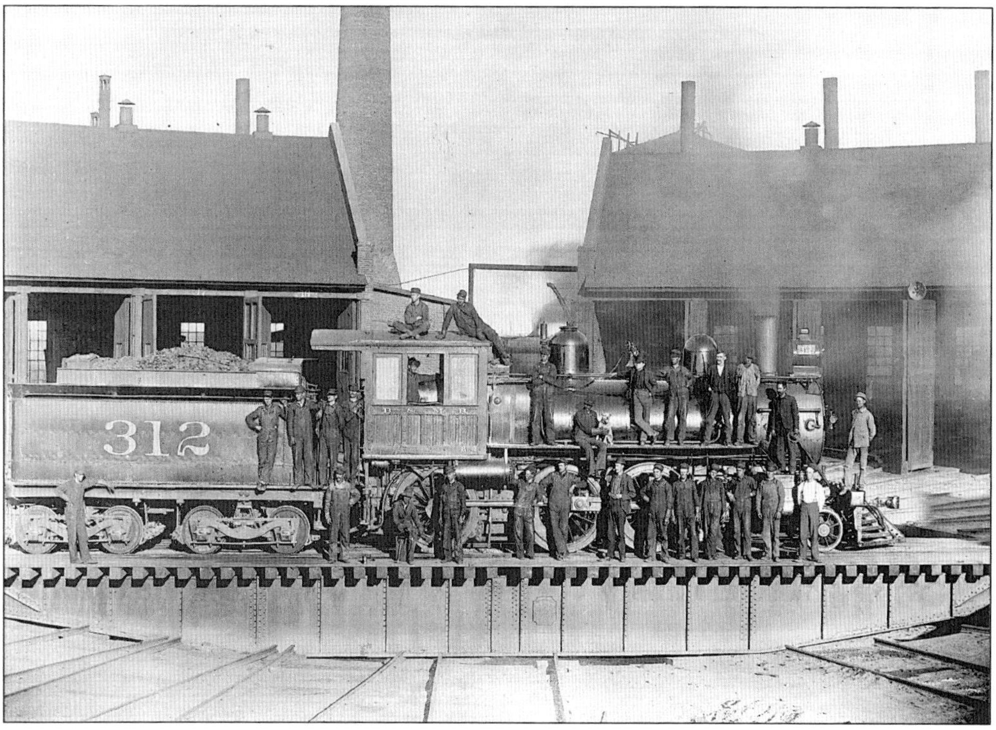

Shown here is Burlington & Missouri Railroad Engine #312, with the Alliance Division Shop workers at the round house. The large turntable in the diesel shop enabled entire engines to be turned around. The turntable was removed, but the diesel shop still employs many railroaders.

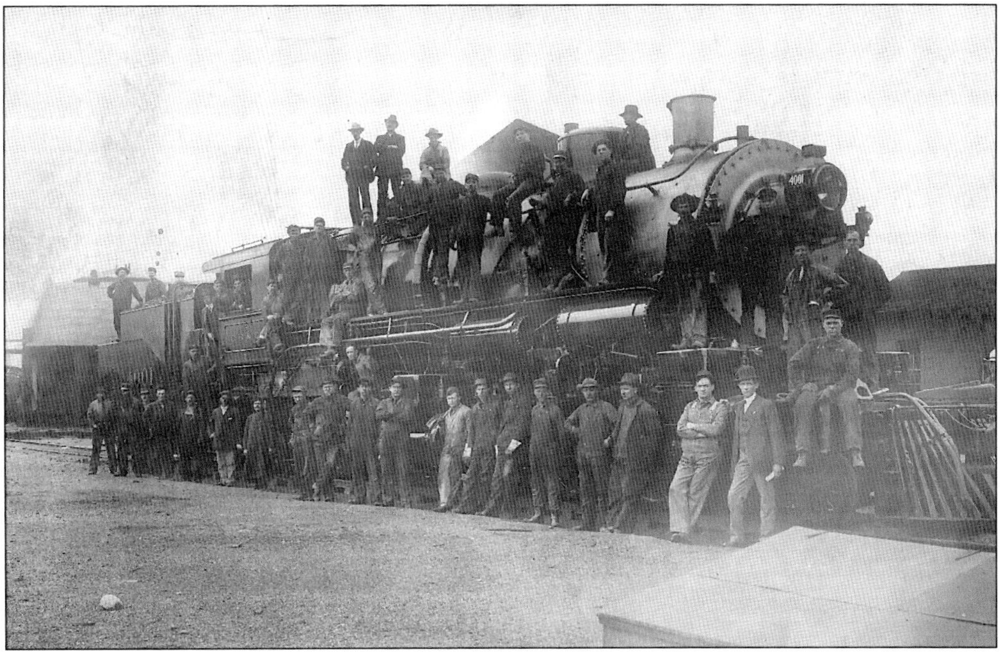

Alliance has been the home of many railroad families, and Burlington Northern Santa Fe Railroad remains the largest employer. Many families have had several generations ride the rails.

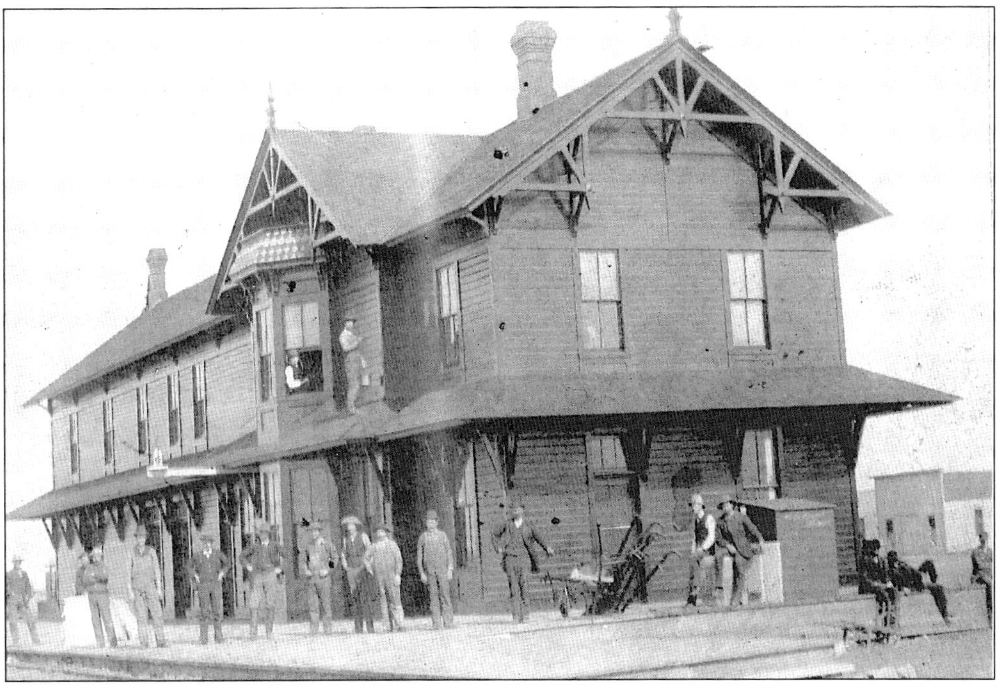

The Burlington Depot in 1905 was a large, red, proud structure with ornate gables and chimneys. A gathering place for tearful farewells and happy returns, the depot was a central part of downtown Alliance. The four chimneys were masterpieces of masonry, but a fire in one of the flues caused the depot to burn down on November 24, 1906.

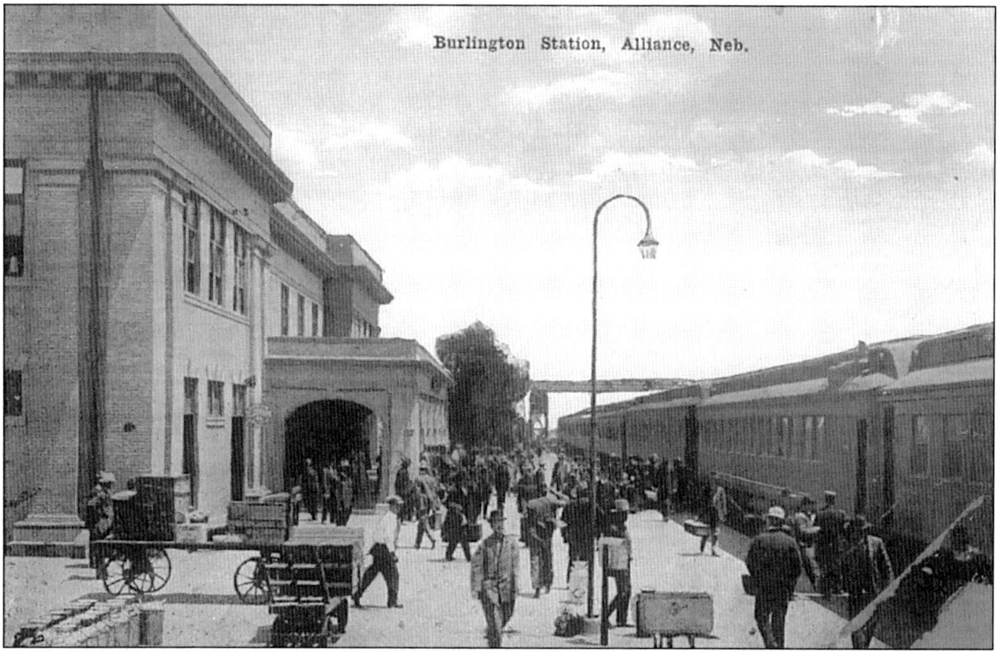

The depot was a busy hub teaming with life. Travelers, salesmen, and people headed in many directions came and went through Alliance. The trains also served the community as a way to ship commodities. Whether retail merchandise or farm products, this was a valuable part of everyday life.

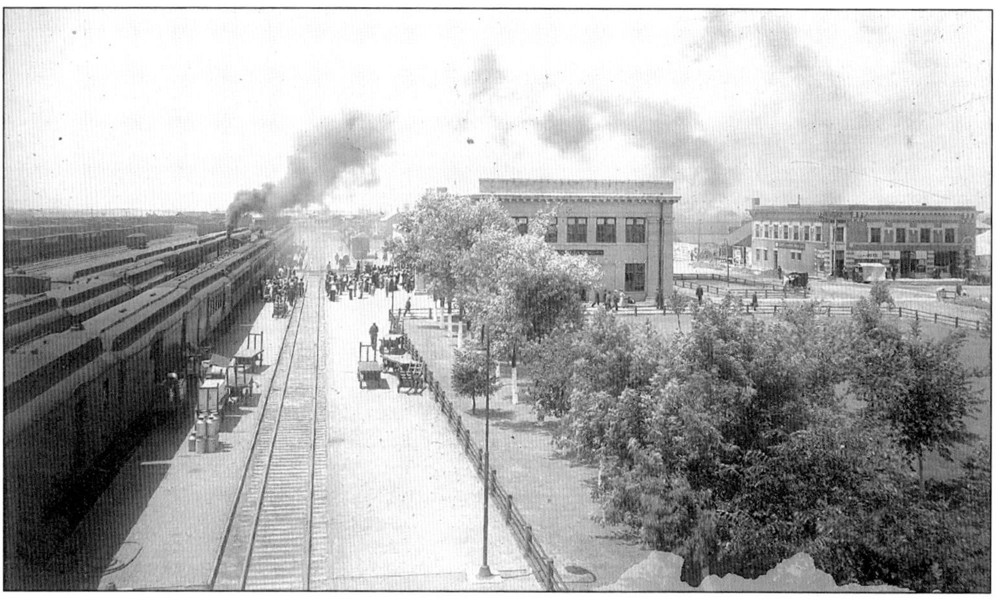

Built in 1917, the gray brick depot became a railway nerve center and landmark for 73 years. The depot contained the main division offices and 23 superintendents. On the east side of the building was a beautiful park that welcomed newcomers to Alliance. The Alliance Hotel sets in the background, and a horse and buggy are in front. The Western Heritage Railroad Credit Union now sits in this park area.

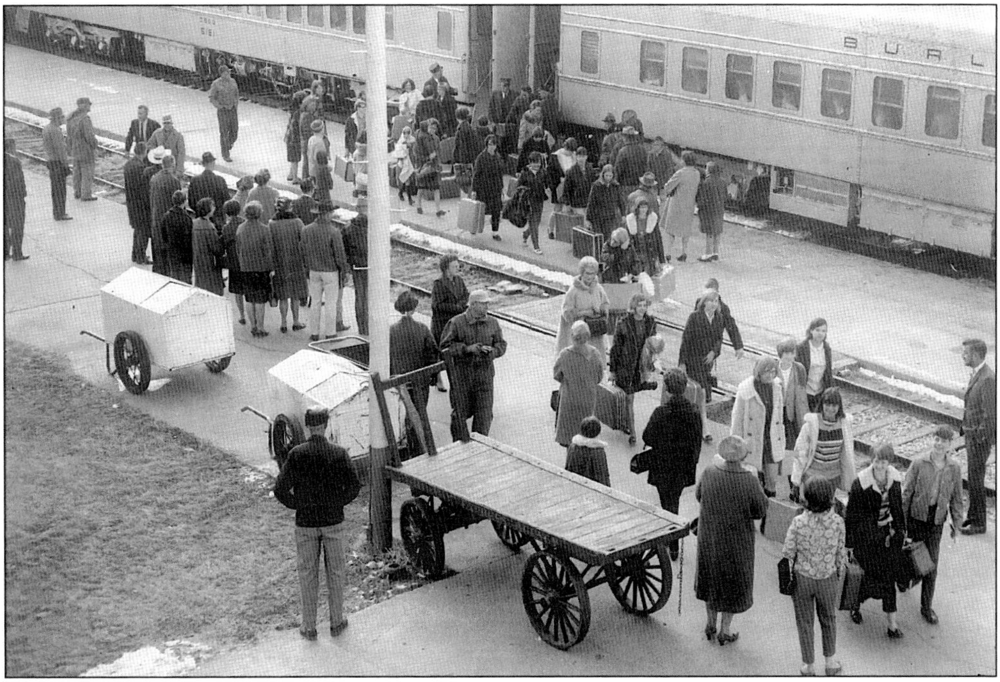

The final run of Passenger Train #43 is shown on the morning of August 25, 1969. The train was made up of two coaches and a baggage car. "Meeting the train," a common social affair, was now a thing of the past. Train travel was a common form of transportation across the U.S. (The baggage cart in the foreground is now at the Knight Museum.)

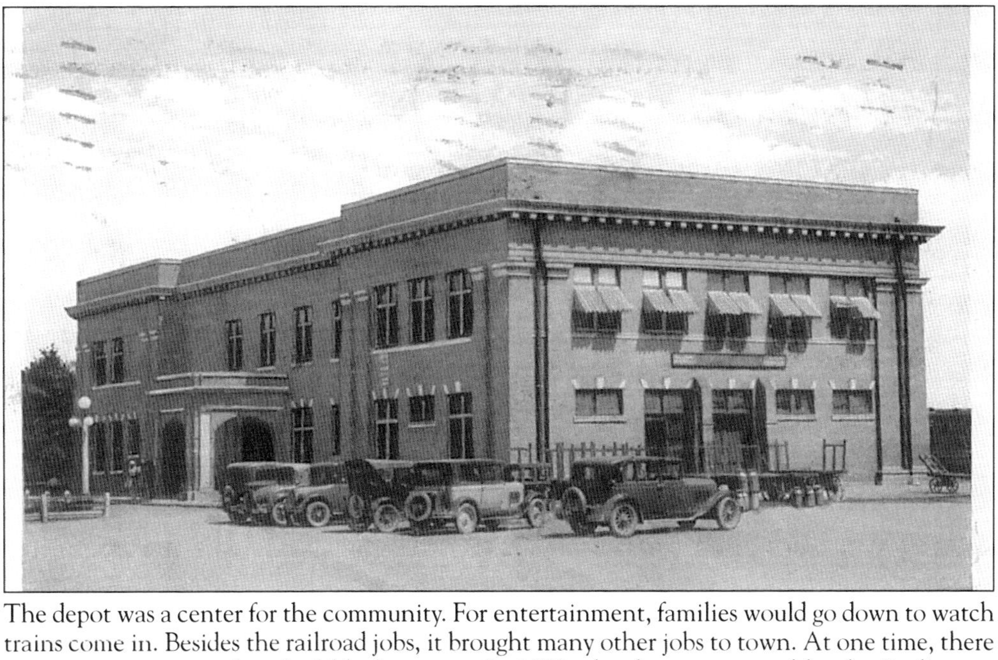

The depot was a center for the community. For entertainment, families would go down to watch trains come in. Besides the railroad jobs, it brought many other jobs to town. At one time, there were as many as two hundred black porters. In 1980, the depot was razed by the Burlington Northern and replaced by a berm of dirt. A new division office building was built to the west of the old depot.

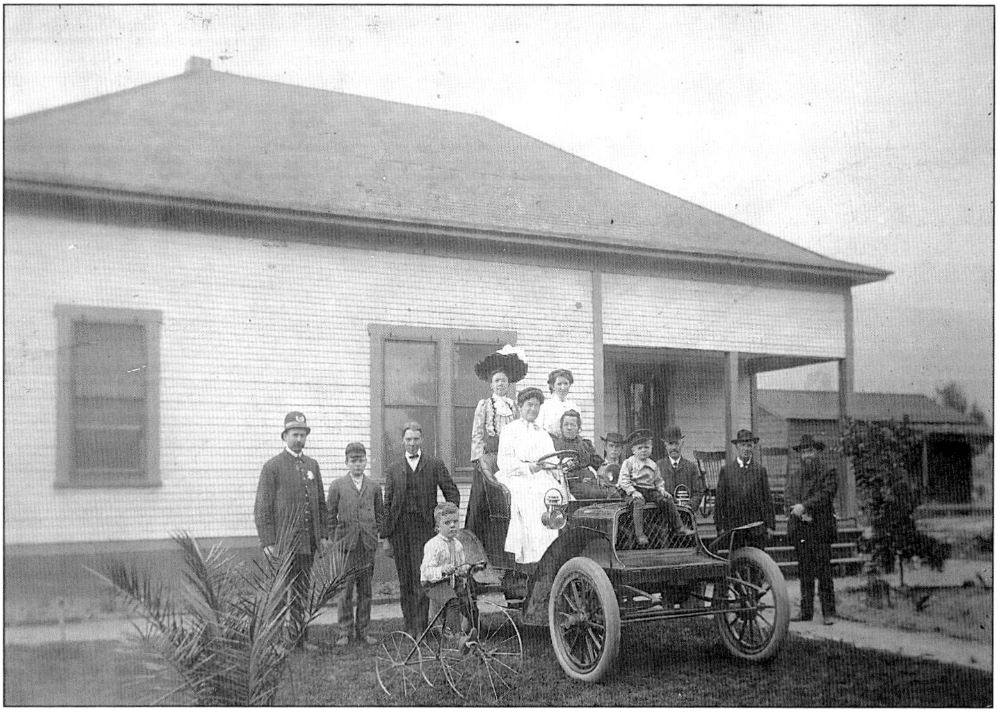

Captain Corbin owned the first automobile in Alliance. He is shown here, second from the right, with his family and friends. The young lad sports a dandy high tricycle in the front, and a local constable is part of the group.

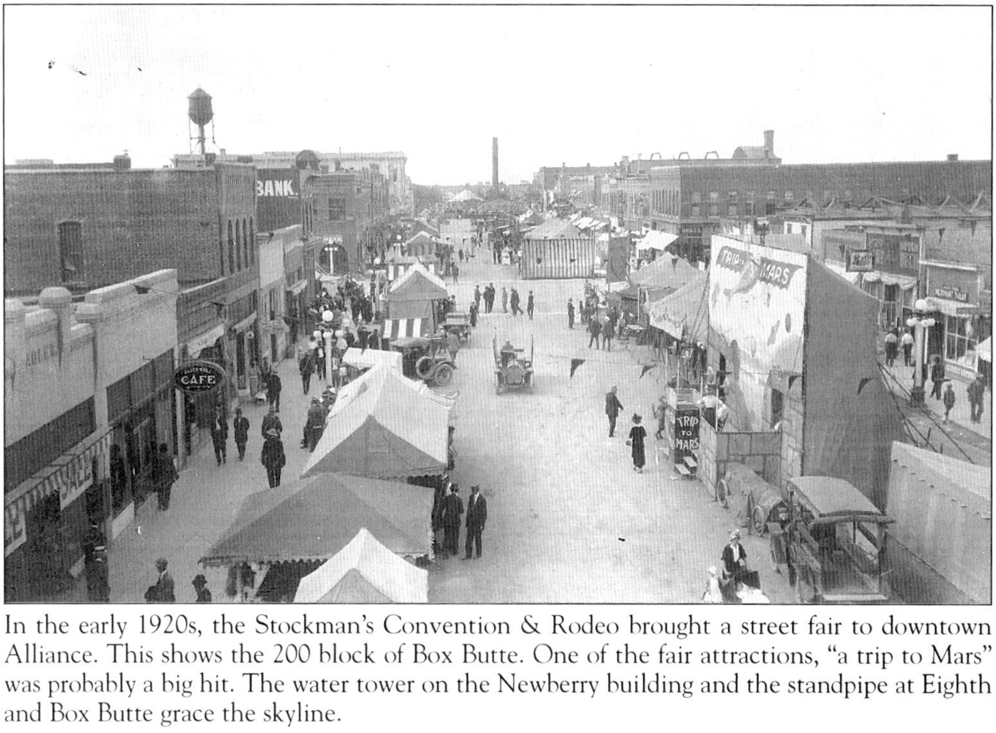

In the early 1920s, the Stockman's Convention & Rodeo brought a street fair to downtown Alliance. This shows the 200 block of Box Butte. One of the fair attractions, "a trip to Mars" was probably a big hit. The water tower on the Newberry building and the standpipe at Eighth and Box Butte grace the skyline.

The first stoplight at Third and Box Butte Avenue also served as a street sign. Note the brick pavement and steps leading to many basement businesses.

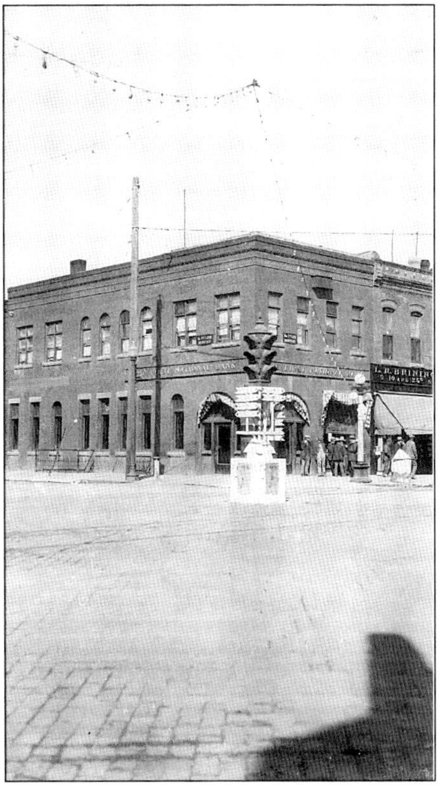

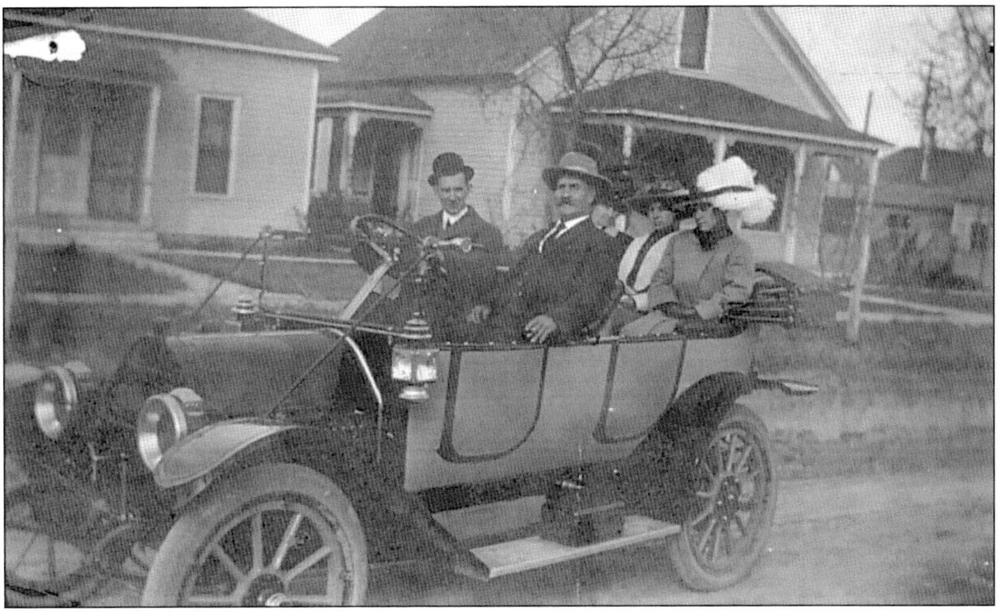

As more cars filled Alliance's streets, life became more bustling. J.S. McCorkle motored around Alliance in 1908 in his Pope-Hartford. This is believed to be the third car in town. Joining him on his jaunt is an unknown fellow, and seated in the rear are Mrs. Harper, Mrs. Ellis, and Mrs. McCorkle. Modern transportation had arrived in Alliance.

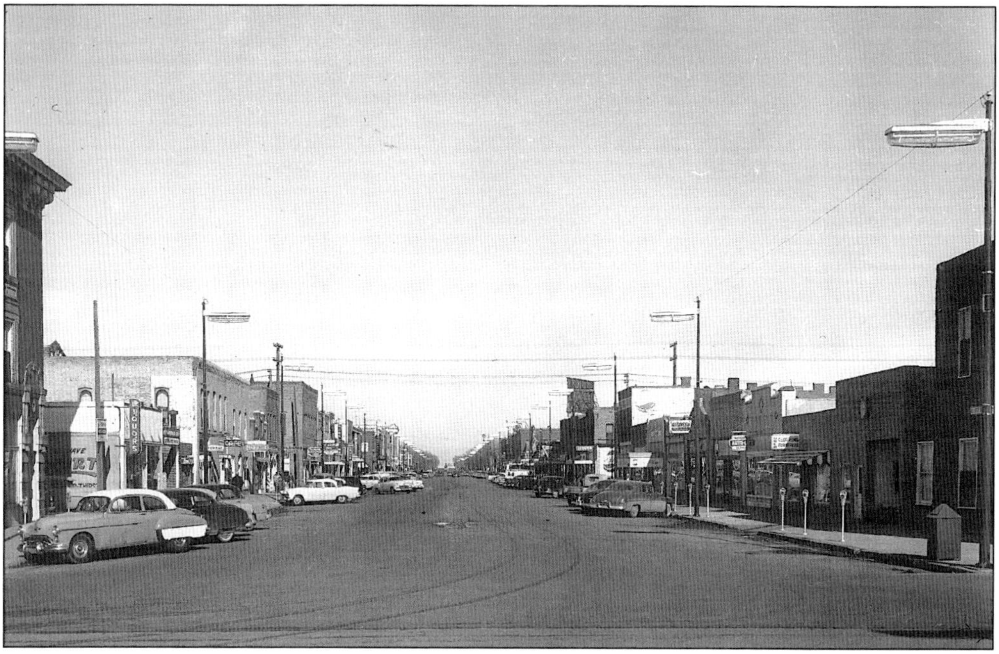

Shown is Box Butte Avenue in 1956, looking north from First Street. The parking meters were a source of revenue that was abolished in 1981. The third building on the left side was Rex's Hamburger Shop, run by Rex Meyers for 42 years. It was home to the best 5¢ coffee in town! North of Rex's is the Western Hotel. The Zurn Taxi Co. was on the east side of the street next to the Alliance Hotel Annex.

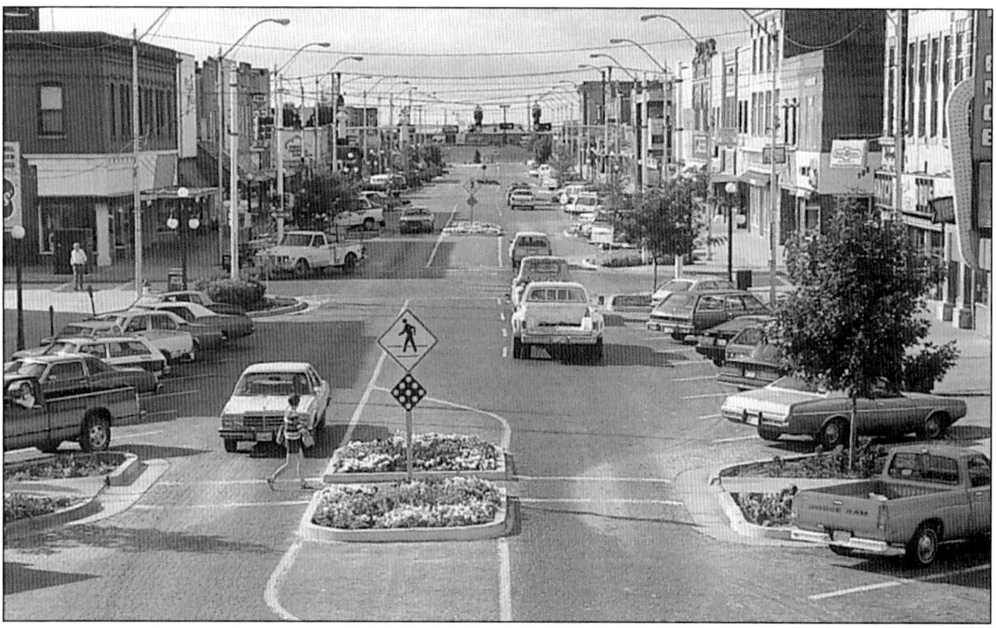

Taken in 1988, this downtown street scene of Box Butte Avenue shows a newer angle of parking and "islands" that were added to make middle of the block walkways. These islands are home to trees and flowers that beautify these quaint brick streets. Wonder what's showing at the theater?

Six

Plowboys, Wranglers, and Entrepreneurs

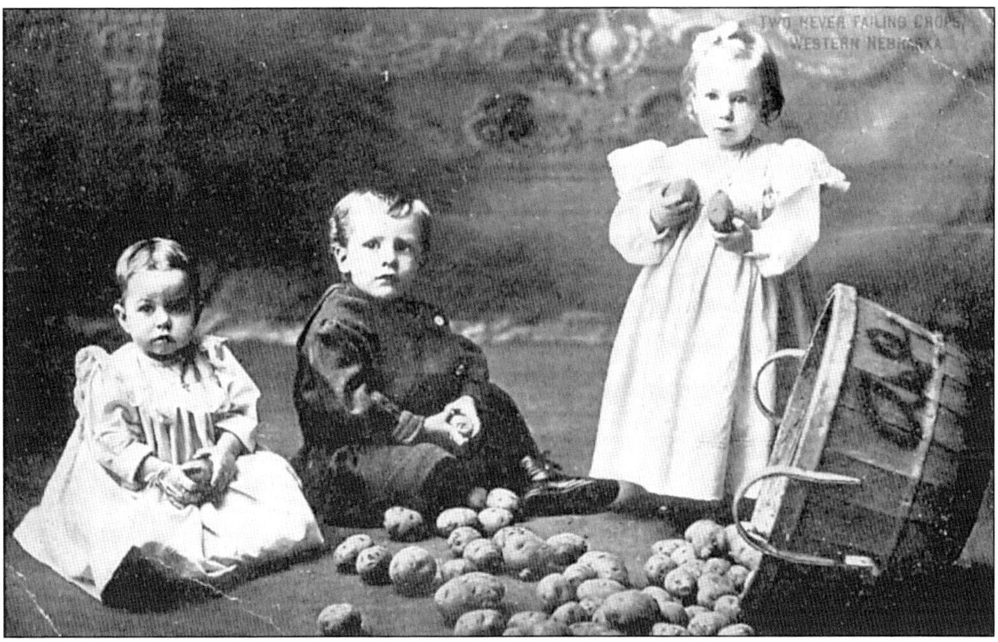

The caption on this favorite postcard reads: "Two never failing crops in Western Nebraska." Children (L-R): Sarah O'Keefe, Glen Miller, and Agnes Newberry mixed with potatoes made your never-fail crops. This incentive brought many pioneer families west to try their hand with the rich, abundant soil. Potatoes thrived on the low summer temperatures and cool nights. Kids did, too.

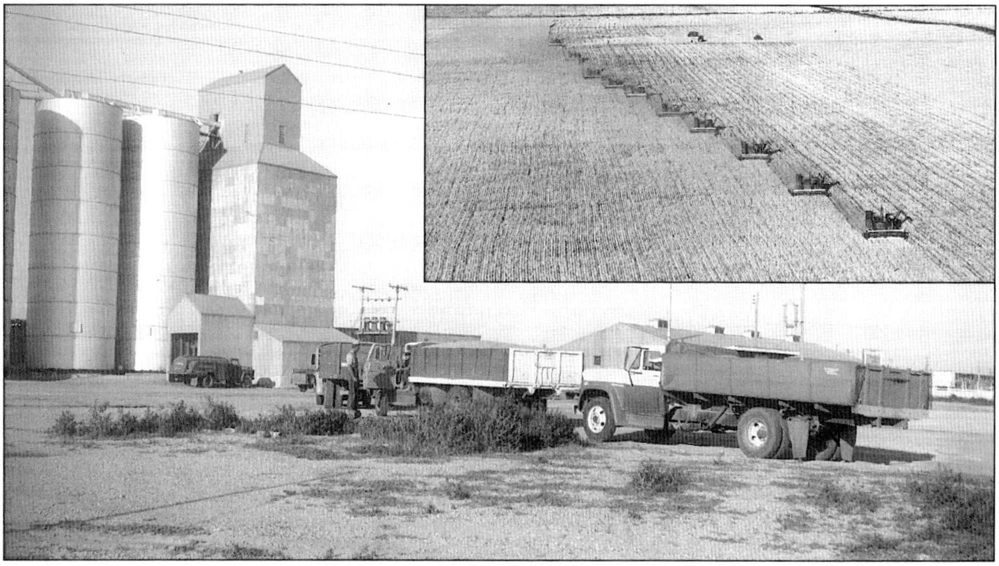

This impressive shot of a fleet of combines was taken in the 1950s on the Bill Riis farm, north of Alliance. Wheat production presented an opportunity to make money, and men in other lines of work attempted to farm on some scale. Men like Riis and James Jelinek were known as "Wheat Kings." The line of trucks at the Neuswanger, formerly Scudders, south elevator was a common site.

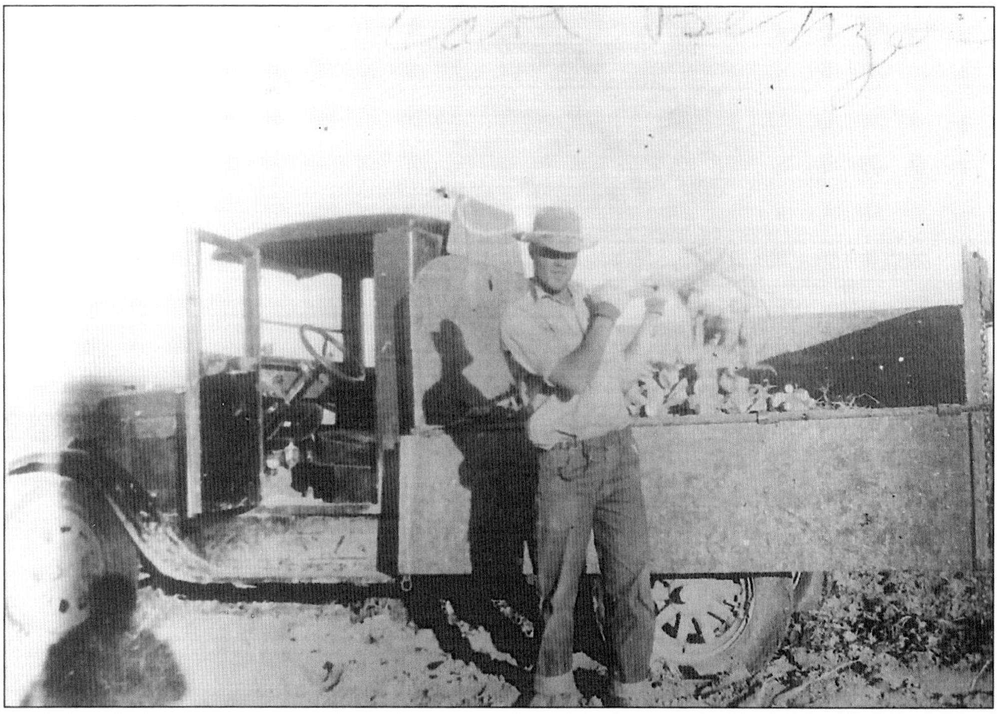

Carl Benzel shows the harvest of sugar beets with his 1928 International truck. Sugar beets were latecomers to this area. Now considered a major crop, most are grown in Alliance and trucked to Scottsbluff to be processed into white and brown sugar. When Carl took his crop to town, he hauled 2 tons at 20 miles per hour. Now 18-wheelers can haul 25–30 tons at high speeds.

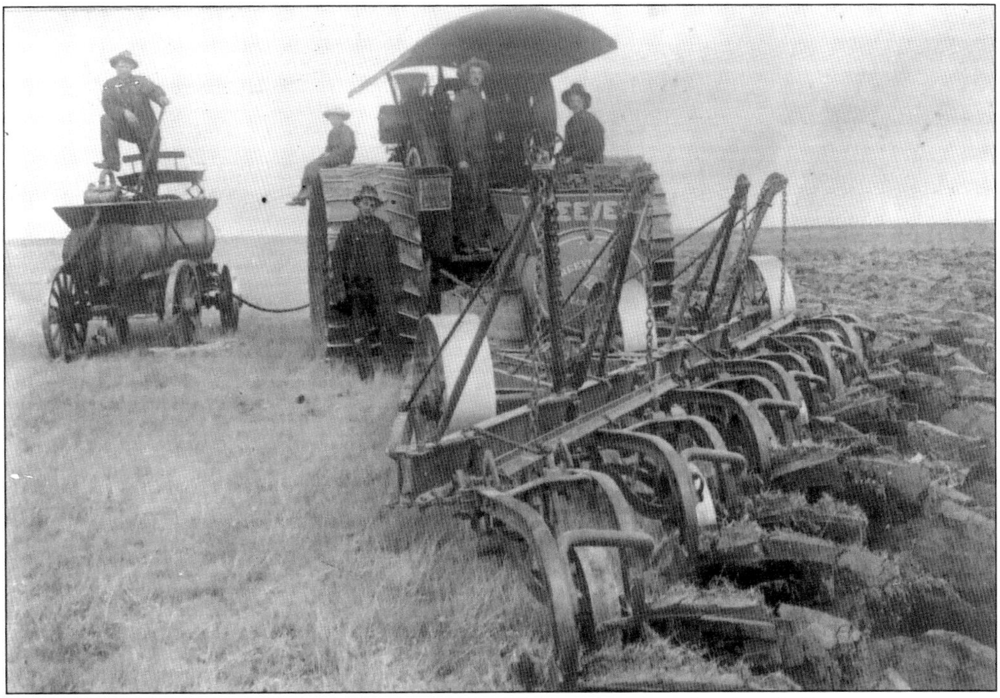

Steam driven tractors and five bottom plows made breaking up the Sandhills prairie an easier task for most homesteaders. After the Kincaid law, homesteaders were permitted a section of land, and free range became a thing of the past. In its stead were patches of grain. When irrigation came to the county, wells were drilled throughout the area. Today we find most crops grown under sprinklers, the modern-day answer to the prairie windmill.

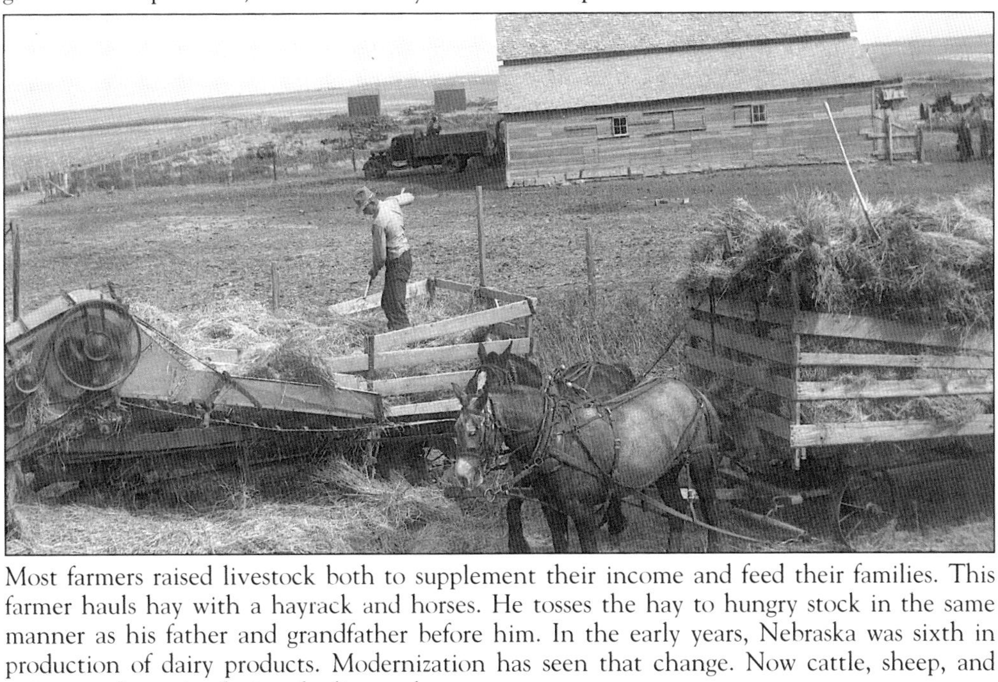

Most farmers raised livestock both to supplement their income and feed their families. This farmer hauls hay with a hayrack and horses. He tosses the hay to hungry stock in the same manner as his father and grandfather before him. In the early years, Nebraska was sixth in production of dairy products. Modernization has seen that change. Now cattle, sheep, and swine are the main choices for livestock.

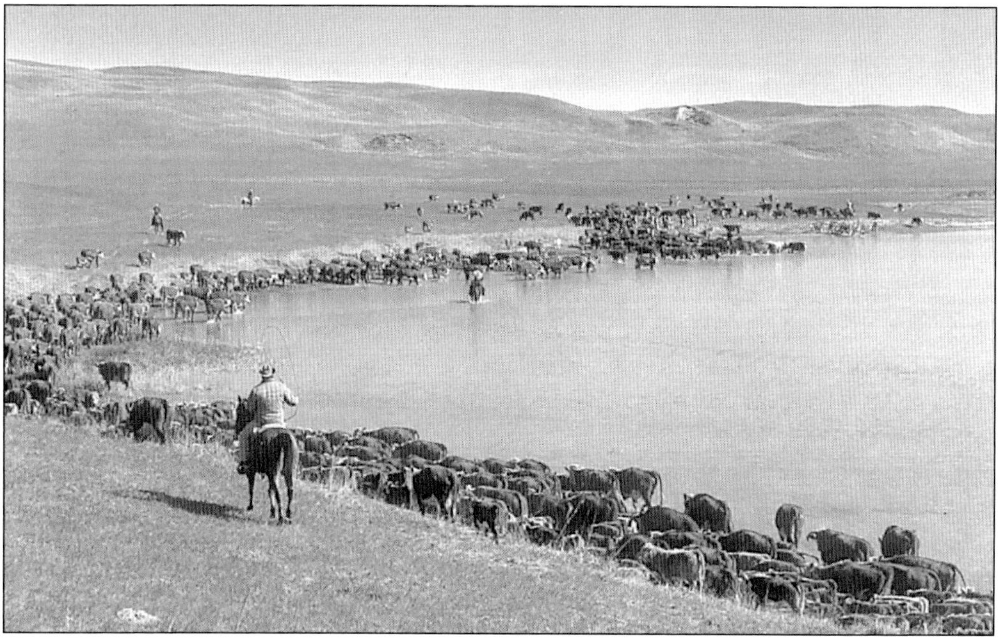

Ranchers had plenty to do before cattle could be taken to market. Winter meant calving. Spring brought the branding season, where herds of calves were marked for ownership. In the fall, cattle were sorted and moved to penned areas, where they waited to be shipped off to local markets. This scene shows Bill Bignell herding cattle on the Hord Ranch east of Alliance.

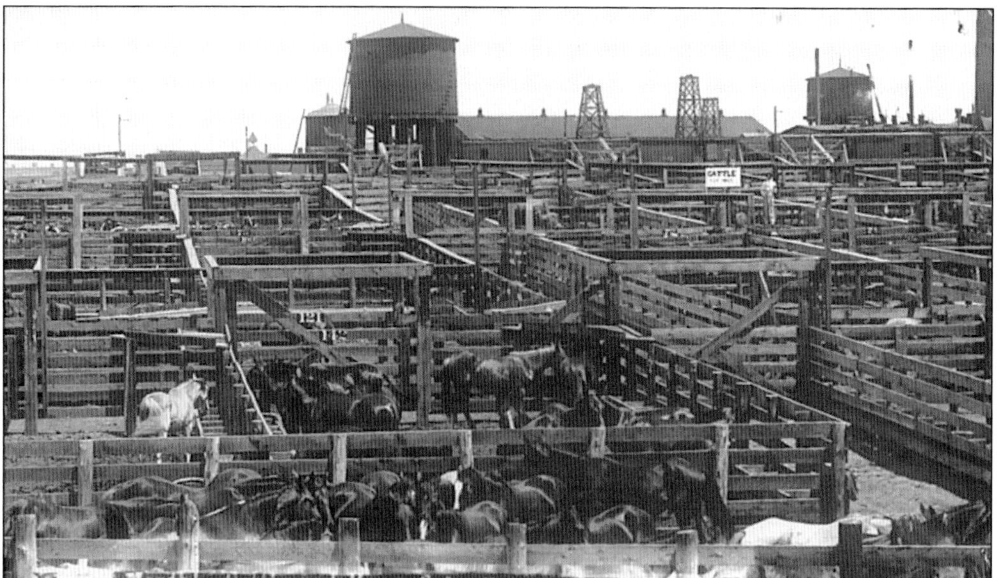

Started by Hans Jaggers and Guy Garrett, the Alliance Livestock held its first sale on April 21, 1939. The yards were always filled to capacity each week, especially in the fall and winter seasons. The Burlington smokestack in the background was torn down several years ago. Closeness to the railroad eventually brought an end to the sale barn. Using the Eminent Domain Statue, the railroad was able to break a 99-year lease when they needed the sale barn land to expand.

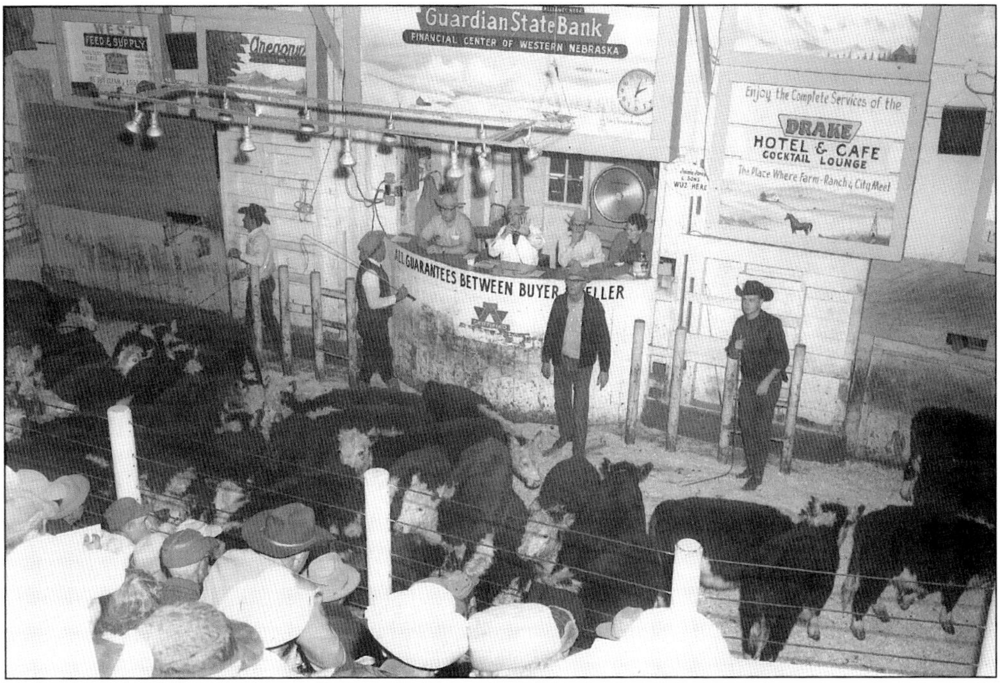

A modern sale ring, seating between five and six hundred ranchers, would wheel and deal for the purchase of over 120,000 heads of stock valued at over $20 million. Hats were tipped to signal ringmen that the hat owner was willing to up the last bid. A restaurant was part of the setup that catered to ranchers all over the Sandhills. Note the advertising for a Feed & Supply store, the Creamery, the Guardian State Bank, and the Drake Hotel.

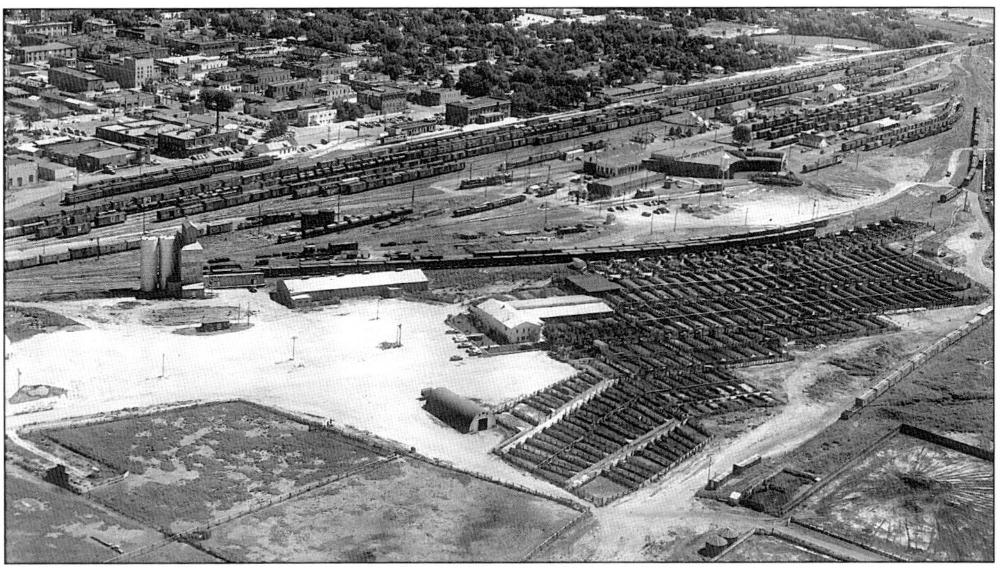

The overall view of the Alliance Livestock Company shows the proximity to the railroad. Holding pens overflowed with the prime beef that helped establish Alliance as the cattle capital of Nebraska. The site was also used by the Alliance Hereford Association for special sales. Some of the last owners include Jack Ressegieu, John Sibbitt, Jack Hunter, and Bill Iodence. The last sale was held December 3, 1976.

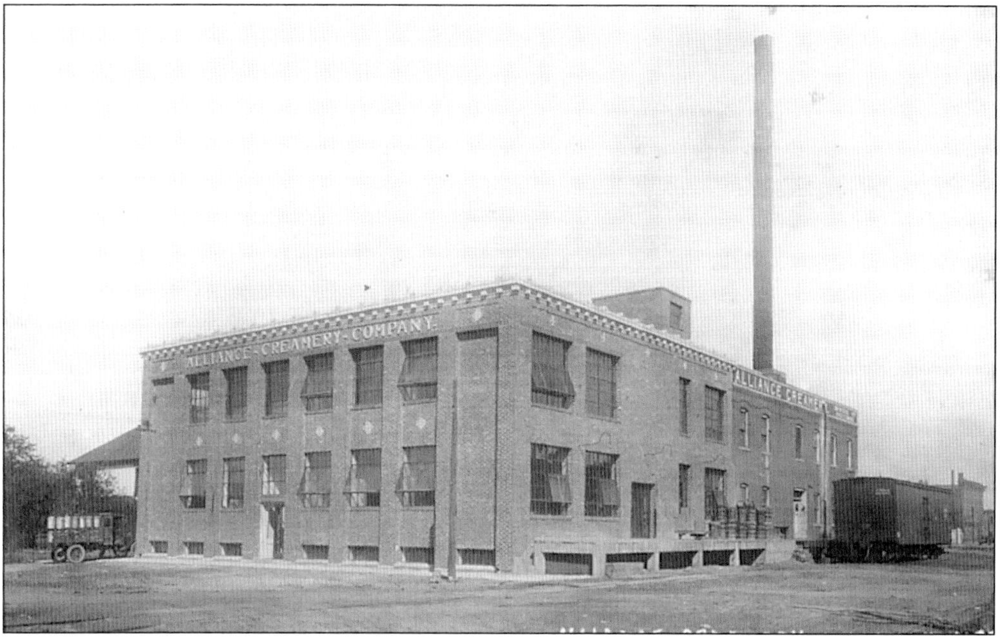

One of the earliest industries was the Alliance Creamery, incorporated in 1907. By 1911, over a million pounds of Diamond A butter were processed from locally produced dairy products. Later they were able to produce up to half-a-million pounds of butter a year. Located next to the railroad for convenient shipping, the $80,000 building employed up to 25 people.

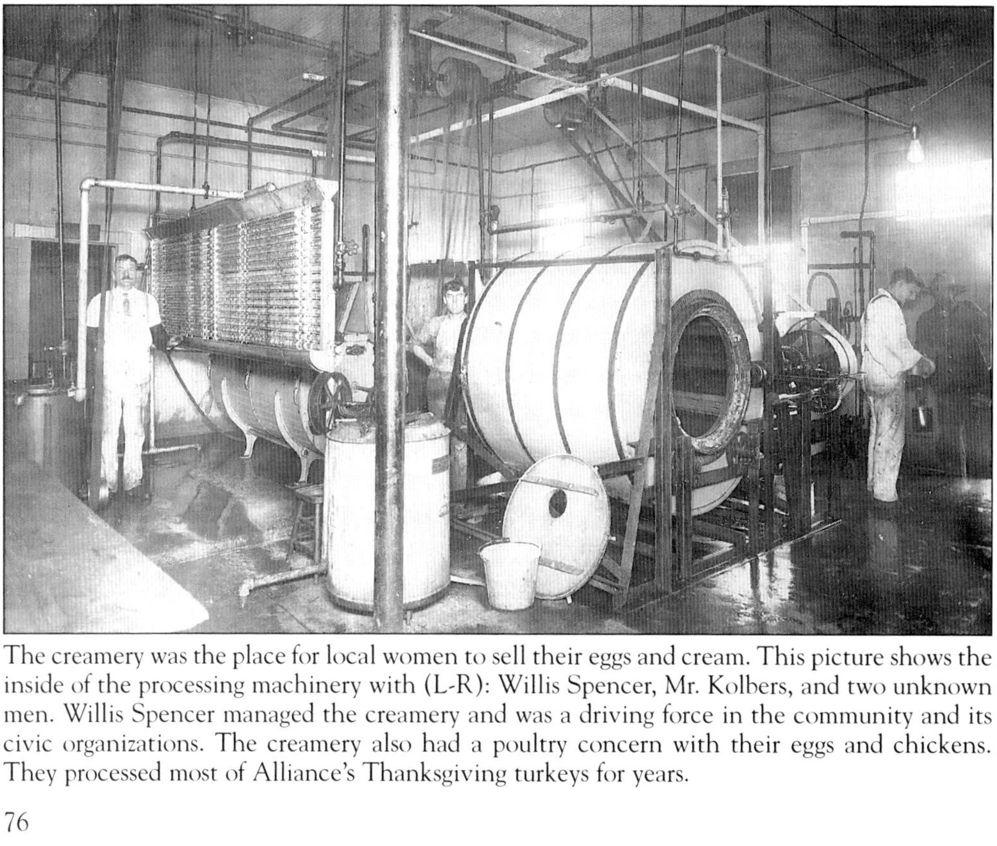

The creamery was the place for local women to sell their eggs and cream. This picture shows the inside of the processing machinery with (L-R): Willis Spencer, Mr. Kolbers, and two unknown men. Willis Spencer managed the creamery and was a driving force in the community and its civic organizations. The creamery also had a poultry concern with their eggs and chickens. They processed most of Alliance's Thanksgiving turkeys for years.

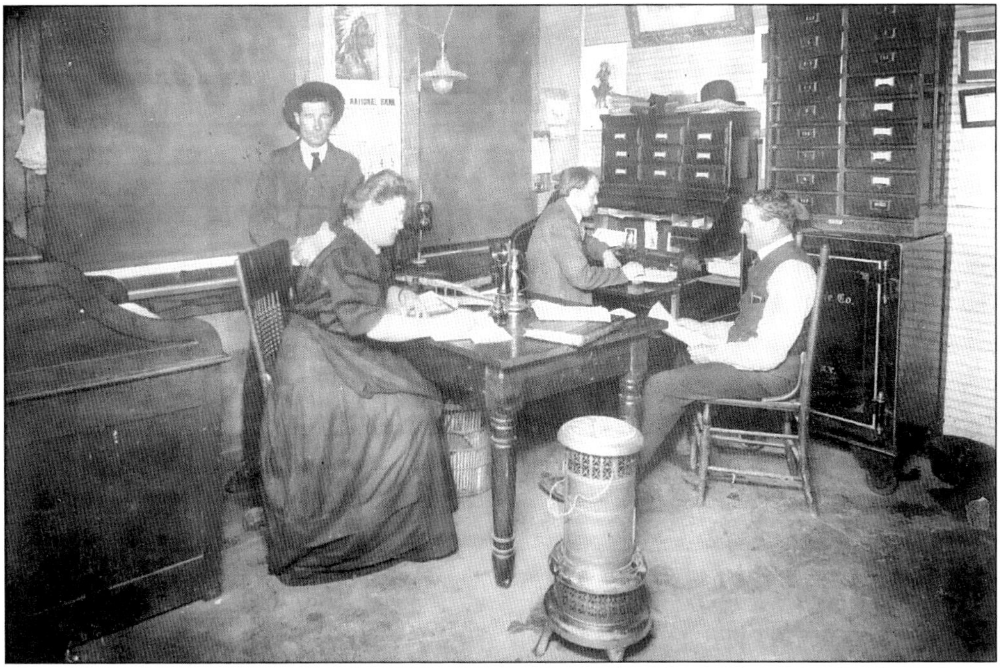

Keeping the books of Alliance Creamery was a major undertaking. The calendar dates this as 1909. From left to right: Link Lowery, Bertha Gregg, Roy Gregg, and Willis Spencer work to keep accounts in order. Every year the creamery sponsored a baseball team for their employees. The machinery came to a stop in the 1950s when the creamery closed. The building sits idle, a tribute to the past with an uncertain future.

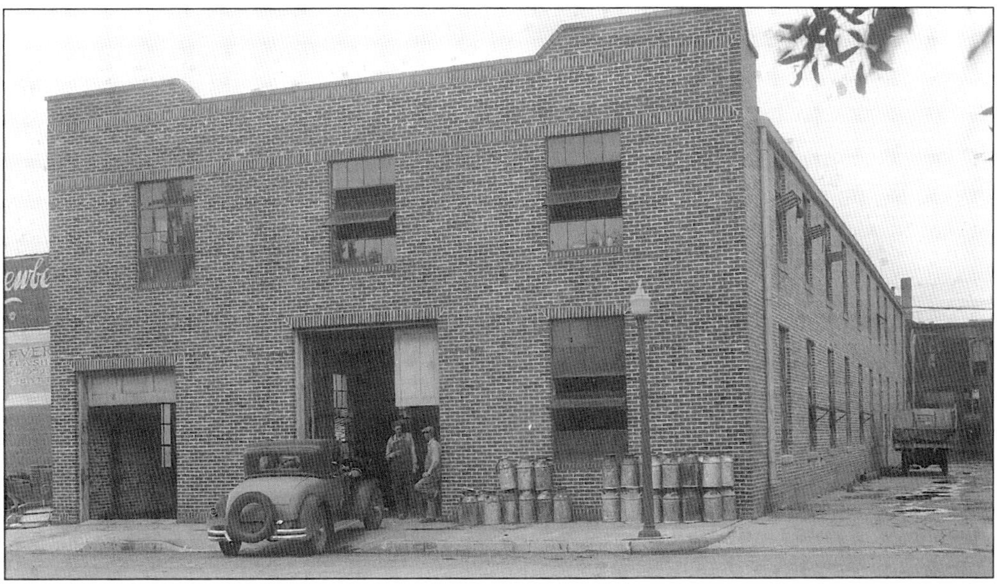

The Newberry Tin Shop, 315 Laramie, now holds the main store for Bernie's Supply. The Tin Shop could fabricate anything from cream cans to chicken candlers. On the left is an elevator large enough to take a car to the second floor. Bernie's Supply is run by Bernie Girard, one of Chenia Newberry's grandsons. Note the stack of cream cans destined for the Alliance Creamery.

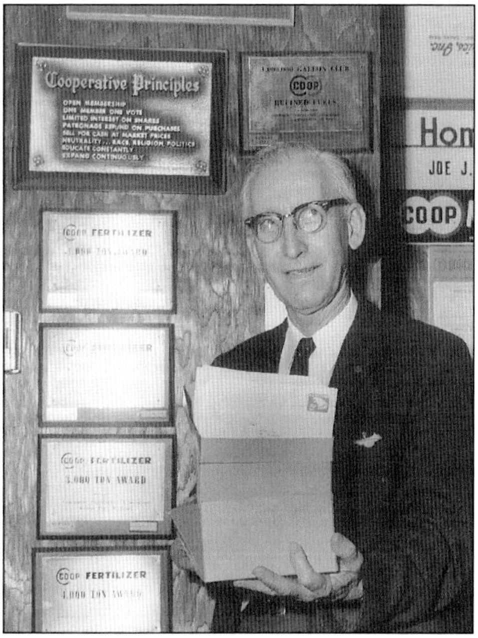

The Alliance Cooperative, now Westco, formed in May 1942, with authorized capitol of $200,000. Joe Kirchner, pictured here, was manager until his retirement. Sons Harold and Richard, and grandsons Joe and Tom, followed in his footsteps of leadership. Today Westco provides many services to Alliance and the farm community. Fertilizer, bulk fuel, car care, a gas station, and an agricultural parts shop have raised the net worth to the about $12 million.

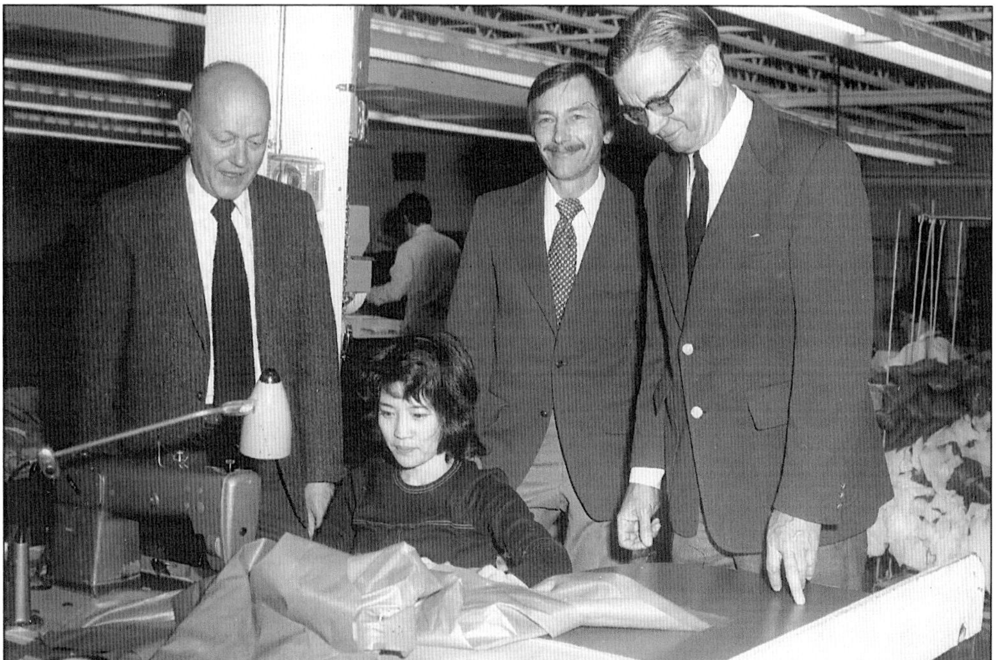

Woolrich started as American Leisure Factory in the former Alliance Creamery building. A new 25,000-square-foot building was built in 1976 in the Alliance Industrial Park. They made sleeping bags, jackets, vests, and other sportswear that were shipped worldwide. Employing over one hundred workers, Woolrich also maintains a retail shop that draws in many Alliance visitors. The factory closed in the 1990s. Farrington's Daughters purchased the building with many future plans.

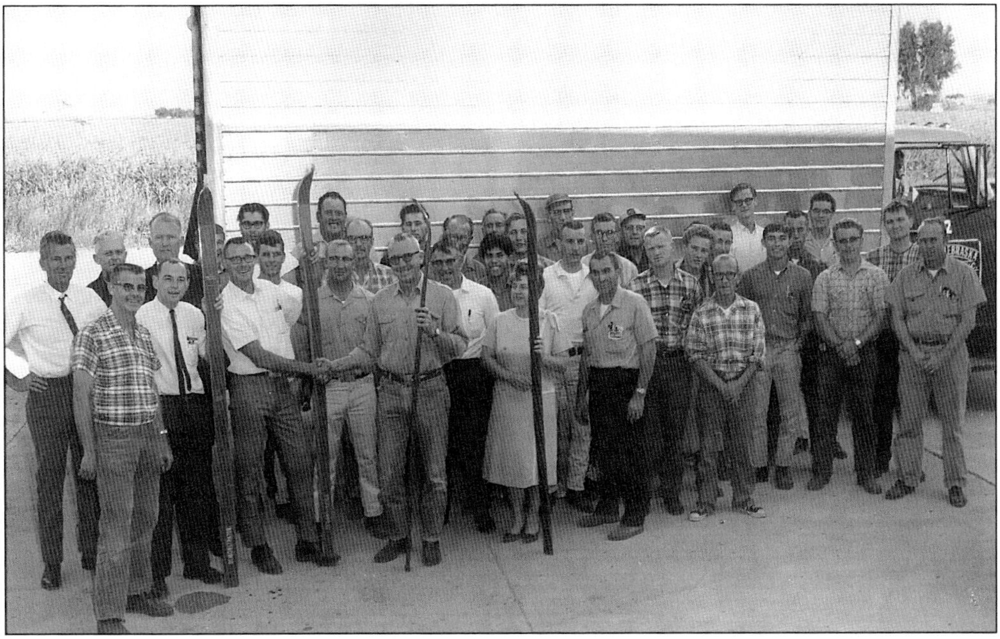

These True Temper workers pose next to a truck loaded with skis made in Alliance. This plant was located in the business industrial site, which was later occupied by Electric Hose & Rubber. Many industries have called Alliance home over the years. One of the most unusual items that was patented and manufactured in Alliance was a Little Sun radiator cover, manufactured by Hartman-Miller Co.

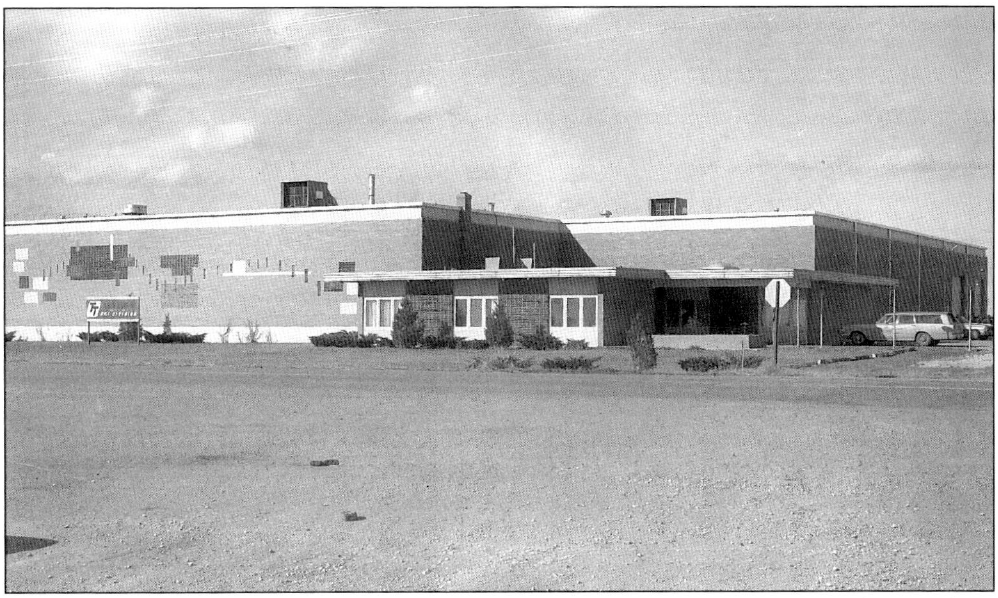

Originally built as True Temper, Dayco is one of Alliance's top five employers. This was built at the Alliance industrial site. Several optimistic-thinking Alliance businessmen had recruited businesses for what they saw as a grand future for Alliance industry. The industrial site houses the former Woolrich (now Farrington's Daughters), Western Potato, Panhandle Rural Electric, and the Nebraska Game Commission.

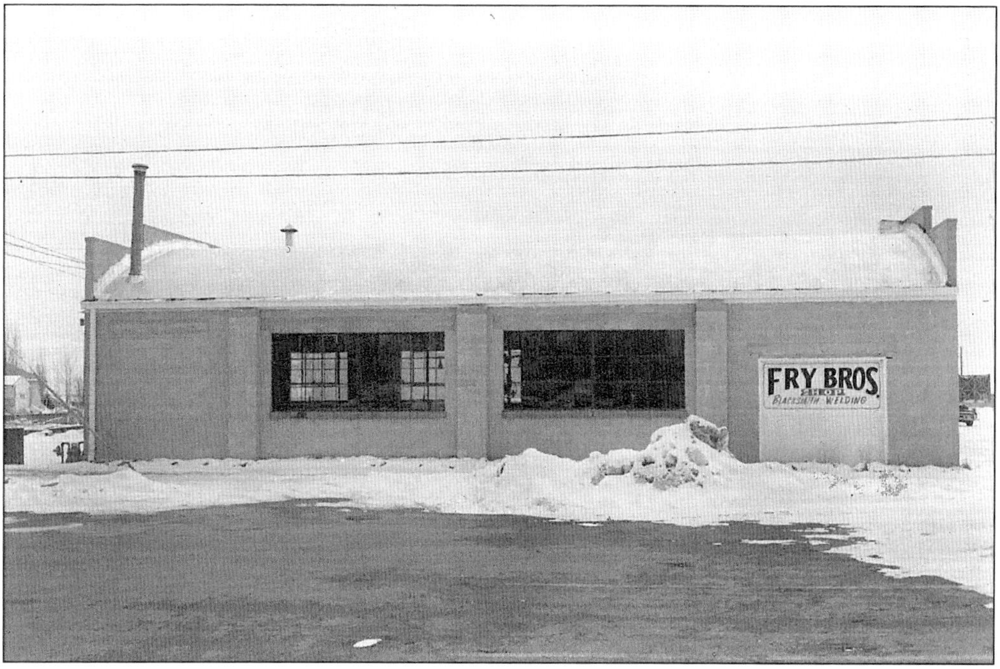

In 1947, Clyde Fry, son of Elmer and Ada Fry, returned from the Army. He and his brother Marvin opened the Fry Bros. Shop at 211 Williamette. They specialized in wrought iron work, sharpening tools, building irrigation equipment, and repairing farm machinery. They served Alliance for over 30 years. Other welding shops included Harley Brooks, Gaines Steel, Tucks, and Berrys.

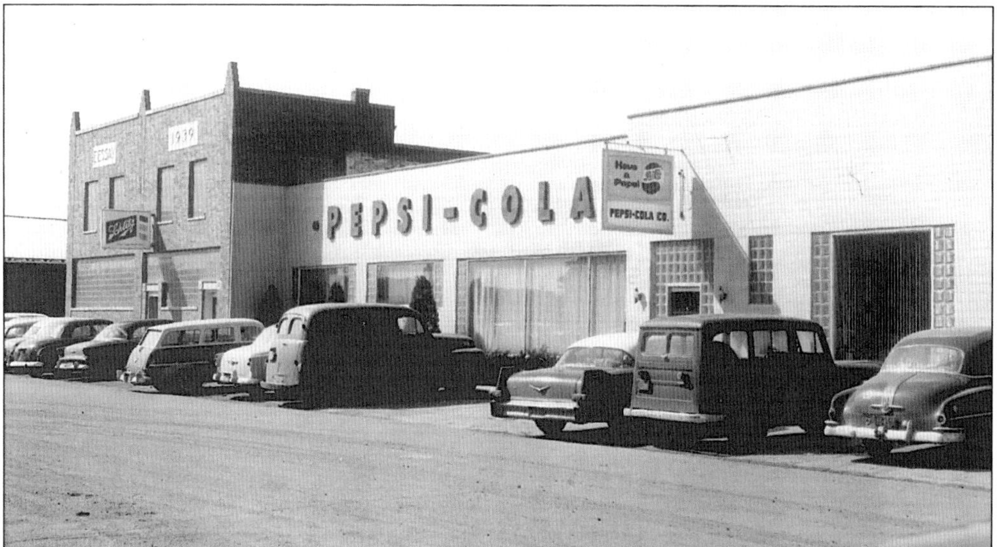

When Elias Essay came to Alliance in 1905, he had been a laborer for the Item Biscuit Company. He started a retail store in 1933, and opened the first wholesale beer distributorship in Western Nebraska. In 1935, he added the Standard Bottling Co., which obtained Pepsi-Cola Franchise charter in 1937. A 12-ounce bottle retailed for 5¢. Now the largest bottler and distributor of soft drinks, it is still a family-run business.

Seven

CITY AT WORK

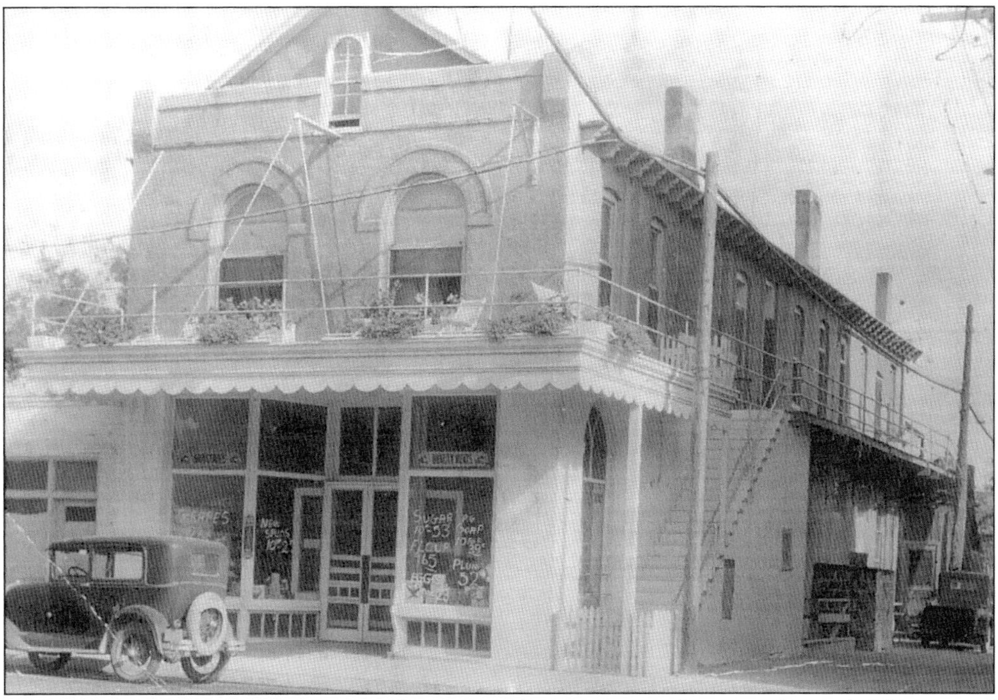

Built in the 1890s at 114 West Fourth Streeet, this was a spot for Saturday night dances and Sunday church services. The First Presbyterians met on the top floor in Bell's Hall. In the 1930s, the top floor was converted into three apartments, called Joe Keegan's Apartments. The bottom floor housed the Food Center Grocery, operated by the Essays. The building was torn down in the 1960s when John Essay, the Food Center proprietor, built at 124 West Fourth.

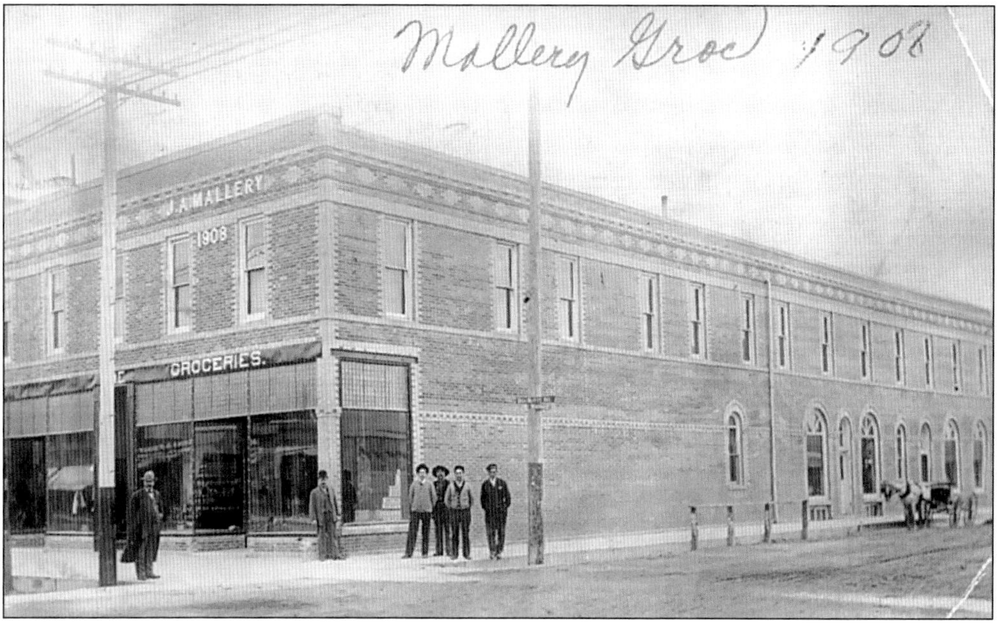

The street sign proclaims Box Butte and Montana Streets, but we know it as 324 Box Butte. Built in 1908 by John Amos Mallory, it housed the Mallory Grocery Store, and later sold to the Stumbaugh's. In later years it housed a Coast to Coast Hardware Store and a book shop. An early ad told shoppers that "Mallory's was the home of Ferndell Brand of Pure Foods." It was torn down in the early 1990s.

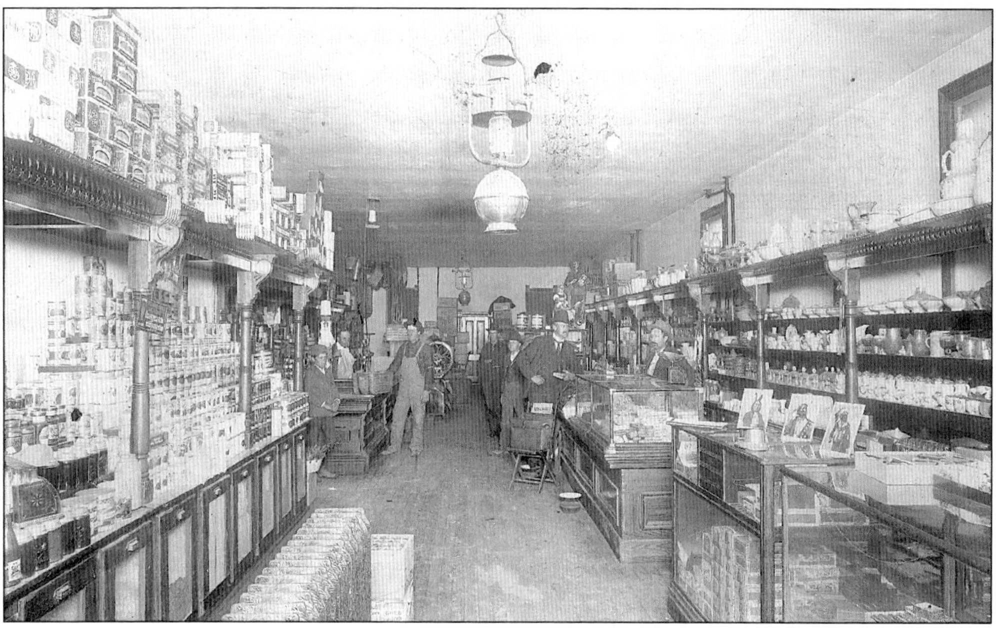

The A.D. Rodgers Grocery Store at 124 Box Butte was a full-service store. A 1915 ad states that the store was "a good place to buy things to eat." They also state that you could phone in your order. How modern! Other grocery stores on Box Butte Avenue included Duncans, Stalos, Essay's Golden Rule, Ryles, Safeway, Piggly Wiggly, and Watsons.

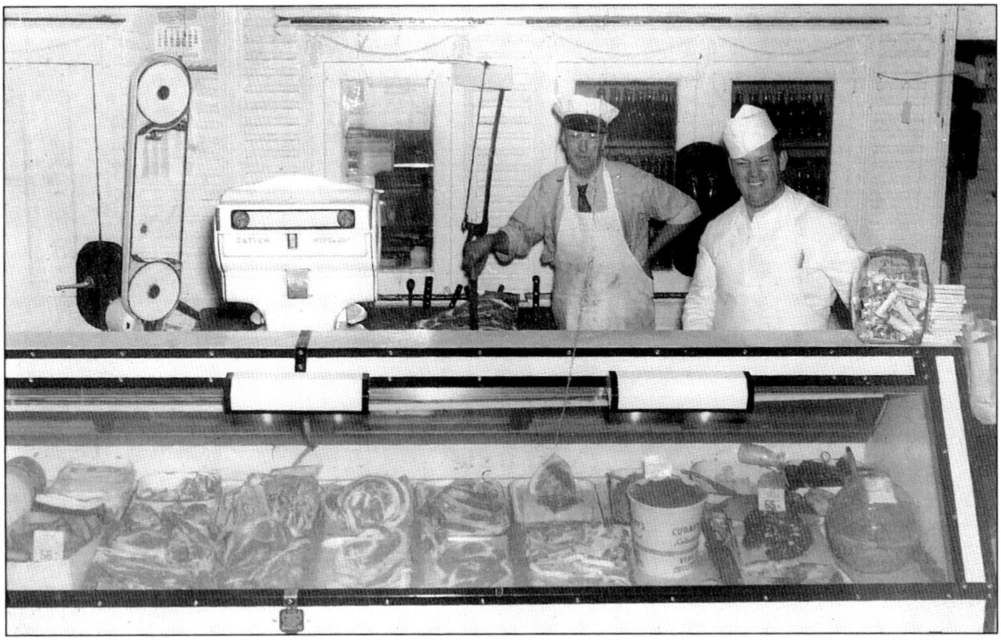

The Palace Meat Market was started in 1909 by Ignatious Herman. Known as "Notsy," he built a slaughterhouse on the east edge of Alliance. They ran it until after WW I, when the family moved to California. Marvin Lee purchased it from the Dole Brothers in 1923. Marvin was famous for his homemade bologna. They delivered groceries for free, with a 1923 Model T. Pictured are Marvin and son Kenneth (Dobby) Lee.

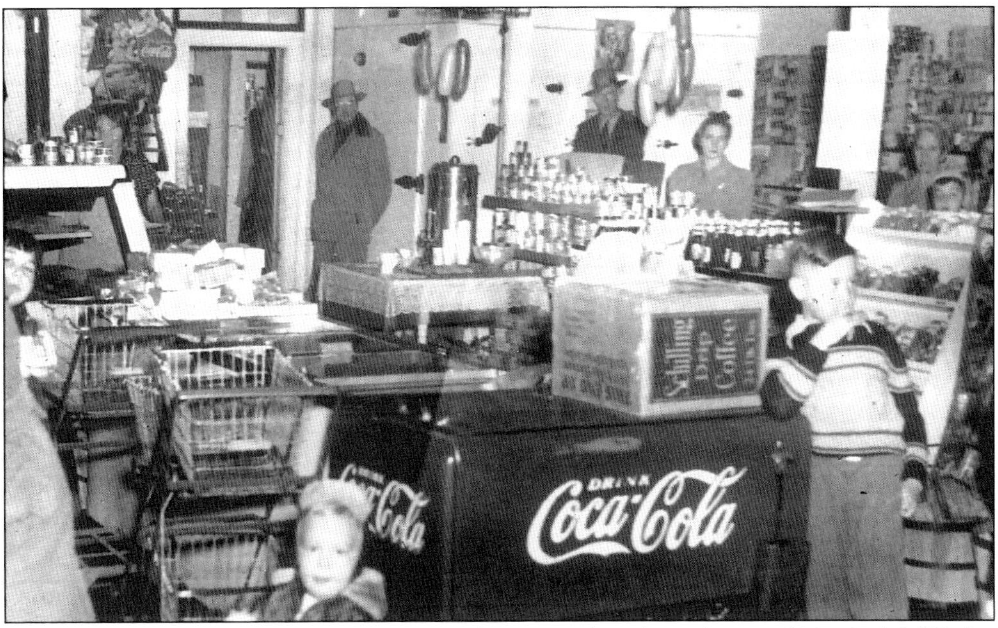

Chimney Town Market was owned by Mr. and Mrs. "Red" Jinks and Mr. and Mrs. Ralph Worley from 1947 to 1949. The grocery store consisted of two housing units combined as one in the Chimney Town housing project east of Flack Avenue. The store was sold to Bailey's at the end of 1949, when both Jinks and Worley moved from the housing project.

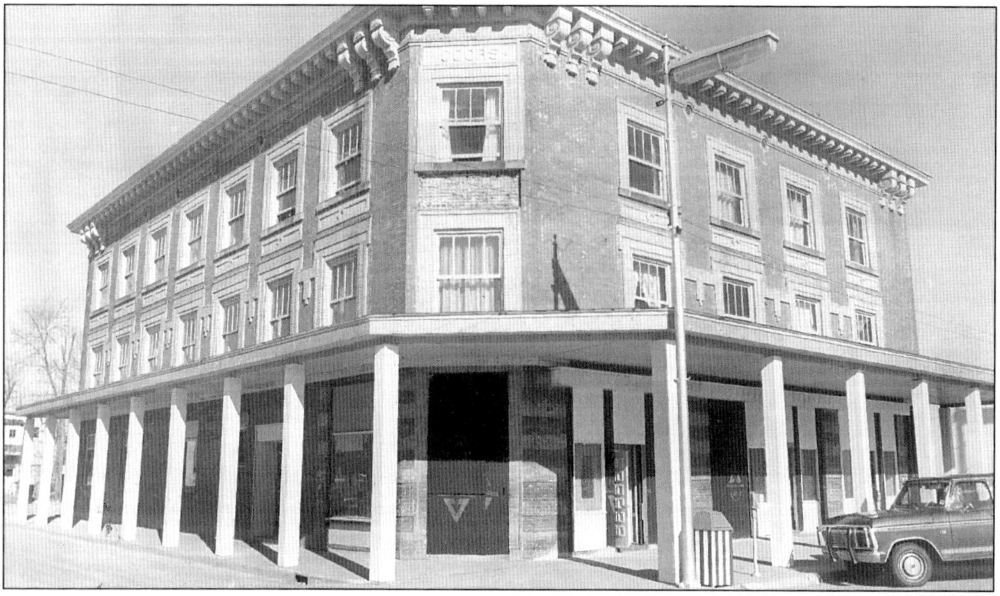

Steam engines headed across the nation, and Adolph Coors built the Alliance Hotel to accommodate early travelers. His vision for a brewery in Alliance didn't happen, but the Alliance Hotel saw much excitement. The proximity to the depot brought many famous guests. The Palm Room was the site for many social gatherings. The Millers ran it from 1908–1945. Coors didn't build his intended brewery because of the hullabaloo stirred up by the Temperance Union.

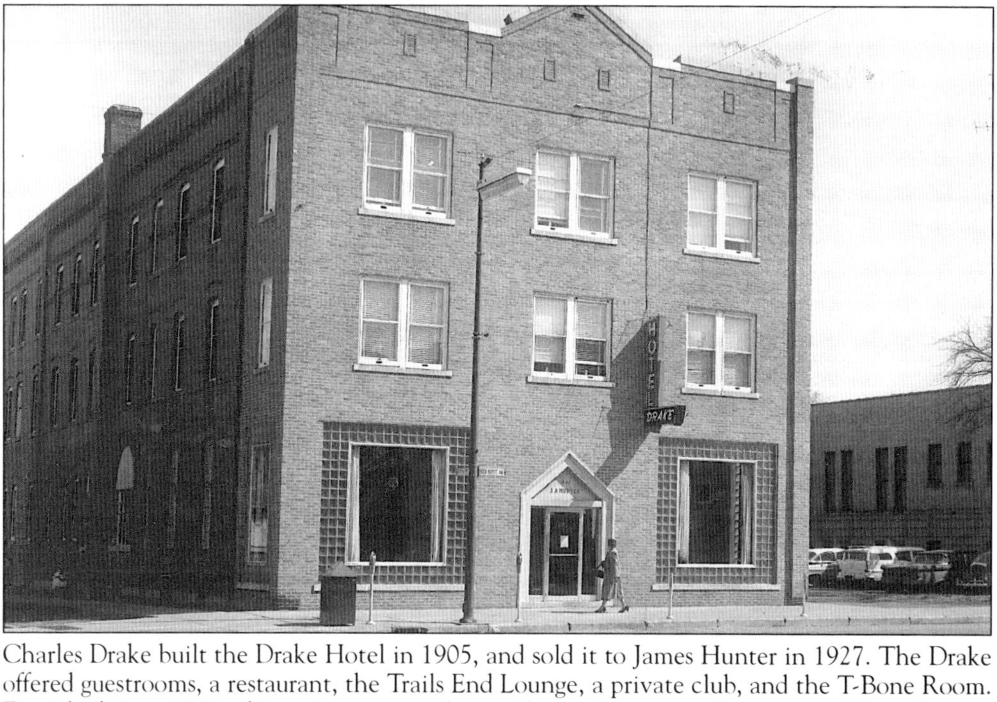

Charles Drake built the Drake Hotel in 1905, and sold it to James Hunter in 1927. The Drake offered guestrooms, a restaurant, the Trails End Lounge, a private club, and the T-Bone Room. Furnished in a 1940s décor, it was complete with an elevator and ramp, used by salesmen to transport their trunks of goods. It closed in 1982, and a shaky future loomed. The new millennium brings hope for the possibility of a fine arts theater.

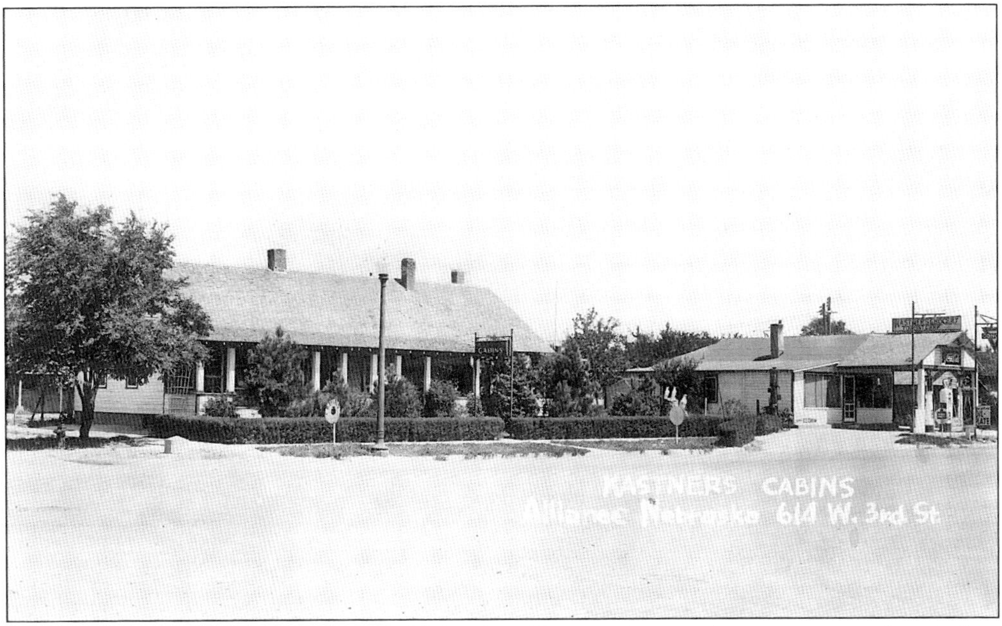

Kastner's Cabins were run by Mr. and Mrs. Leo Kastner. It served as a one-stop shop before convenience stores. The building next to the motel was a grocery/gas station. The cabins were later named the Rainbow Lodge, and were run by Mason Morrills. It still serves as a motel and restaurant for travelers.

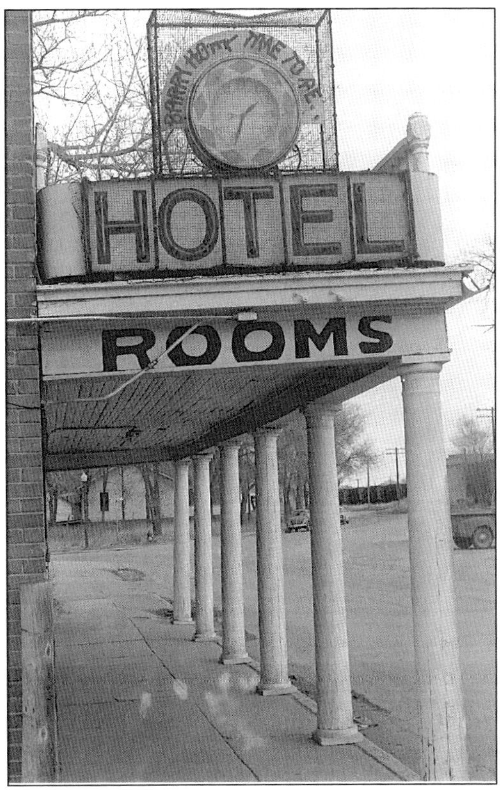

The Barry Hotel was located at 116 East First Street. Its location across from the railroad depot made it a popular place for weary travelers to rest their bones. Built in 1890, the business had a long life until time ran out in June 1987. The look of the Barry Hotel changed very little in all of its years.

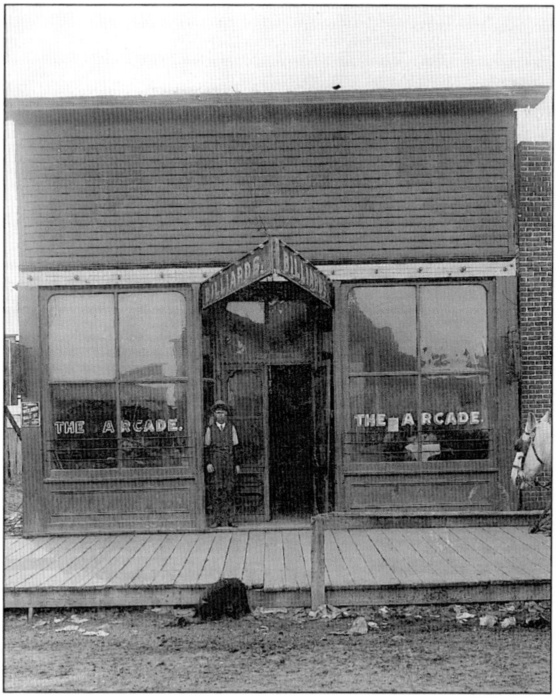

The Arcade Billiard Parlor was a place for early Alliance lads to practice the art of pool. Located on a wooden sidewalk, the Parlor also sported a poster for a coming attraction of "A Wizard of Wall Street." Later, the Joe Smith Snooker Parlor was the local lads' hangout.

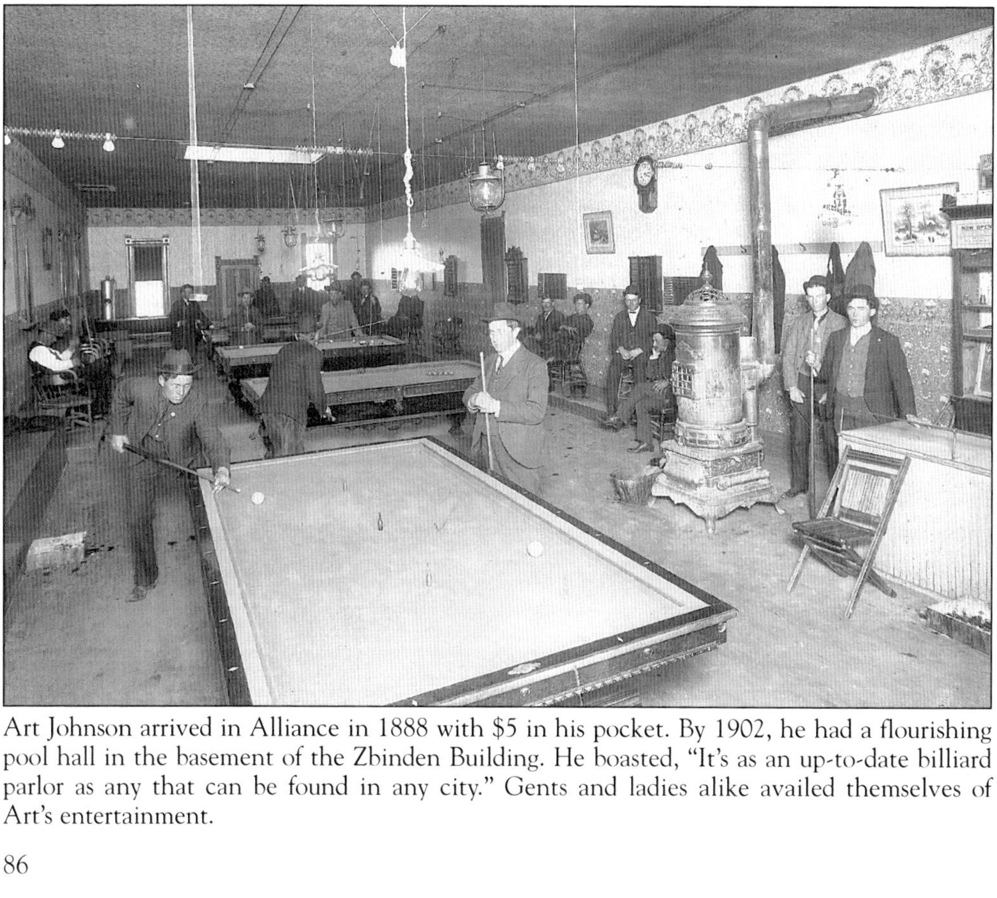

Art Johnson arrived in Alliance in 1888 with $5 in his pocket. By 1902, he had a flourishing pool hall in the basement of the Zbinden Building. He boasted, "It's as an up-to-date billiard parlor as any that can be found in any city." Gents and ladies alike availed themselves of Art's entertainment.

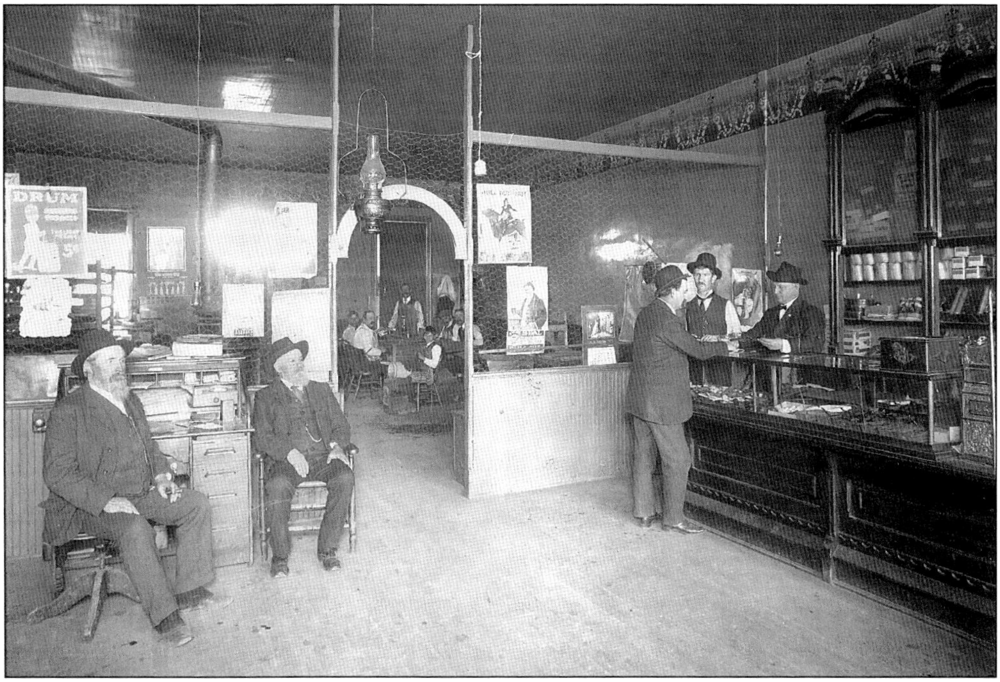

In early Alliance, a good 5¢ cigar was easy to find. There were as many as three cigar factories, with the Buechsenstein factory being on the 200 block of Box Butte in 1904. Louis Buechenstein was also known as the "Father of the Alliance Fire Department" which he helped found in 1891.

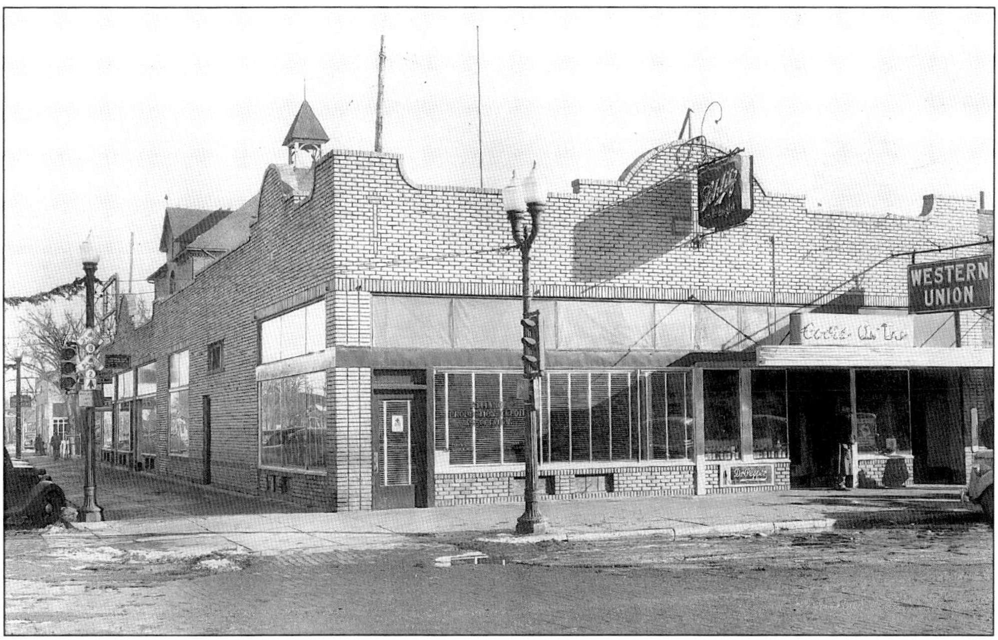

Originally the home of Kings Corner, a local pub, the southeast corner of Third and Box Butte has seen many changes. Production Credit, Western Union, First Federal Savings & Loan, and now Chuck Langford & Associates are some businesses that have called this corner home.

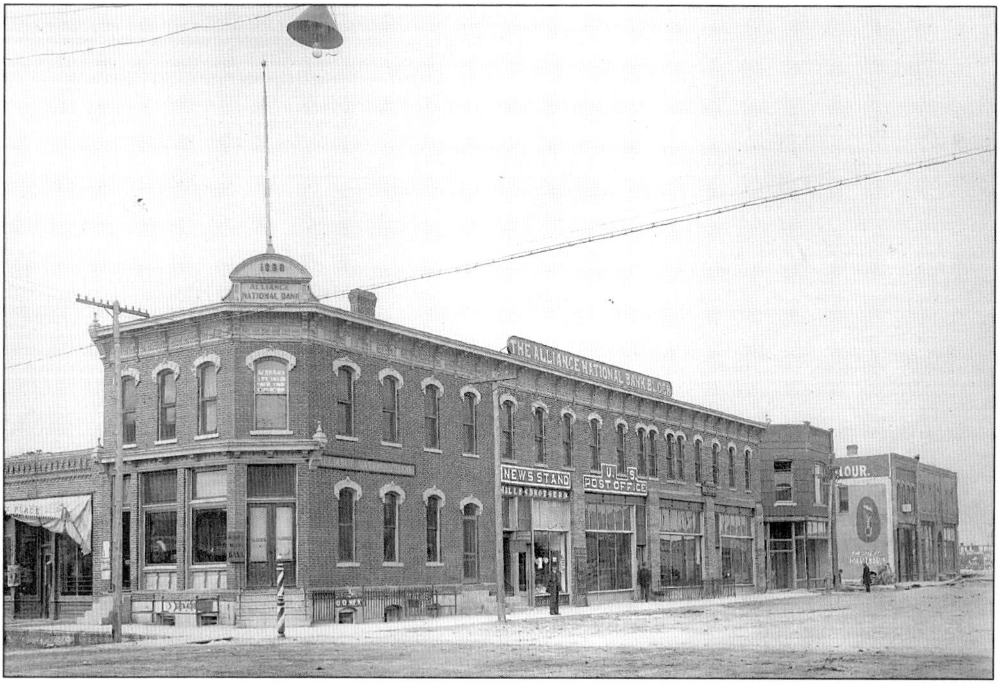

Dr. F.M. Knight founded the National Bank/Bank of Alliance in 1888, at the corner of Wyoming and Box Butte Avenue. The original structure was rebuilt after an 1893 fire, and later the bank moved across the street. In 1966, a new building at Third and Laramie was built which still flourishes today. The bank remained in the Knight family until the mid 1990s. Note the many businesses that shared that second building.

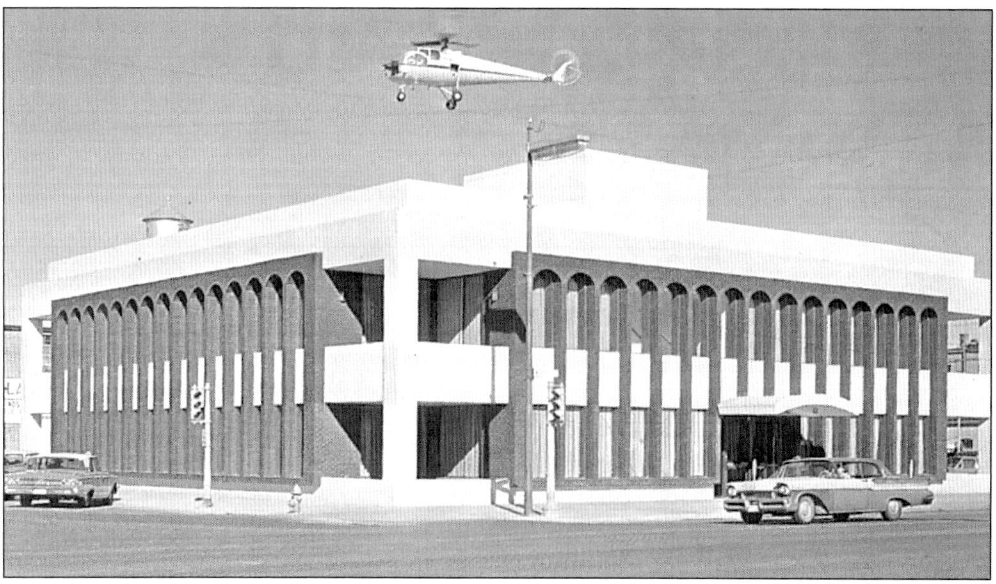

The new Alliance National Bank was completed at Third and Laramie on August 15, 1966. A unique feature of a heliport on the roof prompted the advertising slogan, "Walk in, drive in or fly in for all your banking needs." The bank has been in continuous business since 1888, now named First National Bank.

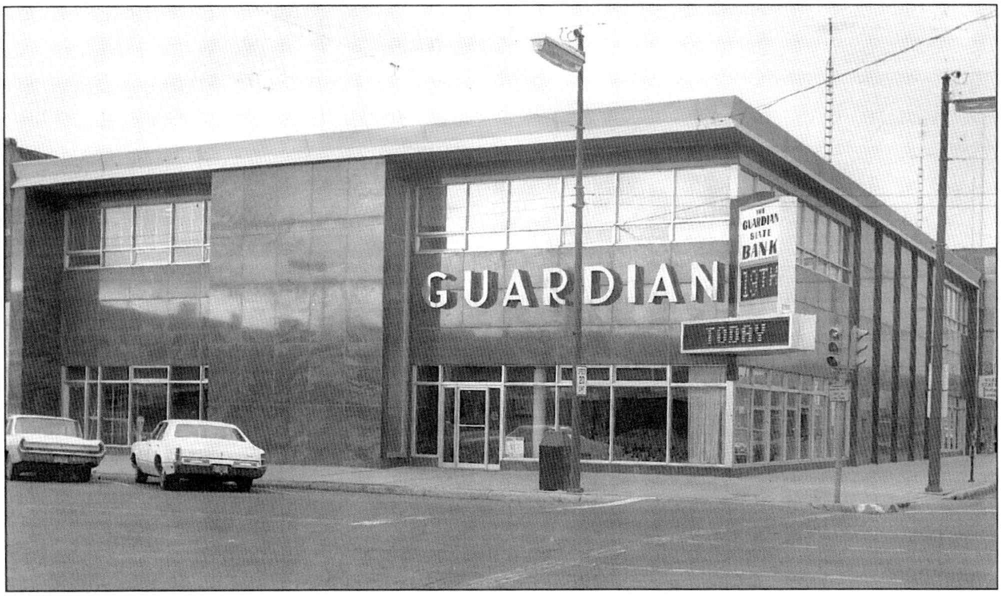

The Guardian State Bank at Third and Box Butte was built on the site of the original Bank of Alliance. It was built July 14, 1919, as a successor to the business of the Guardian Trust Co., which was started in 1916. Arthur J. Abbott, and sons of Hyannis, assumed ownership in 1927. In the 1980s, the name was changed to Abbott Bank, and today it is known as Community First National Bank.

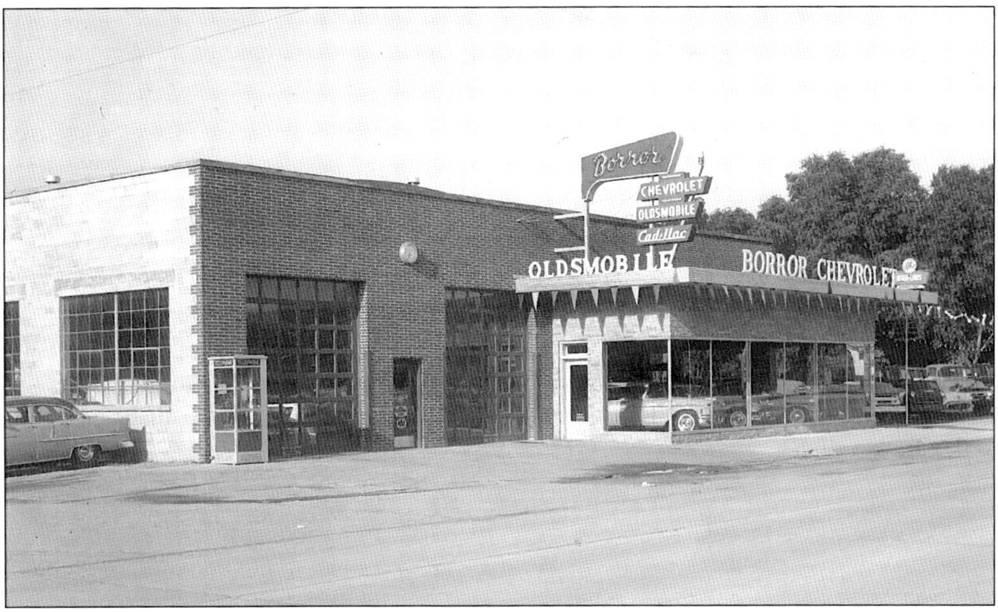

Car dealers have changed many times over the years. The Keeler Coursey Garage, the Lowery-Henry Garage on Box Butte, Dobson Dodge, Cover-Jones, A.H. Jones, and many others catered to the transportation needs in Alliance. This photo shows the Borror Chevrolet business on East Third Street. Later, names like Campbell, Masid, and Wegner were associated with the Chevrolet line. Wegners closed in the mid-1990s, and the building is used by the BNSF as a training center.

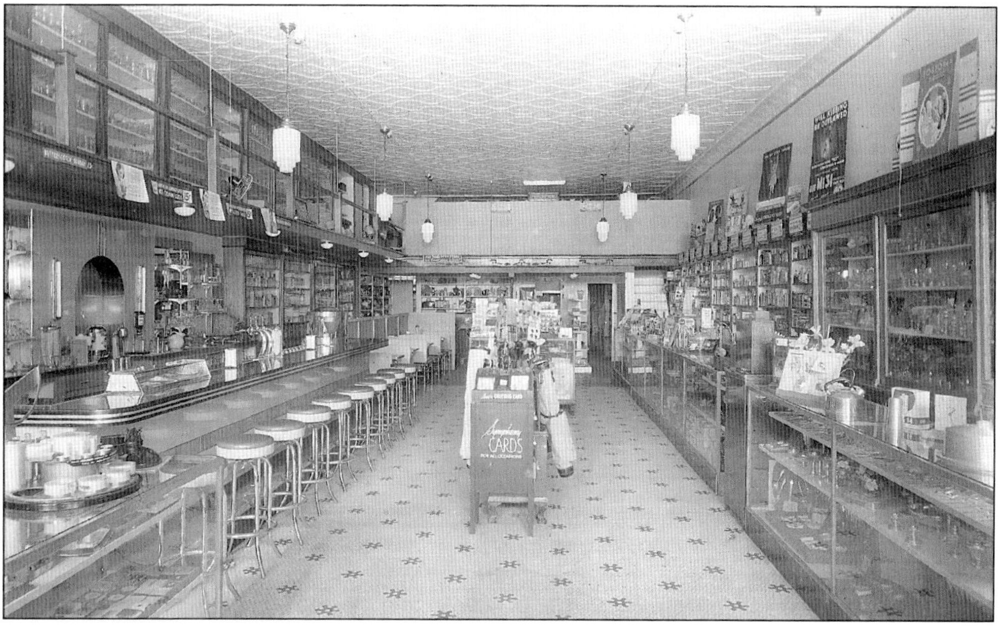

The Holsten Drug Store was started in 1892. When Fred Holsten bought the business from H.C. Akin, located at Fourth and Box Butte, it only carried jewelry. In 1898, he invested in a drug stock and moved to 316 Box Butte. Owen Farrington later took over and served as druggist until the close of business in 1968. A luncheonette was also available at the time this photo was taken.

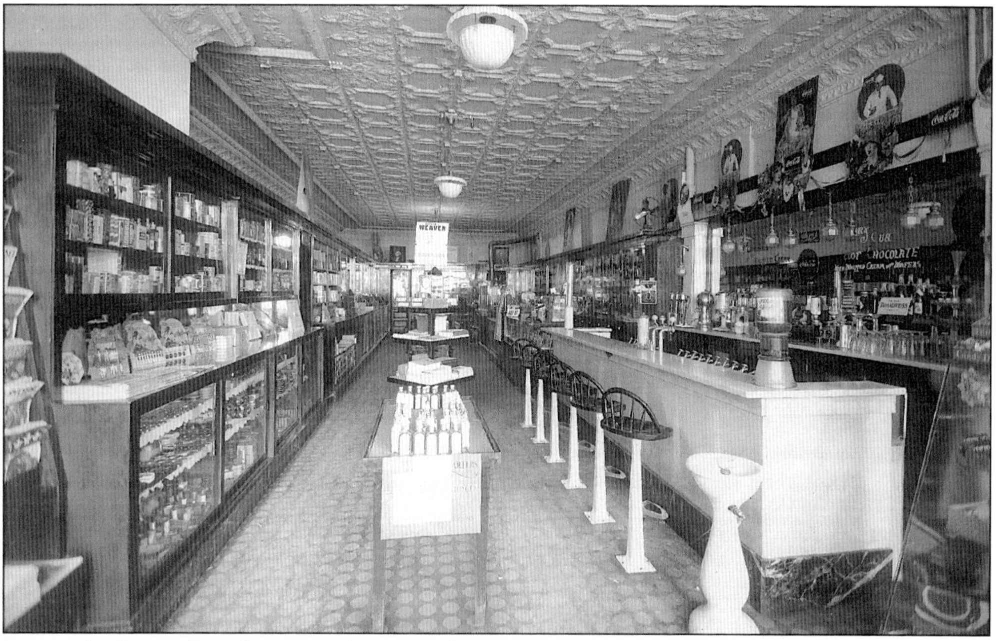

Harry Thiele purchased a going drug store business in 1902, and later bought out W.O. Barnes retail jewelry store next door. The name Thiele was now associated with both. In the late 1940s, Harlan Gorder invested in the business with Mr. Thiele. "Swede" V.E. Lierk, son Charles, and Charles' wife Ellen combined both stores after phasing out the jewelry. It now carries the name Thiele Pharmacy & Gifts.

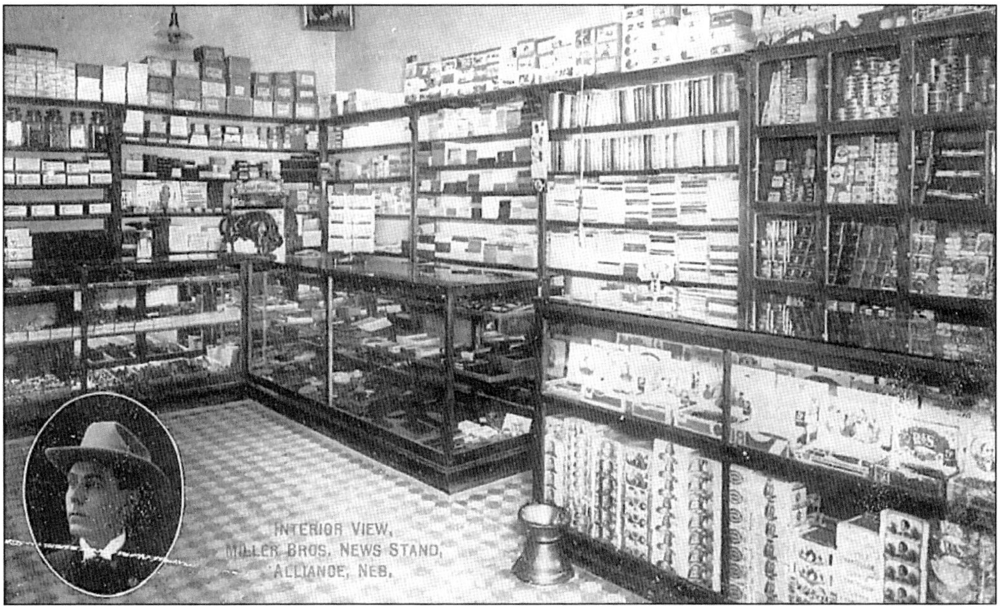

J.B. Miller and his brother were the owners of the Postoffice News Stand and Confectionery, one of the most creditable institutions of its kind. It had all the periodicals and novels of the day, and most of the great dailies of this continent. Also kept on hand was a fresh line of confectionery, nuts, popcorn, and other dainties. Miller Brothers also owned a furniture store, and J.B. was a representative of Old Line Bankers Life Insurance Company.

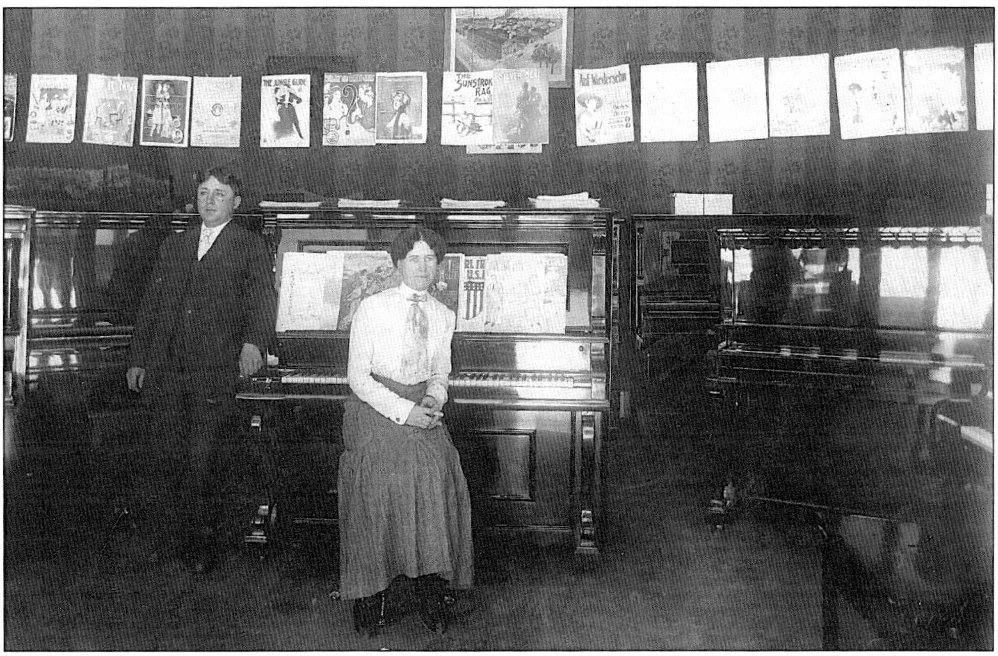

John and Minnie Wiker were two of Alliance's most musical residents. They ran a local shop on Box Butte Avenue. Minnie played for many local dances and other occasions, and also was part of the Spacht Orchestra. These early day musicians brought a touch of culture to the oasis called the Sandhills.

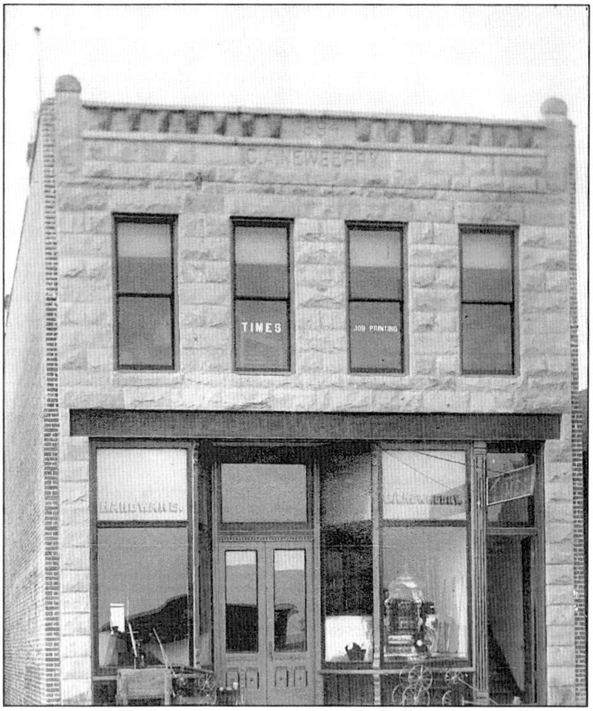

After the 1893 fire, Chenia Newberry rebuilt his brick building at 312 Box Butte. The *Times Herald* had one of its many homes upstairs, and Newberrys was on the main floor. Chenia later moved to the new 402 Box Butte building in 1914. The *Times* moved to the Ellis building at 423 Box Butte, and in 1930 moved again to their present location at 114 East Fourth. This building still stands as a retail store in downtown Alliance.

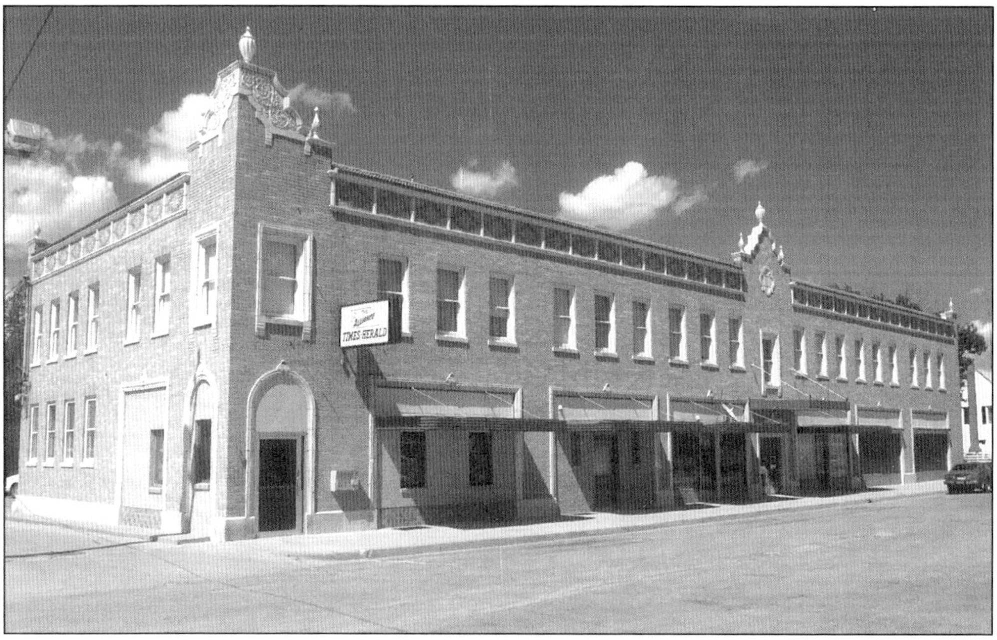

In 1930, Ben Sallows felt a move was in order for the *Alliance Times Herald*. He commissioned C.C. Coursey as the architect and built at 114 East Fourth Street. The cream-colored brick with terra cotta trim was very unique. Urns adorned the roofline. An unusual entrance in the southwest corner made this building a visual delight. Medical offices of the Copsey Clinic were upstairs for many years.

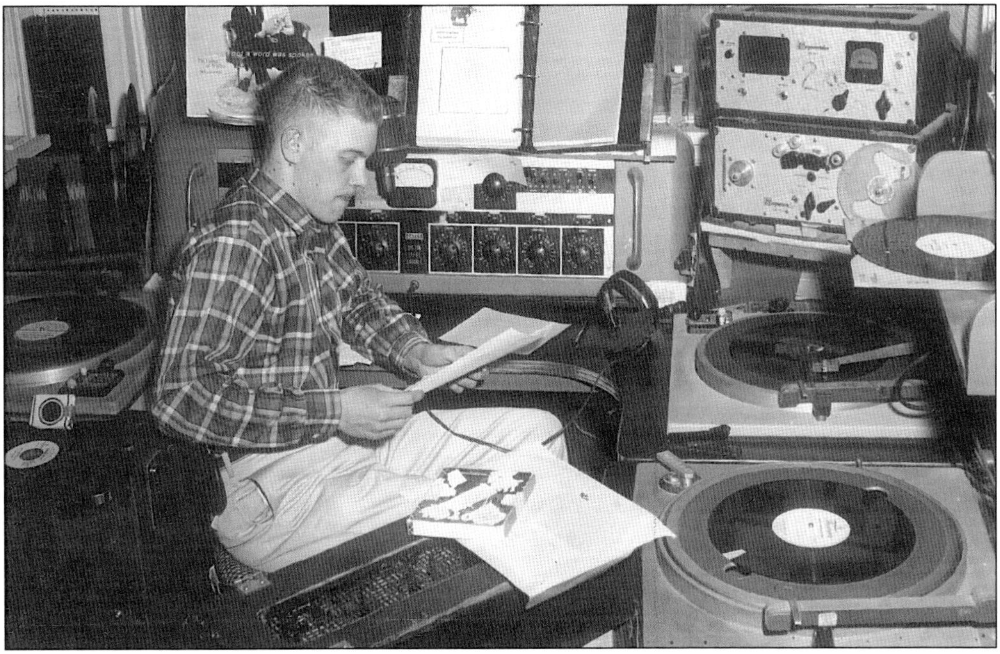

Over the 50-year history, there were many KCOW employees. Don Gill went from station manager to broadcasting Nebraska Cornhusker Radio for ten years. After that, he spent a long career in public television. In this picture, disk jockey Skip Stevenson spins albums while reading news clips. He went on to star on *Real People* on T.V. The albums, album cover, and Lucky Strike cigarettes date the picture.

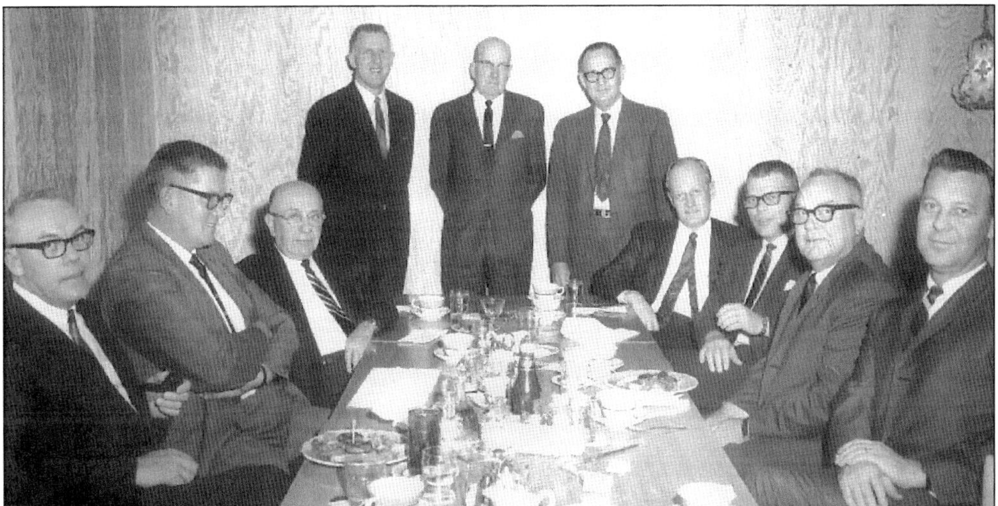

The exchange of KCOW Radio from Sandhills Broadcasting Company to Kloe, Inc. took place in the Drake Hotel private dining room in 1966. The details of the exchange were determined over lunch with a handshake to seal the deal. An official written contract was not even considered. (L-R): Bauman, Metz., McKibbin, Gill, Gregory, Beach, Schmidt, Cover, Jeter, Melia. KCOW Radio went on the air in February 1949. Today, known as Eagle Communications and teamed with Double Q Country (KAAQ and KQSK), it is an employee-owned operation.

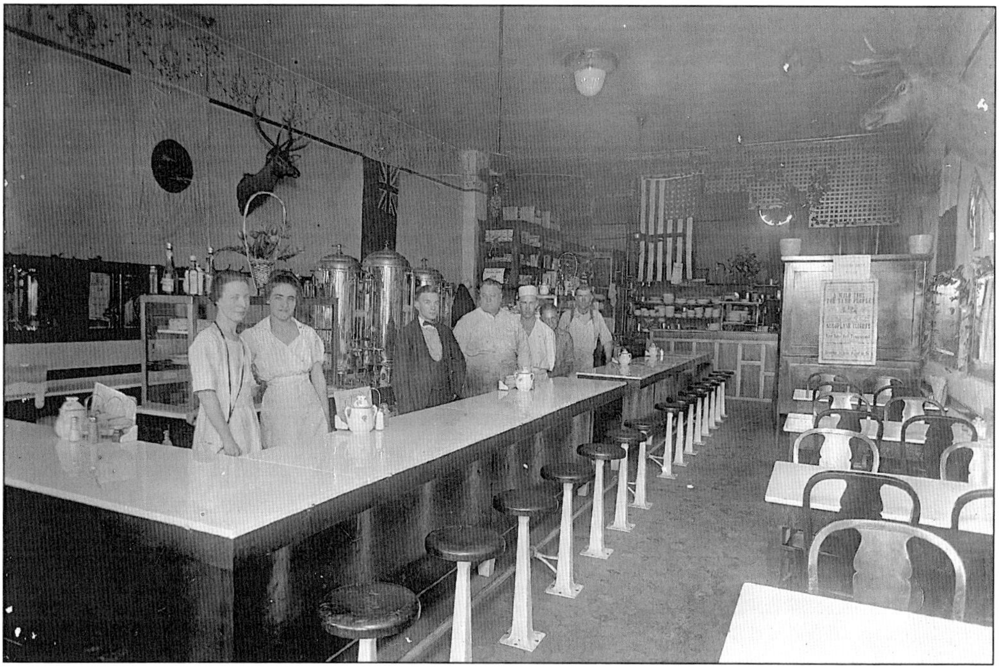

This café in early 1900 Alliance was probably in the 200 block of Box Butte. As the cheerful crew lined up for this photo, one has to wonder if the diners took offense to the mounted animal heads over the food or table area. The poster in the back tells of a coming "Aeroplane Flight" show. Framed and decorated mirrors took the place of windows on the right side.

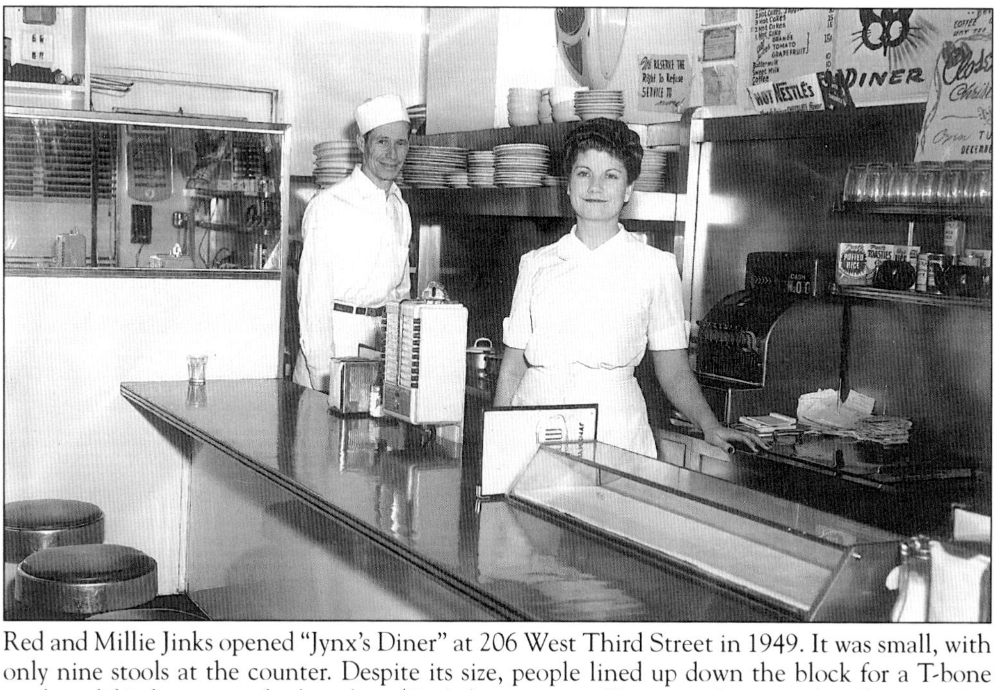

Red and Millie Jinks opened "Jynx's Diner" at 206 West Third Street in 1949. It was small, with only nine stools at the counter. Despite its size, people lined up down the block for a T-bone steak and fried potatoes for less than $3. A large piece of homemade pie and coffee was 20¢. Sold in 1951, the building was moved to Mullen, Nebraska. Note the jukebox on the counter.

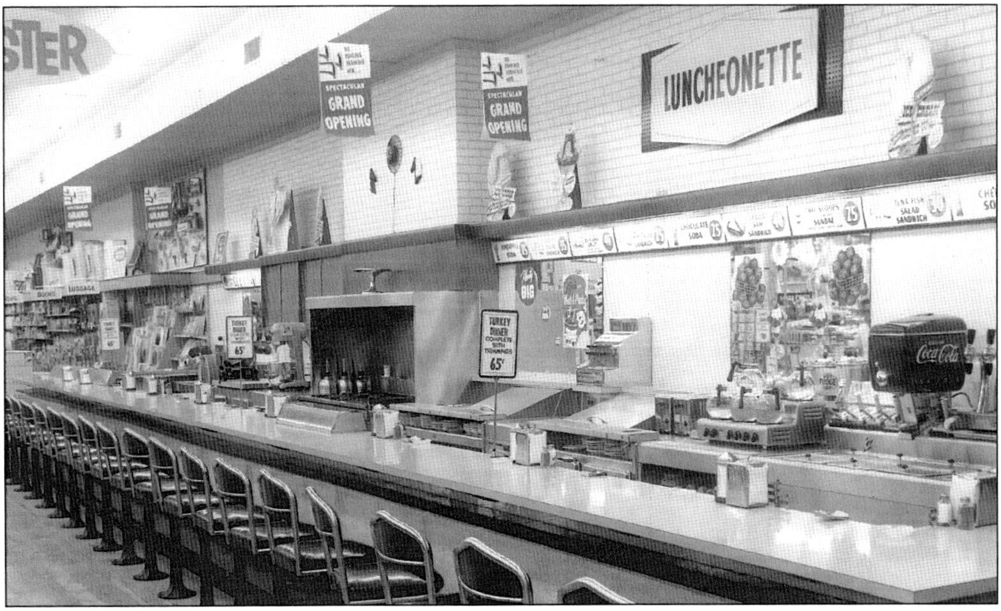

Luncheonettes were very popular in many retail stores. This counter in the local Hested's Variety Store at 310 Box Butte was a common eatery for everyday folks. The sign proclaims a turkey dinner with all the trimmings for 65¢, or a chocolate soda for 25¢. This photo was taken in 1957. The building was built in 1903, with two stories in front and one in back. The upstairs had a dance studio, photographer, and offices.

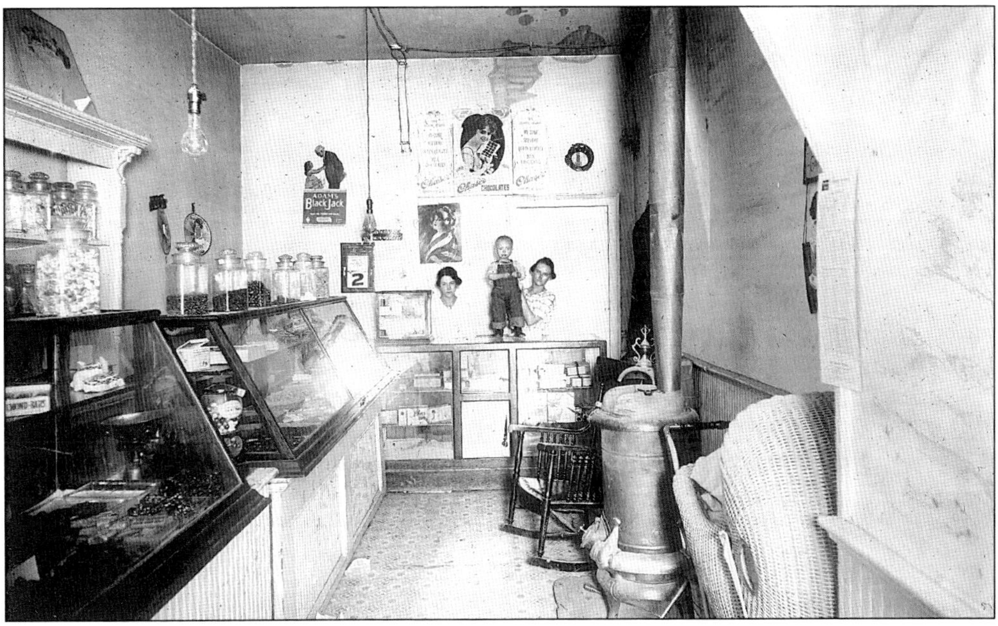

The Sugar Bowl was a popular candy store in 1914. In 1920, Visna Watteyne Steinman purchased the business, relocated, and renamed it The Kandy Snap. Pictured here are (L-R): LaVelle Watteyne Rodgers, Fritz Steinman, and Visna Watteyne Steinman. Visna's son Jim bought the business and continued the fine tradition of making confections until 1955. It was then bought by Eloise Hill who kept the candy pots boiling until 1976.

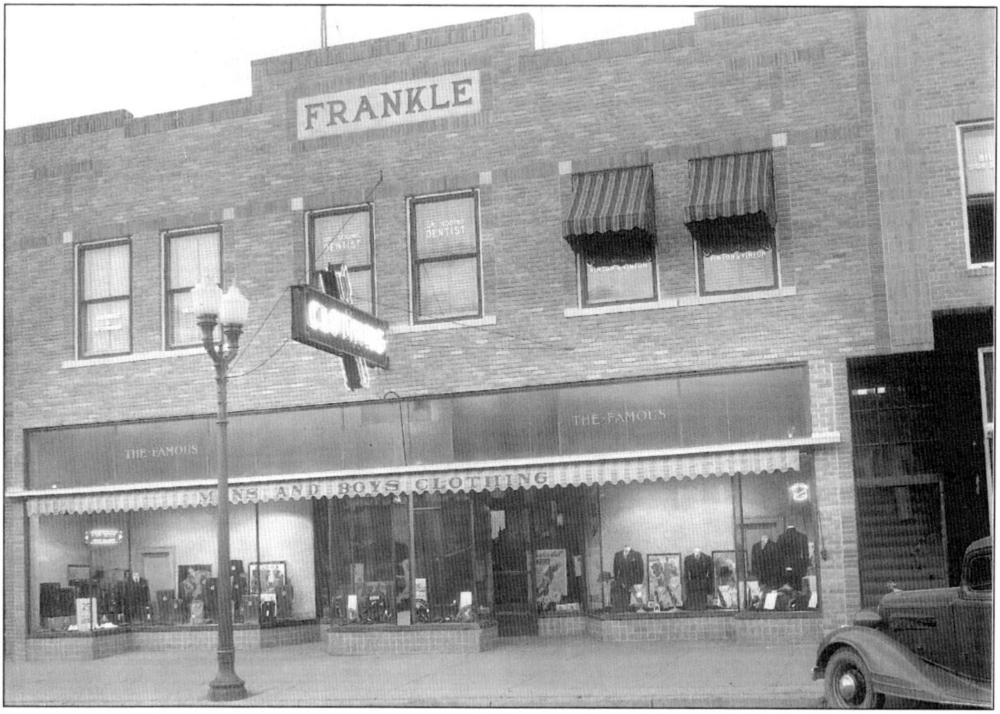

Marcus Frankle started the Famous Clothing House in 1902 at 307 Box Butte, which was constructed out of local brick made by George Fox. Percy Cogswell, managed the store after Frankle's death and J.W. (Hook) Keebaugh and Edward Knight purchased the store in 1952 with other later partners. The store ran continuously as a clothing store for 80 years, until it closed in 1982. Early ads state: "The largest establishment between Lincoln and Billings; selling exclusively men's and boy's wearables."

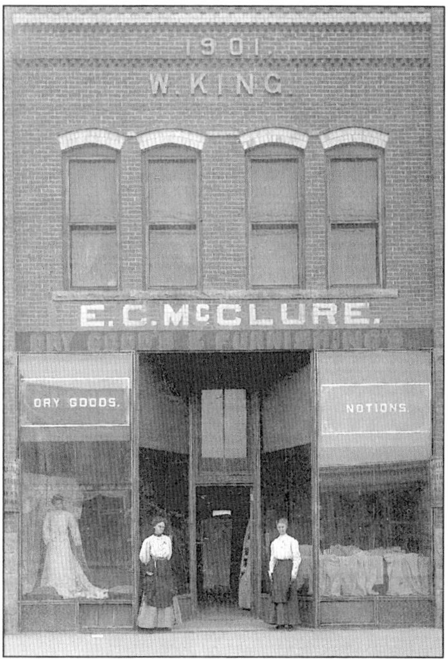

E.C. McClure had a dry goods store in the King Building. Dry goods stores were the old time equivalent of today's ready-to-wear and department stores. The clerks, ready to serve you, were (left to right): Marie Rodger and Miss Mosher.

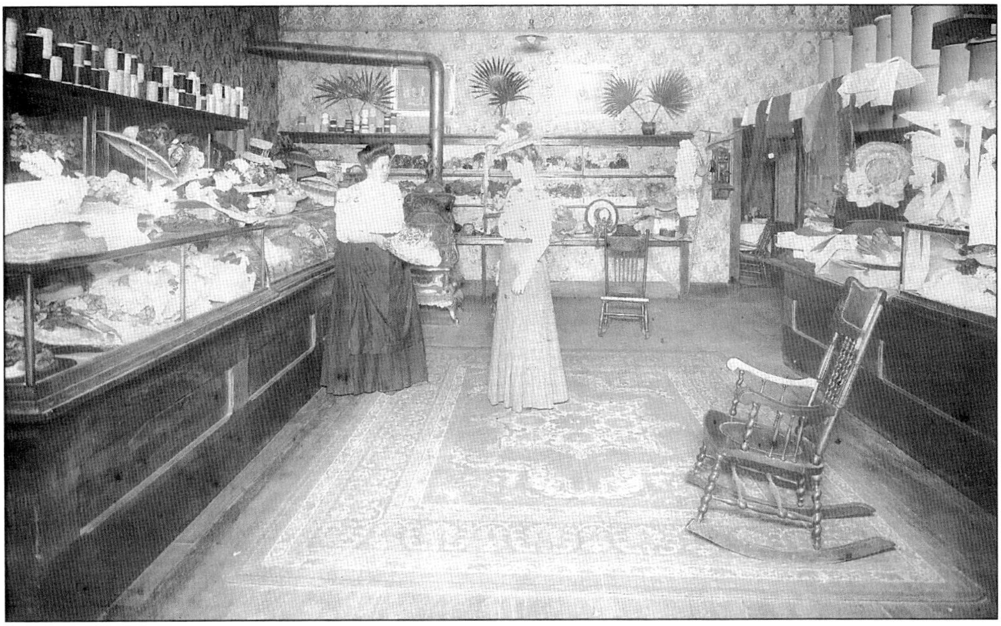

An up-to-date milliner, Mrs. Holdredge had a decked out shop that would have pleased any turn-of-the-century lady. Her store was on 411 Box Butte, where the post office sits now. Here she is shown selling a fancy confection to Mrs. Hacker. The sturdy pioneer women were still conscious of proper fashion.

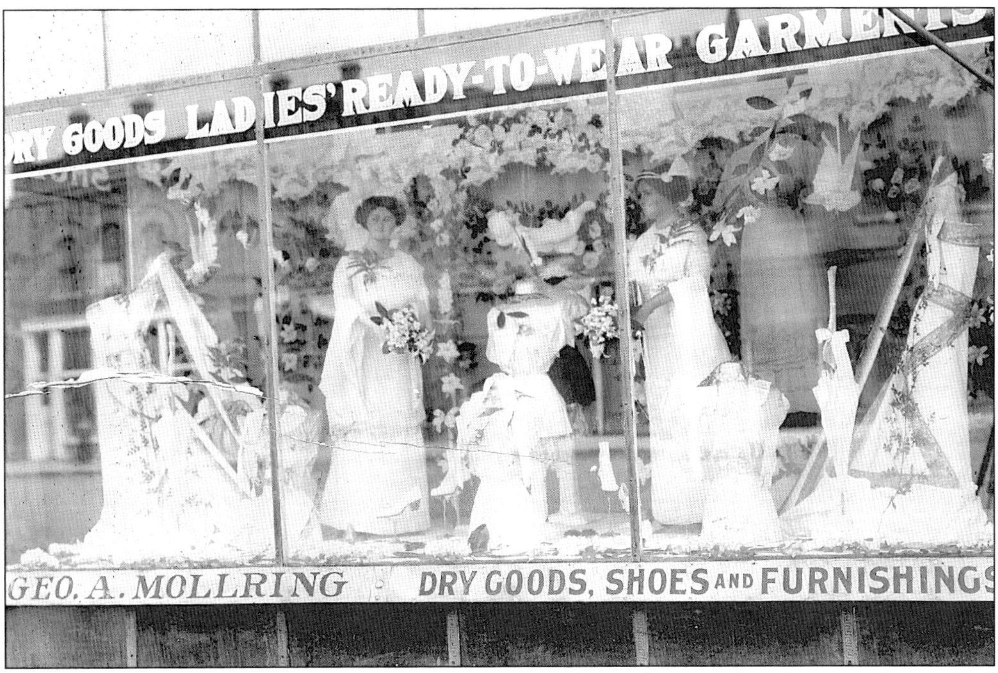

The Mollring Dry Goods, Shoes and Furnishings was located at 301 Box Butte and carried all the ready to wear for busy families. They advertised that they were "a store of quality." In later years, this corner was the Montgomery Wards Building. In the late 1960s, it was torn down and has since been turned into a mini-park.

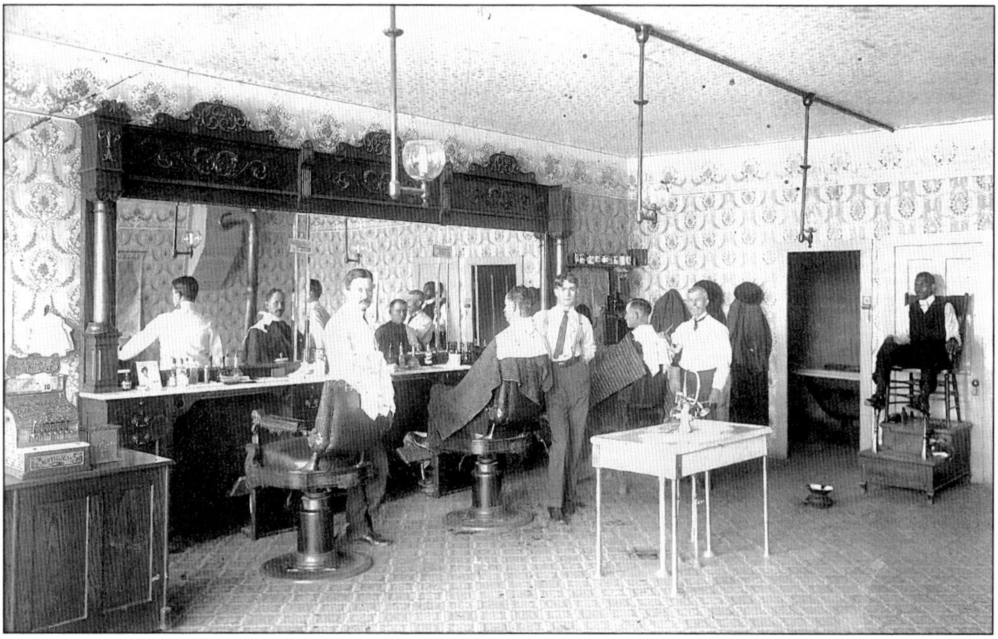

The Service Barber Shop at 220 Box Butte was the place for all fashionable gents. The gas lighting and sink in the middle of the room show this to be an upscale business. You could get a shave, haircut, and shoe shine for a small amount. The ornately carved mirror and spittoons were signs of the times. Ross Sampson ran the Service Barber Shop at one time. There was also a ladies beauty shop in the rear.

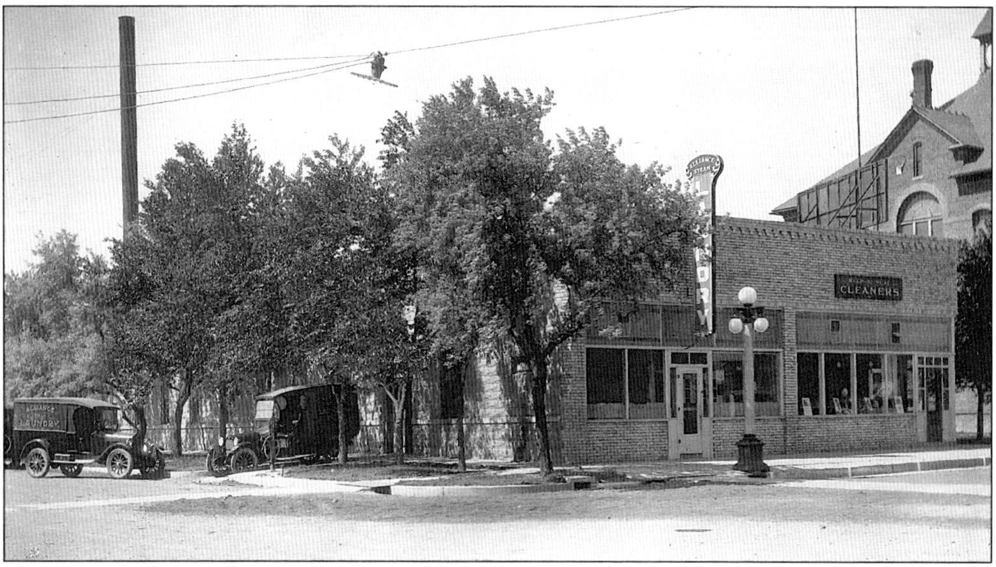

The Alliance Steam Laundry at 121 East Third Street was built in 1910. It's owners included: Charles McCreay, Charles Hill, the Smith Brothers, and in 1946 it was purchased by Mr. and Mrs. Noah Steinman. In 1920, Keep-U-Neat Cleaners were moved next door to the laundry. Jack and Fritz Steinman purchased the cleaners in 1966. When both businesses were combined, new equipment made this a fine and efficient establishment. The late 1970s saw the demise of the building.

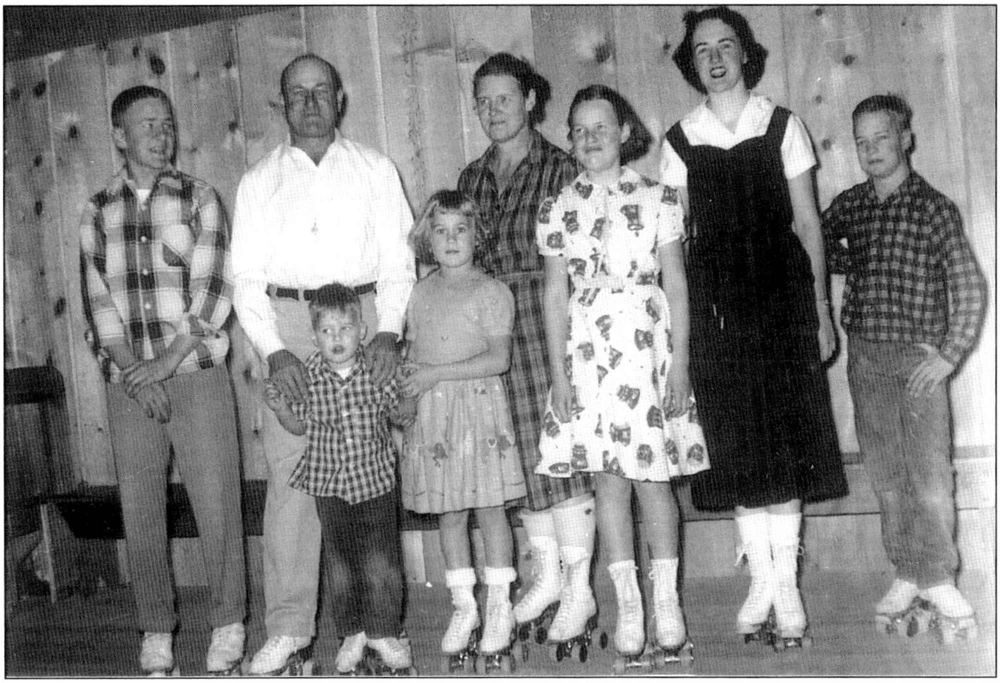

Anthony and Margaret Yeager married and raised 6 children in Alliance. Anthony had his hand in many businesses, including hauling coal, plumbing, and carpentry. His son Ralph runs the Yeager Construction Company today. One of his most unique businesses was the Roller Rink he built on West Third Street in 1951, which was run as a family business for 26 years. From left to right are: Ken, Anthony, Ralph, Dorothy, Margaret, Kathleen, Phyllis, and Glenn.

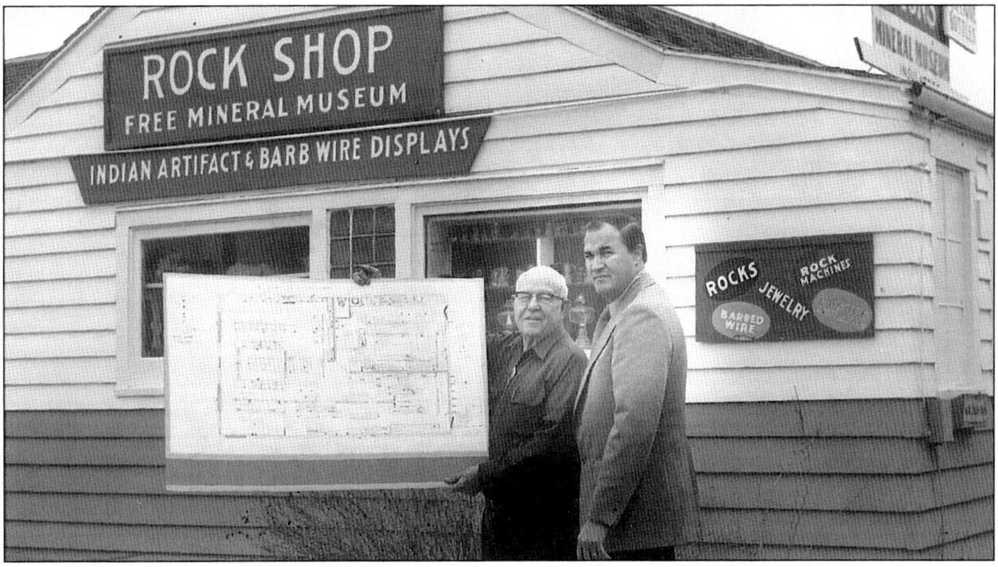

Bill Zieg, commercial sign painter, rock hunter, and all-around community helper holds a floor plan for the New Pamida store to be built at 304 Flack Avenue, the location of Zieg's Rock Shop as shown. Blaine McVicker, on the right, bought the lot from Mr. Zieg. The site for the new Rock Shop was 608 Flack. Mr. Zieg enjoyed putting a smile on the visitors face by giving each a small polished stone.

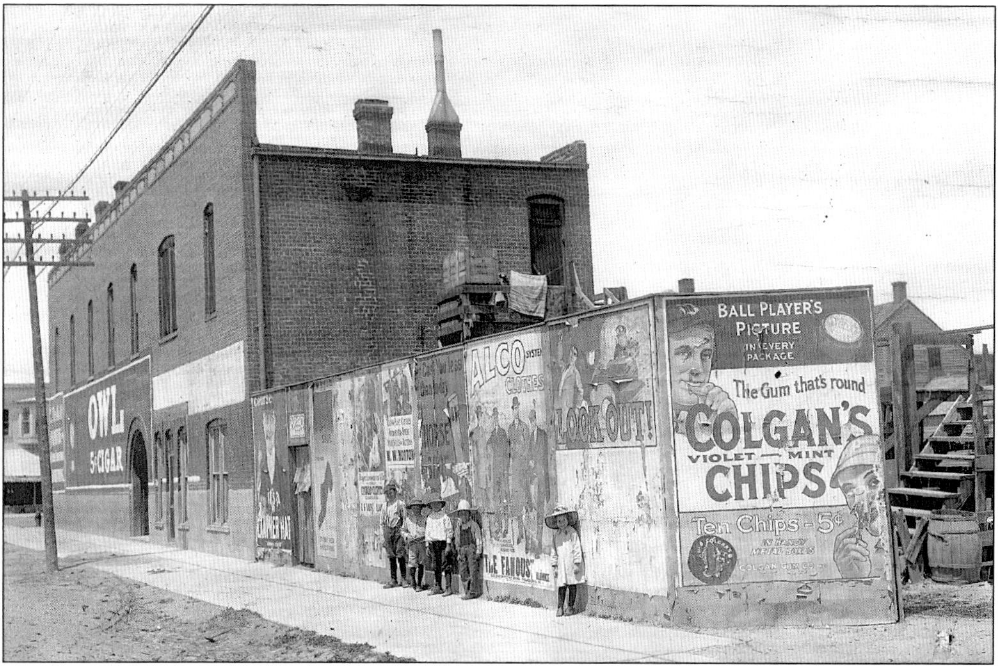

This building at 201 Box Butte once housed the Watson Grocery Store. Billboard walls like the one shown were used for a dual purpose; to advertise and conceal unsightly clutter. The children in this photo seem more than happy to interrupt their play to pose for the photograph.

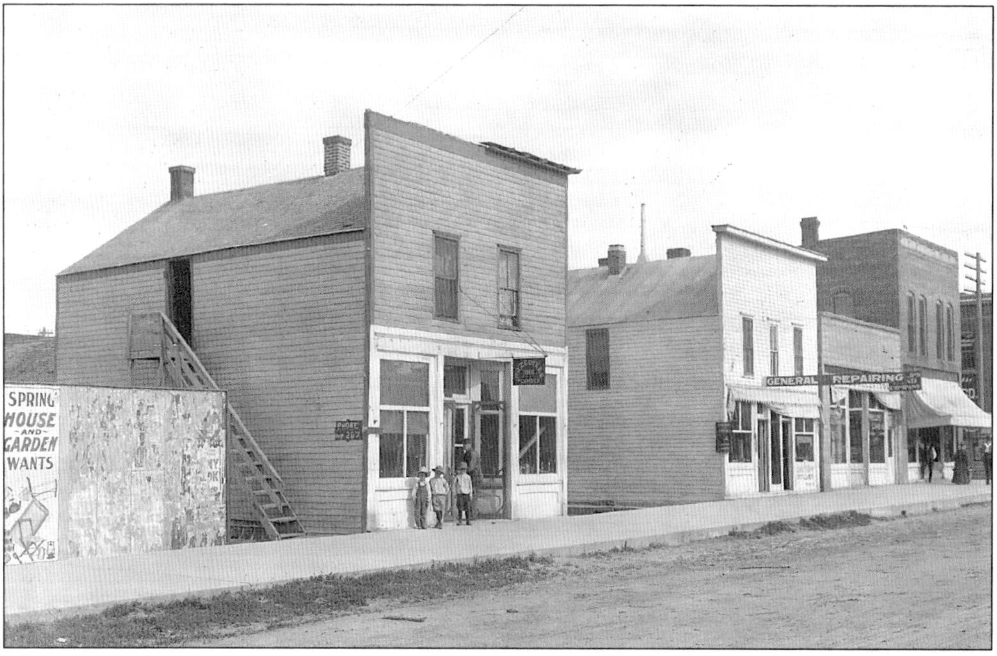

This turn-of-the-century street scene on 112 Box Butte shows three young boys posing while Mr. Zediker unlocks his plumbing business. Further up the street is a general repair shop, an unknown shop, and Rodgers Grocery. This photo was probably taken before 1893—note the dirt streets. Alliance is one of the few towns left with brick streets. Bricking was completed in 1920.

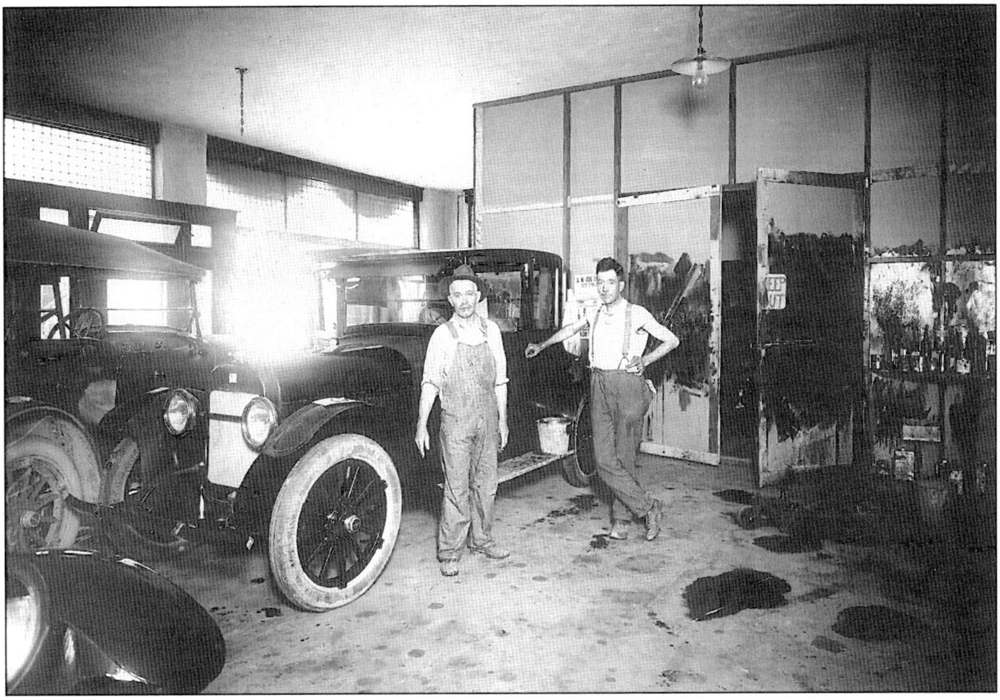

Chet Moore inherited the paint business from his father-in-law William Zehrung. Besides painting, they also wallpapered and stenciled. During WW II, they worked extensively at the air base with a crew of as many as 25 men. Shown here are Lou and Nate Cook in 1923. Great cars, guys!

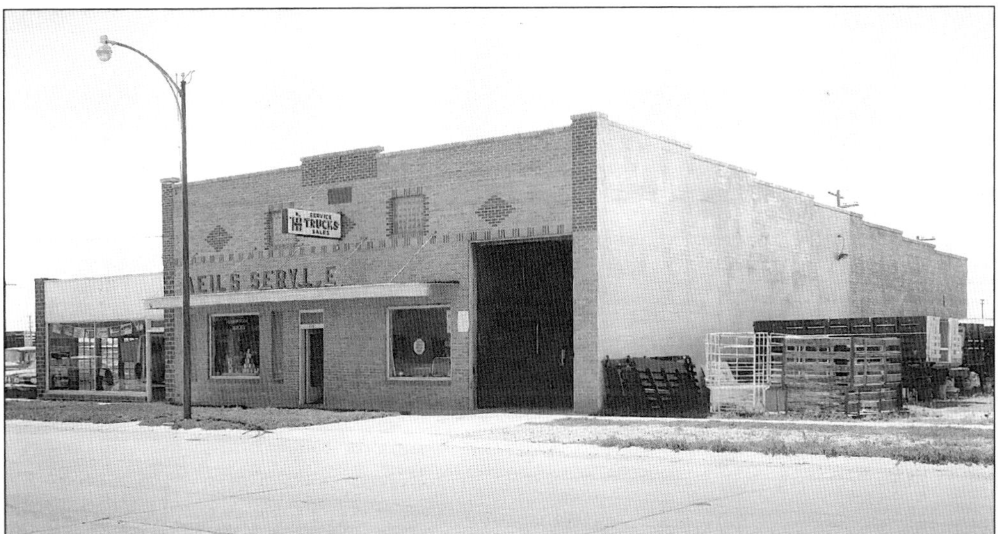

Neil Colerick was born and raised in Antioch. When he was 13 years old he rebuilt a Model T-Ford, and his future with transportation was sealed. He worked for Mandlebergs, Empire Construction, and Propers until 1950, when Neil bought the international dealership from Dodd DeBolt. The first location at 115 Box Butte was quickly outgrown, and they moved to 412 Black Hills. Neil retired in 1984, and Westco now owns the building and lot.

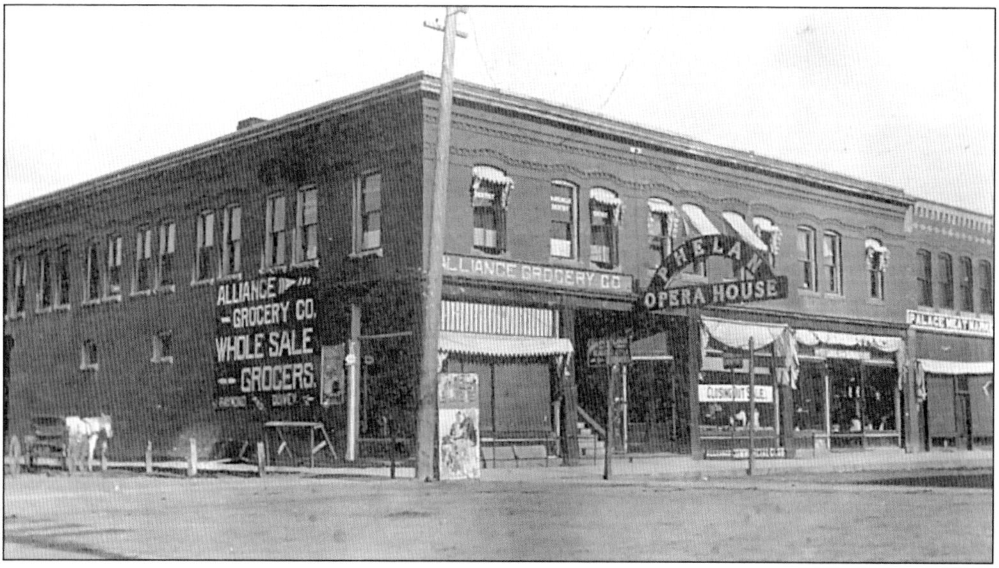

J.R. Phelen built the Phelen Opera House in 1893. With an opera house on the second floor, operas and plays were performed there until 1920. It was also used for graduations and civic functions. L.H. Highlands Alliance Grocery filled the corner slot for many years. Will Rhodes opened a ladies wear store that rivaled any big city store. The phrase "All roads lead to Rhodes" can still be seen on the ghost sign on the north wall.

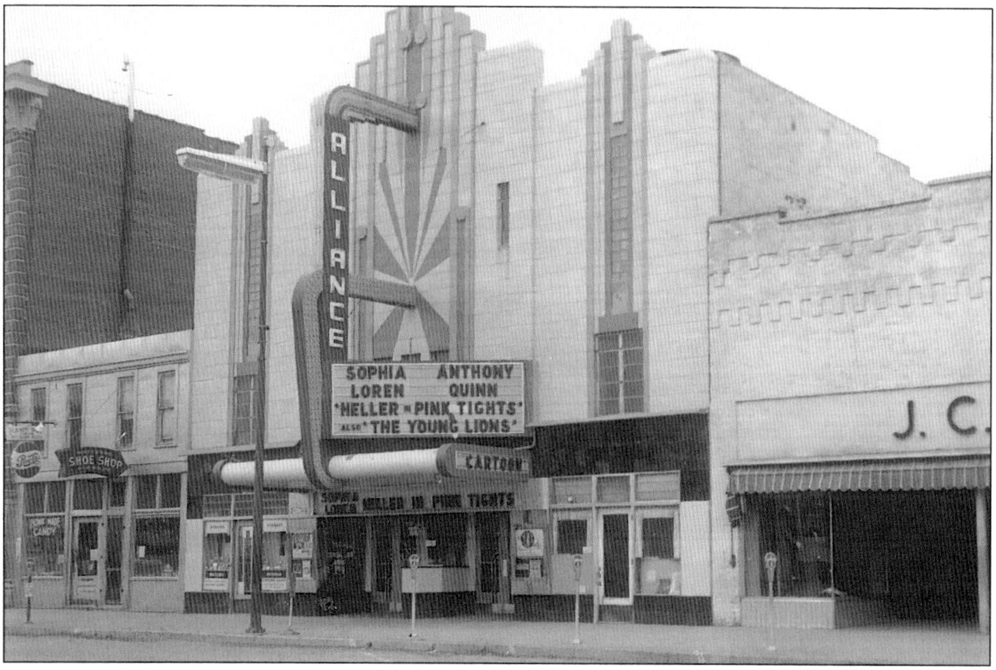

When the Alliance Theater was built in 1937, the cost was $140,000. Designed by Walter Simon, the front was covered with structured glass imported from Belgium. More than two carloads of steel were used in its construction. The ornamental grills, convectors in the lobby, and handrails were all made locally by Newberry's Hardware Company. The Kandy Snap was two doors away for gooey movie treats! There are now three screens to serve more patrons.

Eight

Celebrating a Way of Life

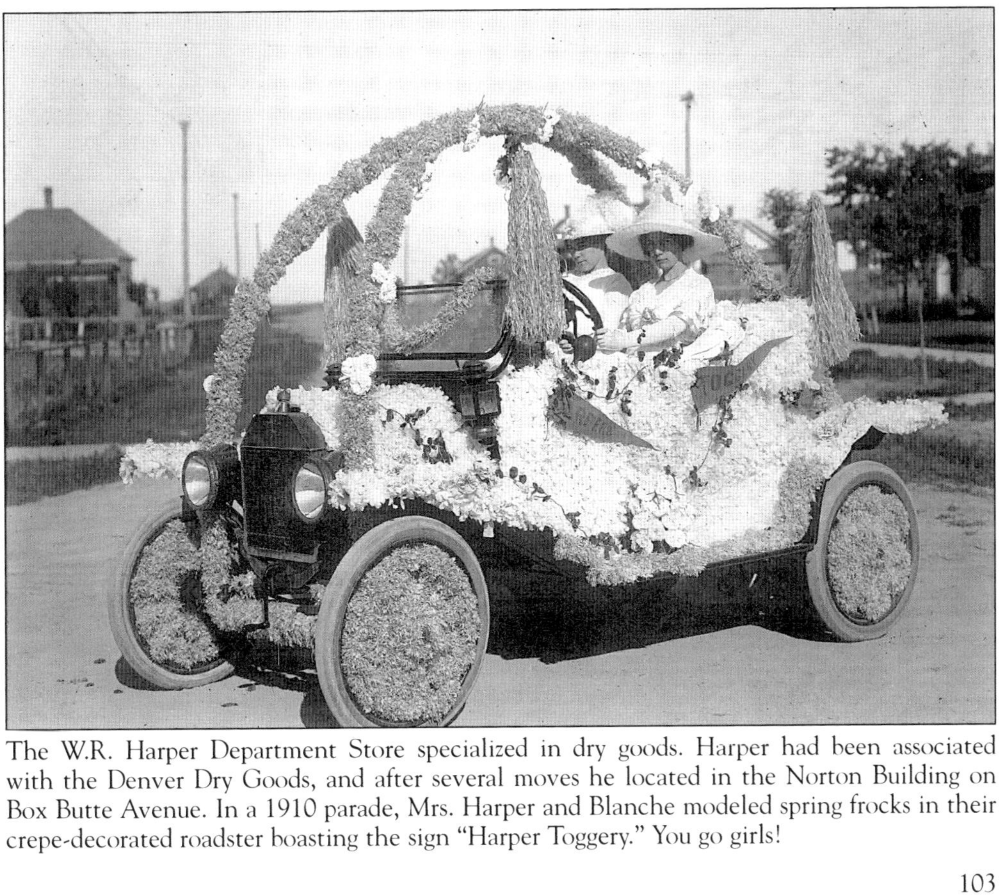

The W.R. Harper Department Store specialized in dry goods. Harper had been associated with the Denver Dry Goods, and after several moves he located in the Norton Building on Box Butte Avenue. In a 1910 parade, Mrs. Harper and Blanche modeled spring frocks in their crepe-decorated roadster boasting the sign "Harper Toggery." You go girls!

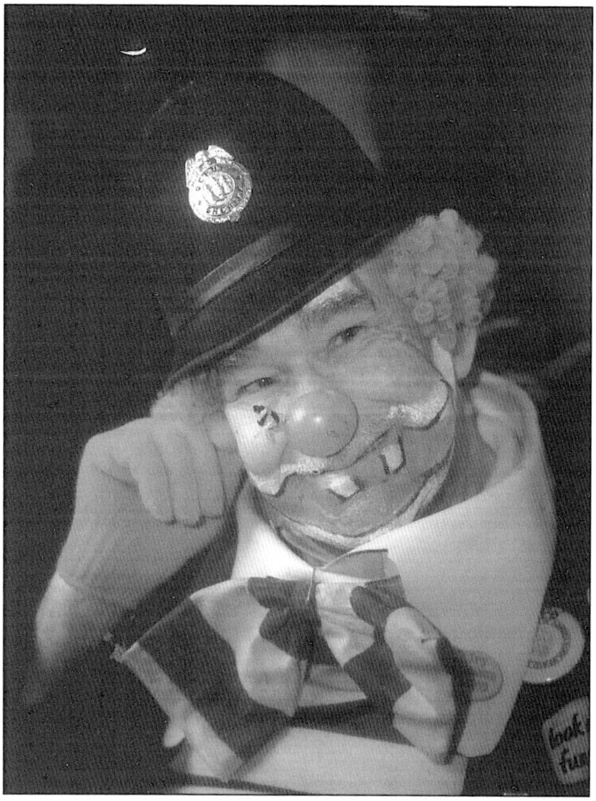

Leonard Glarum, known as "Pepe the Clown," was a local sign painter, entertainer, and entrepreneur. His cheerful antics provided many smiles for young and old alike. Whether performing for a store opening or a parade, "Pepe" was always a hit. Leonard's wife Juanita was a longtime high school teacher. The Glarums are an asset to the community.

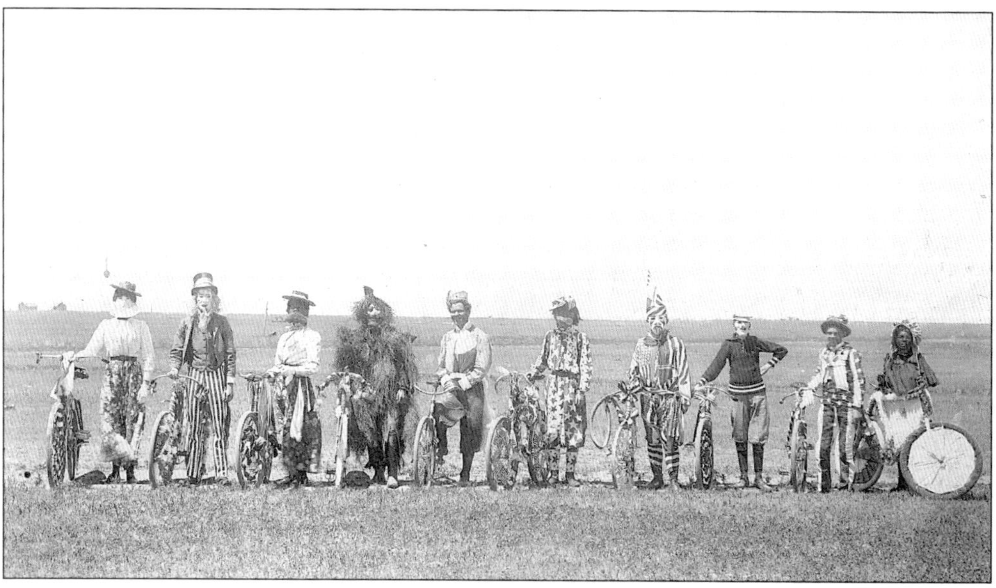

Everybody loves a clown! These turn of the century clowns in their unusual costumes were ready with decorated bicycles to join the Fourth of July parade. While the names are unknown, we can see "Uncle Sam," a gorilla, a gypsy, a sailor, and a clown in black face. Pioneers were hard working from sunup to sundown, and enjoyed what little playtime they had. Always patriotic, they celebrated every July Fourth with a parade.

Rodeos were a highlight of each summer when local cowboys competed in events such as calf roping, bareback riding, bulldogging, bull riding, saddle bronc riding, and steer wrestling. The cowgirls had their events also with barrel racing usually being the favorite. These local cowboys carry the flag for the Rodeo Parade in 1962. From left to right are: Charles Dingman, Henry Neafus and Floyd Stone. The parade always included the rodeo queen and cowboys that were entered in the rodeo.

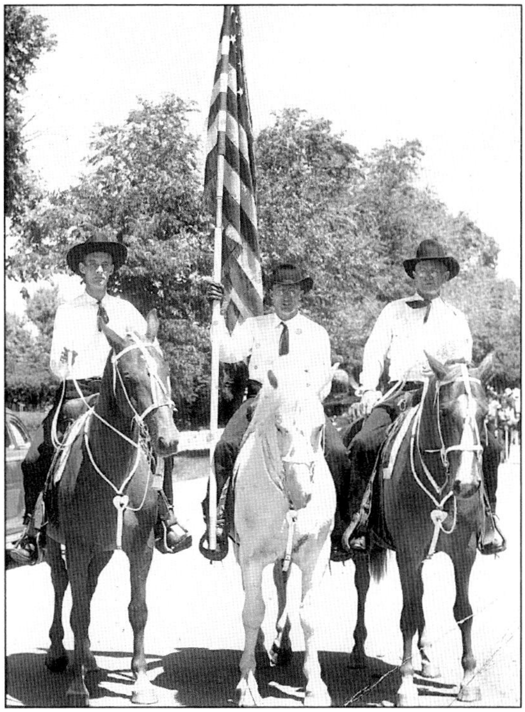

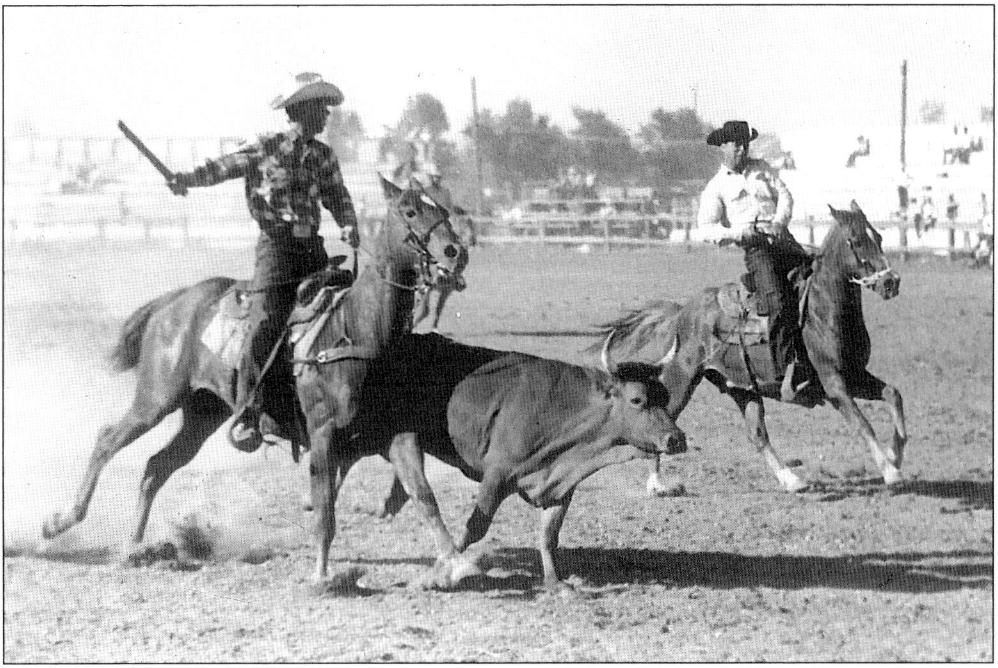

Started in makeshift pens on local ranches, rodeos grew to be major Sandhills sporting events. These unknown cowboys take part in the steer wrestling events. Huge crowds packed the grandstands at the rodeo grounds located at the airport. Peanut vendors, rodeo clowns, pretty rodeo royalty, and the Grand March were all part of this celebration of cowboy life.

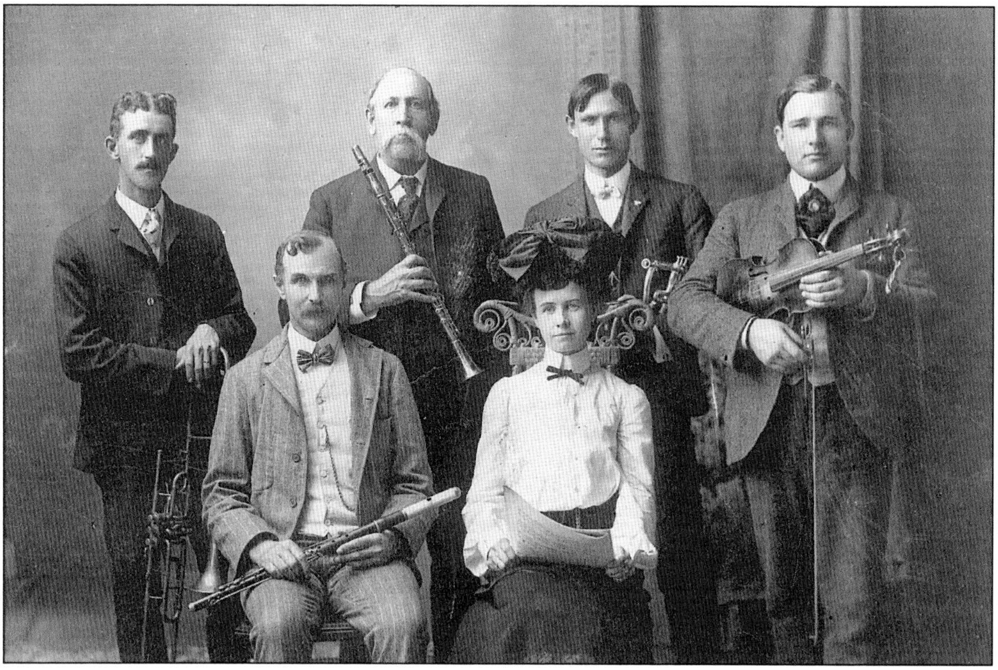

Bringing Eastern culture to the barren plains, the Spacht Orchestra drew large crowds of homesteaders hungry for a glimpse of nostalgia. The only identified musicians are Daniel Spacht with the clarinet and Mrs. Minnie Wiker as the pianist.

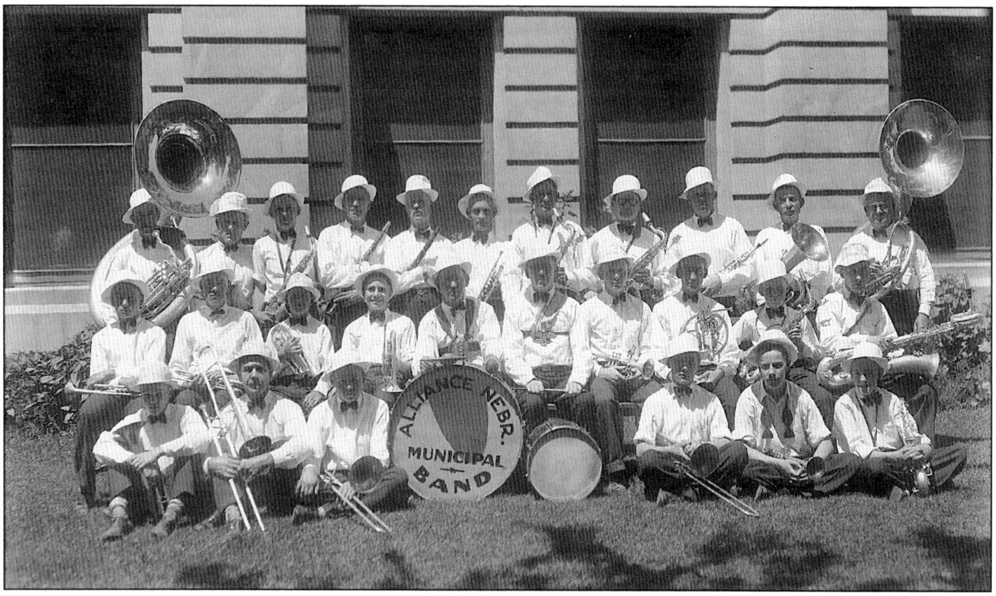

Alliance had depended on a handful of elderly musicians for its celebrations. In 1939, the city had no band for the Fourth of July parade. Since the schools had no music program, City Manager Clarence Hoper proposed that a band director be hired to work for the school ten months, and for the city two months. Young and old alike joined the band and music was once again heard on summer nights in the park. The municipal band posed on the south side of the courthouse for this picture.

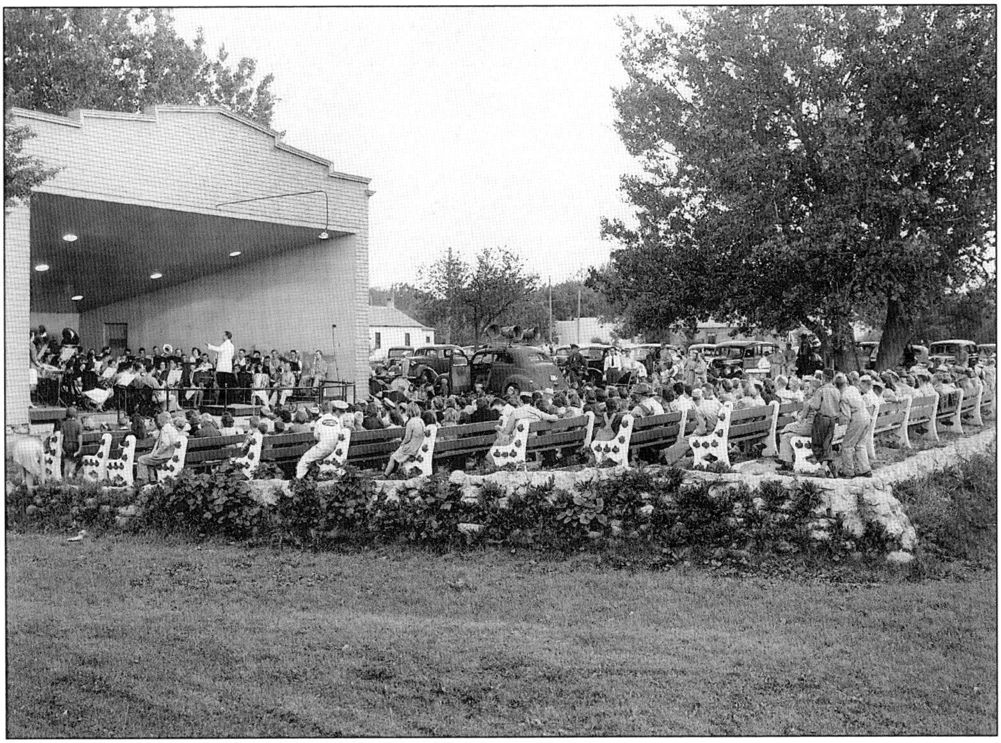

The Band Shell is a fond memory for many in Alliance. The war years brought overflowing crowds that filled the park at Seventh and Sweetwater. Cars lined the streets as music filled the air. Vallette Hill directed a quality band for many years for $150 per month. Musicians were paid 50¢ for rehearsals and $1 for concerts. The band shell fell into disrepair and was torn down in the 1960s. There is talk about replacing it, so music may still be in Alliance's future.

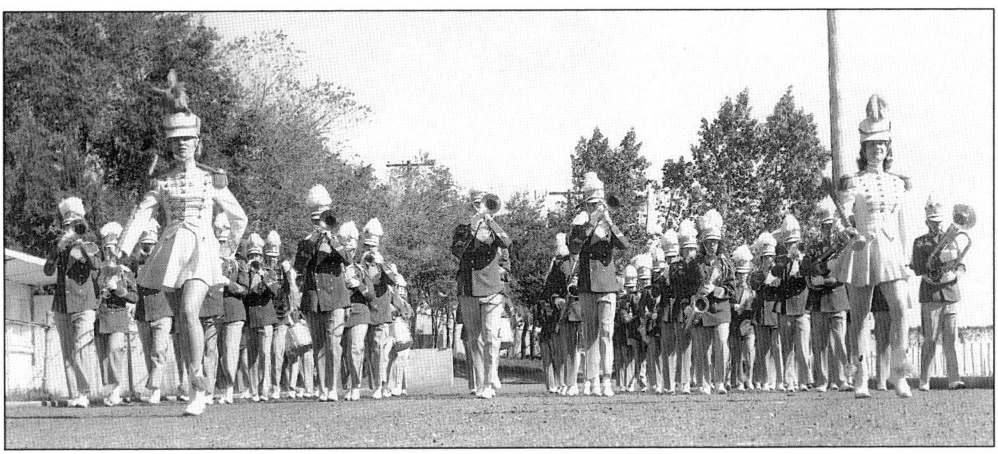

The bands now in Alliance are part of the schools. The AHS Marching Band continues to be a regular in area parades. The 21st century saw them parading in Washington D.C. for July Fourth. This group pictured was from 1963. From Washington to county fair parades, these smart stepping youngsters bring a feeling of pride to Alliance.

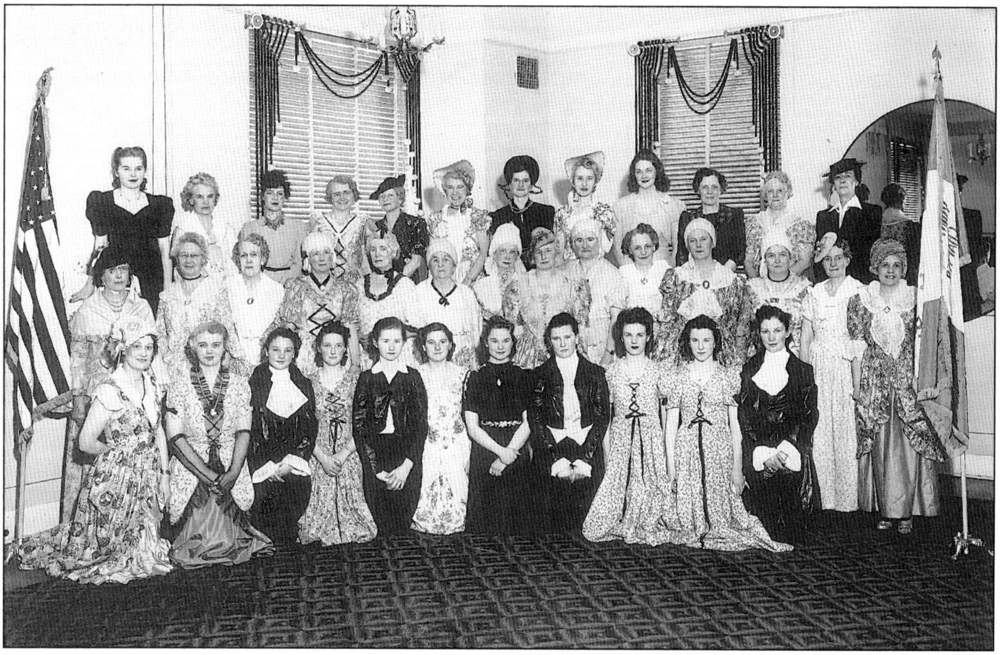

The Point of Rock chapter of the Daughters of the American Revolution was founded in Alliance on February 22, 1919, with 18 members. The chapter name commemorates a historical landmark west of town on the Sidney-Deadwood Trail. This civic organization promotes patriotism in the community and schools. They were instrumental in helping start the museum. The group pictured celebrates their revolutionary heritage in the Palm Room of the Alliance Hotel.

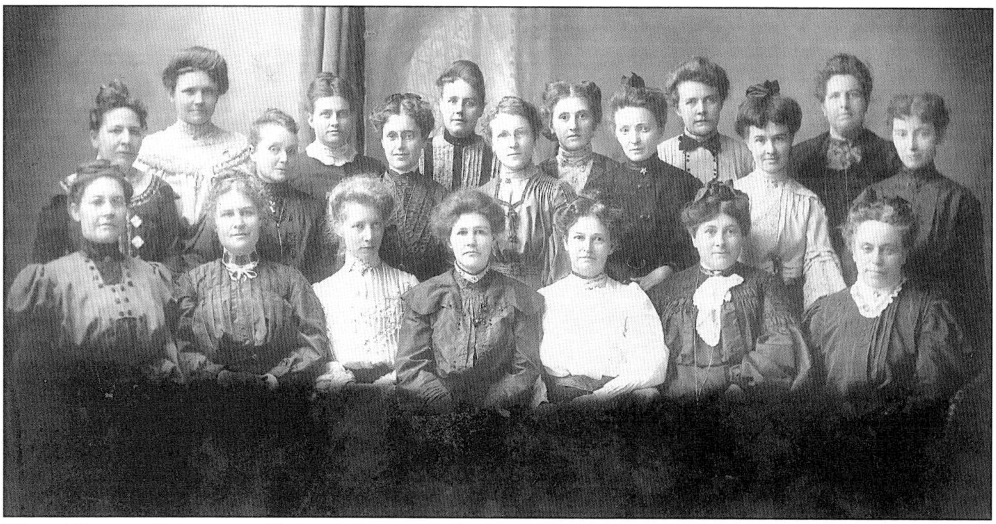

The Alliance Women's Club was organized in 1903, when social life was very limited. Their crowning accomplishment was the founding of the Alliance Library. It was first organized at their clubroom in the basement of the Syndicate Block with donated books. They paid $10 a month rent, including utilities. An application to Andrew Carnegie Foundation brought a grant for a new building. What a wonderful legacy for the Woman's Club! Pictured here are the members in 1906.

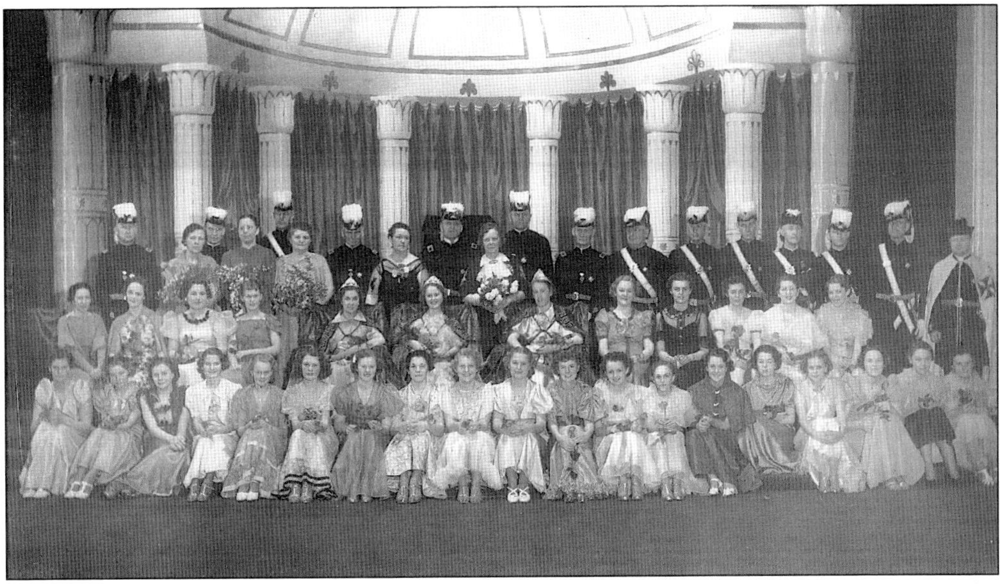

Bethel #3 of the Job's Daughters organized on June 24, 1921, and is the third chapter in the world. With an original membership of 33, the group has been a part of young womanhood for many years. The first queen was Mariellen (Beagle) Peters. This group posed in 1937, with Edith Knight as queen.

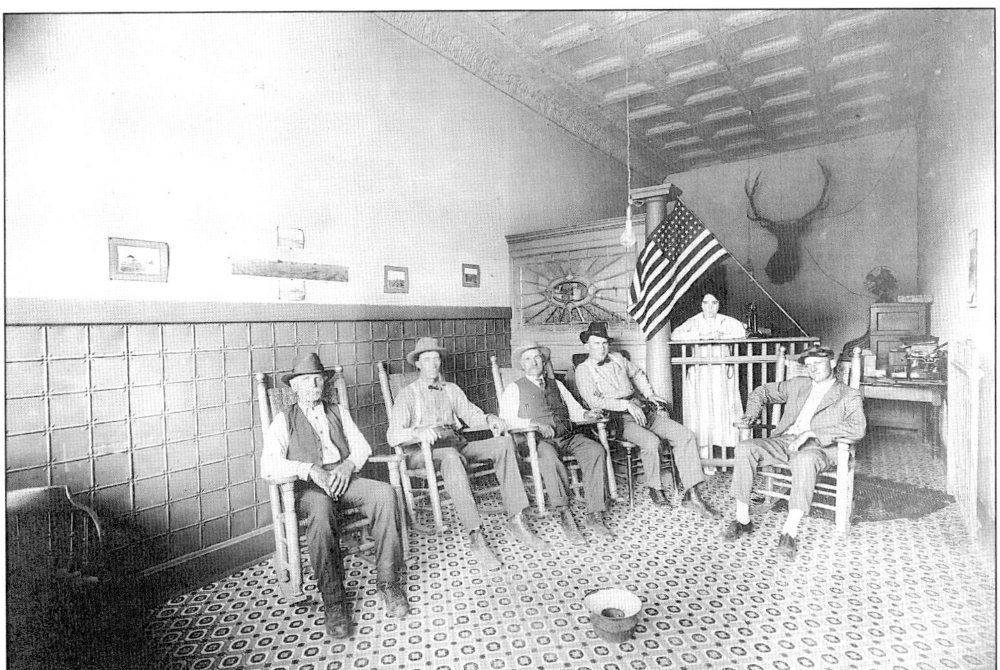

The Alliance Lodge #961 BPOE was granted a charter in 1905. Local attorney William Mitchell led the original 47 members at the room on the second floor of the Zbinden Building at 202 Box Butte. From left to right are: Fred O'Bannon, Oscar O'Bannon, Mac McCorkley, Dick O'Bannon, and two unknowns in the entry of the First Elks Lodge. The 48-star flag dates this at about 1912, before they moved into the new lodge at 417 Box Butte.

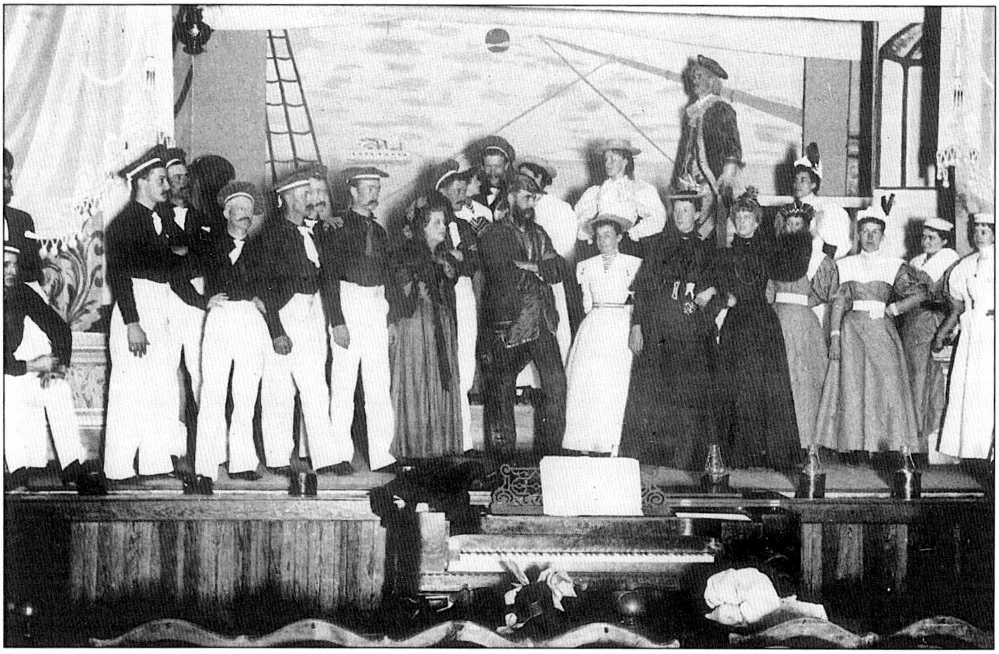

This cast of the Pirates of Penzance performed at the Phelan Opera in 1895. Clever costumes and scenery wowed audiences who came from all walks of life. Entertainments such as this were popular fare at the Opera House.

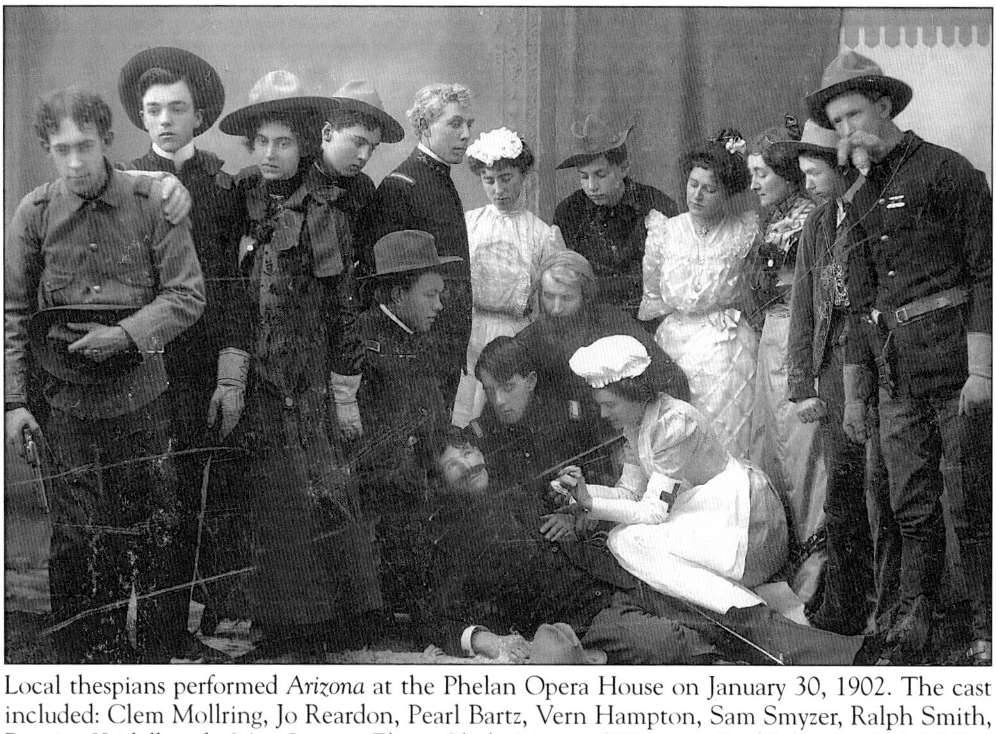

Local thespians performed *Arizona* at the Phelan Opera House on January 30, 1902. The cast included: Clem Mollring, Jo Reardon, Pearl Bartz, Vern Hampton, Sam Smyzer, Ralph Smith, Bernice Kridelbaugh, Mrs. Smyzer, Elmer Clark, Martin O'Conner, Fred Johnson, Jack Miller, Della Weber, Anna Wills, and Ed Reardon.

Nine

IN THE GOOD OLD SUMMERTIME

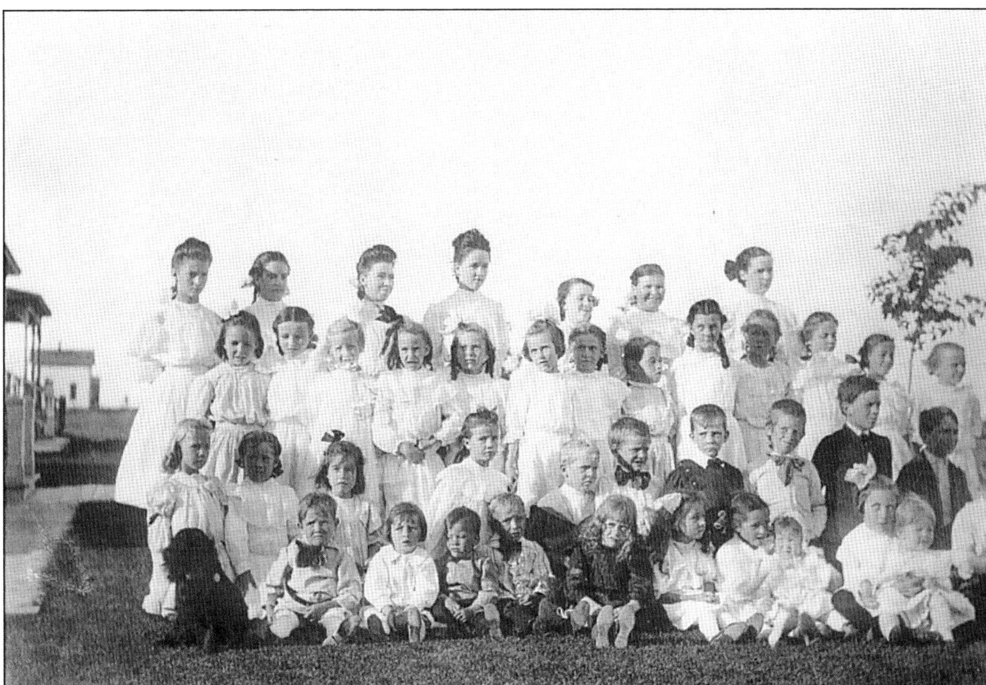

Summertime brought white lawn dresses, knickers, and frolicking puppies. Taken at the George Griggs home at 916 Box Butte in 1906, this picture includes the neighborhood kids. They are, from left to right: Sutton, Nation, Graham, Johnson, Hayes, Chruikshank, Griggs, Cotant, Frankle, Albro, Lotspeich, Mollring, Grassman, Raby, and Stewart. Constance Chruikshank is the young child on the lap of the last girl in row one. The Spencer's dog "Patsy" rounds out the group.

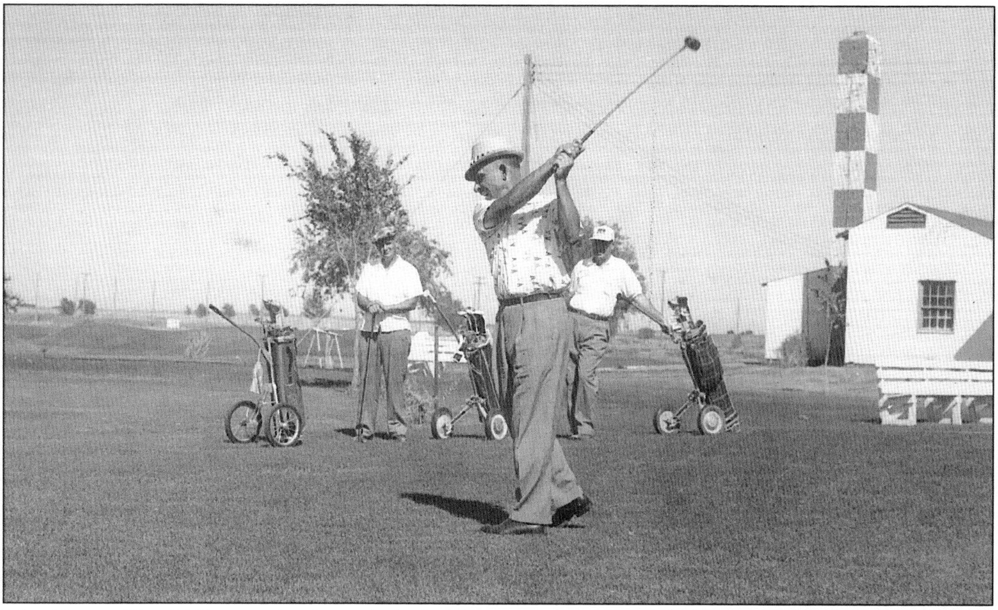

The Ec-na-Illa (Alliance backwards!) Golf Course was one of the first in the Panhandle in 1953. A nine-hole grass greens course was laid out over the cantonment area of the abandoned air base. The facilities included a three-barracks clubhouse/proshop with an apartment for the live-in pro, latrines, and a bar. Memberships cost $25, and anyone could join. The 18-hole greens are now a backdrop for golfers young and old.

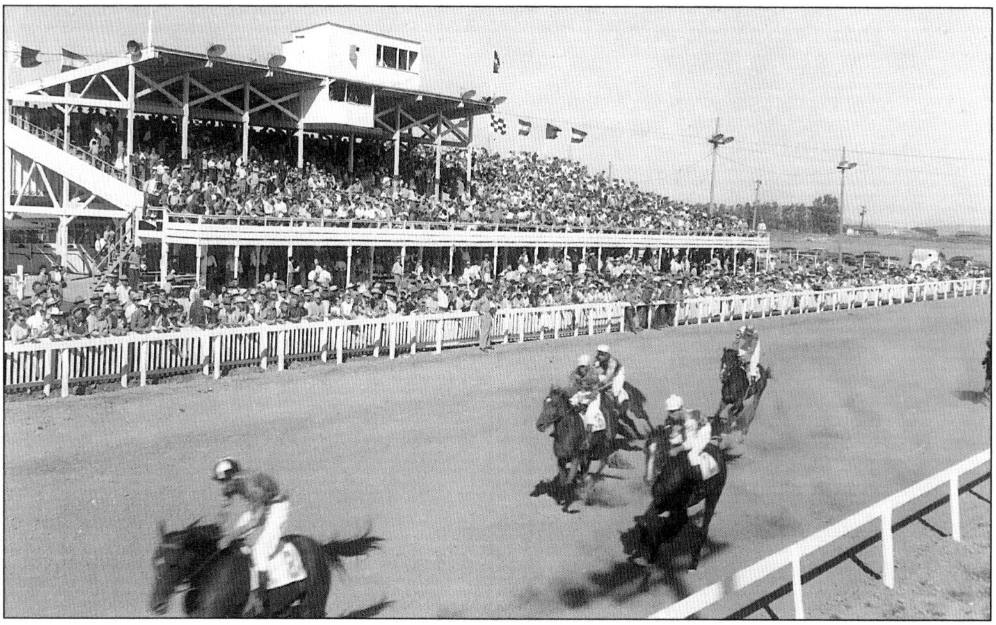

The Sandhillo Race Track was a half-mile circle track and rodeo grounds built at the air base. Para-mutual horse racing was held in the fall, and rodeos were held every June. The covered grandstands seated over three hundred people, with the betting booths below. Behind the stands, the Turf Club became a popular social club during the races. Racing lasted 1958–1964, with the rodeos lasting much longer.

One of the most popular summertime entertainment was the Drive-In Theater at Sixth & Flack. Started in the 1950s, stars twinkled above while young families watched movies with sound coming from the box hanging in the window. This spot is now a Pizza Hut & Dairy Queen, but a new Sandhills Drive-Inn shows flicks at the old rodeo grounds. This is one of only three remaining in Nebraska.

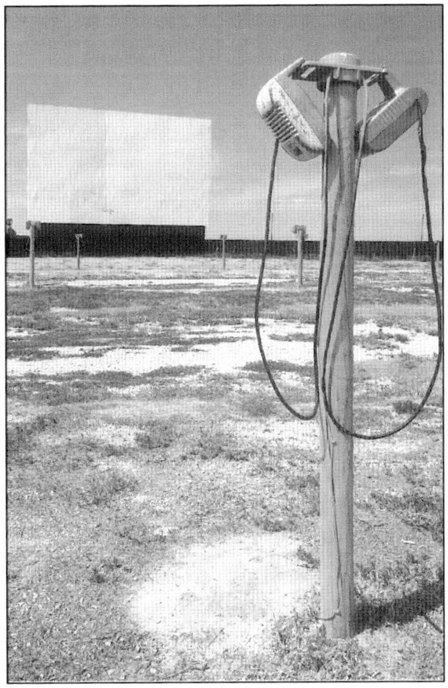

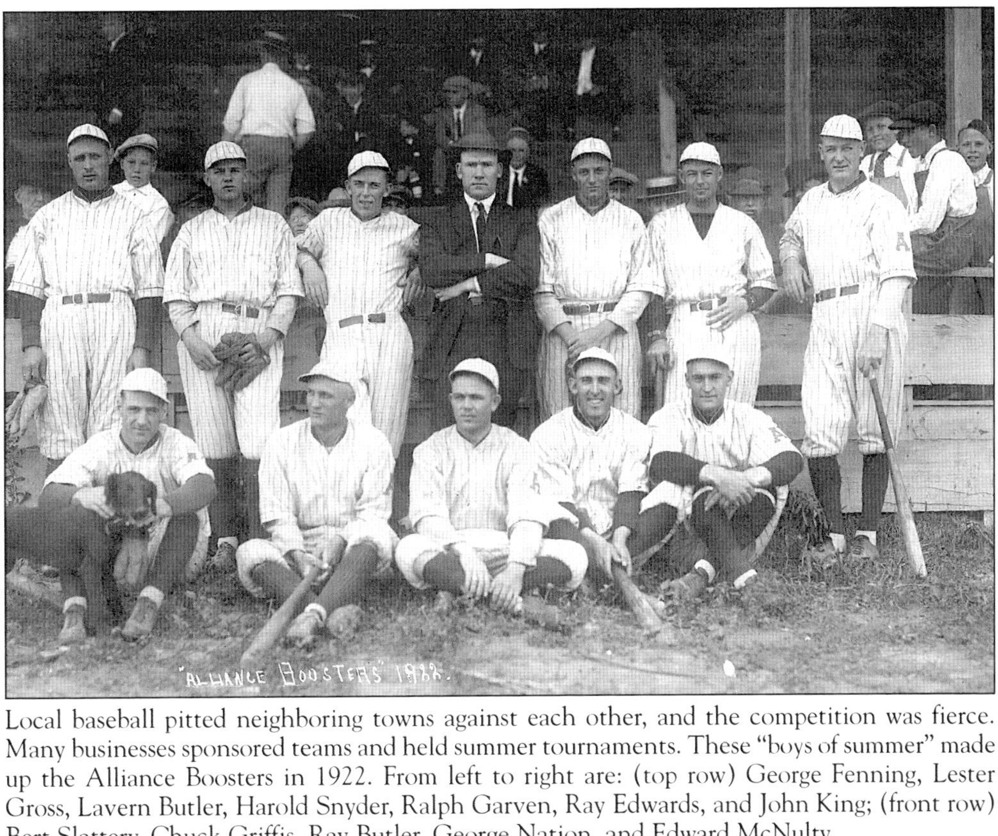

Local baseball pitted neighboring towns against each other, and the competition was fierce. Many businesses sponsored teams and held summer tournaments. These "boys of summer" made up the Alliance Boosters in 1922. From left to right are: (top row) George Fenning, Lester Gross, Lavern Butler, Harold Snyder, Ralph Garven, Ray Edwards, and John King; (front row) Bert Slattery, Chuck Griffis, Ray Butler, George Nation, and Edward McNulty.

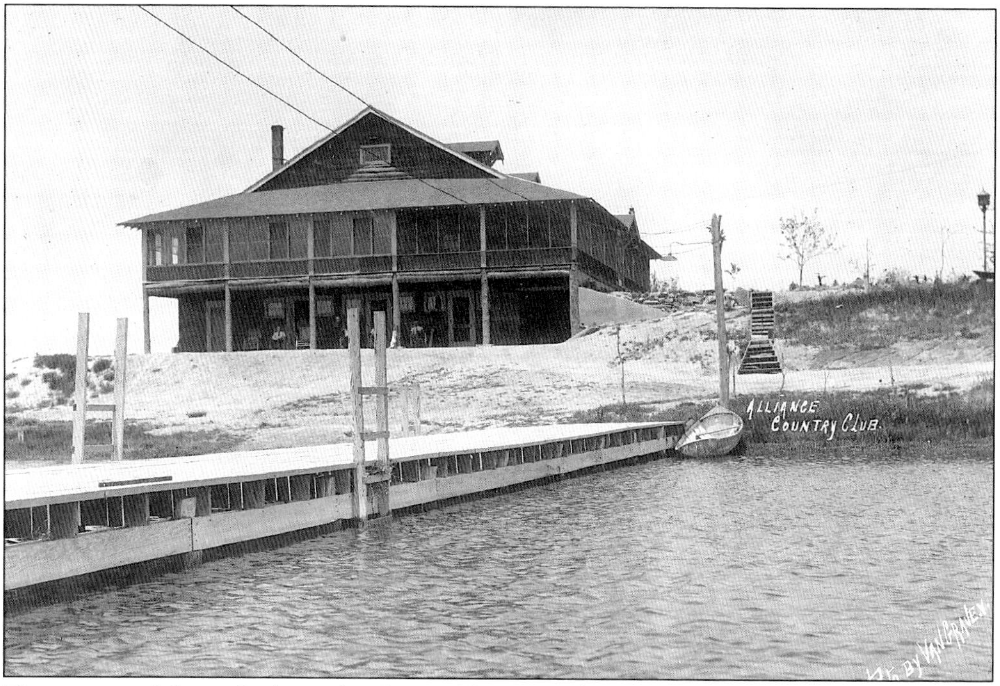

The country club was built on the shore of Bronco Lake in 1923. As irrigation became more popular, the lake mysteriously dried up in the 1950s. Despite two fires, the club remains as an important social gathering place. It was the scene of many beach parties, with three piers in use at all times. Besides the restaurant, entertainment consisted of swimming, canoeing, boating, tennis, dancing, and golf on the nine-hole course.

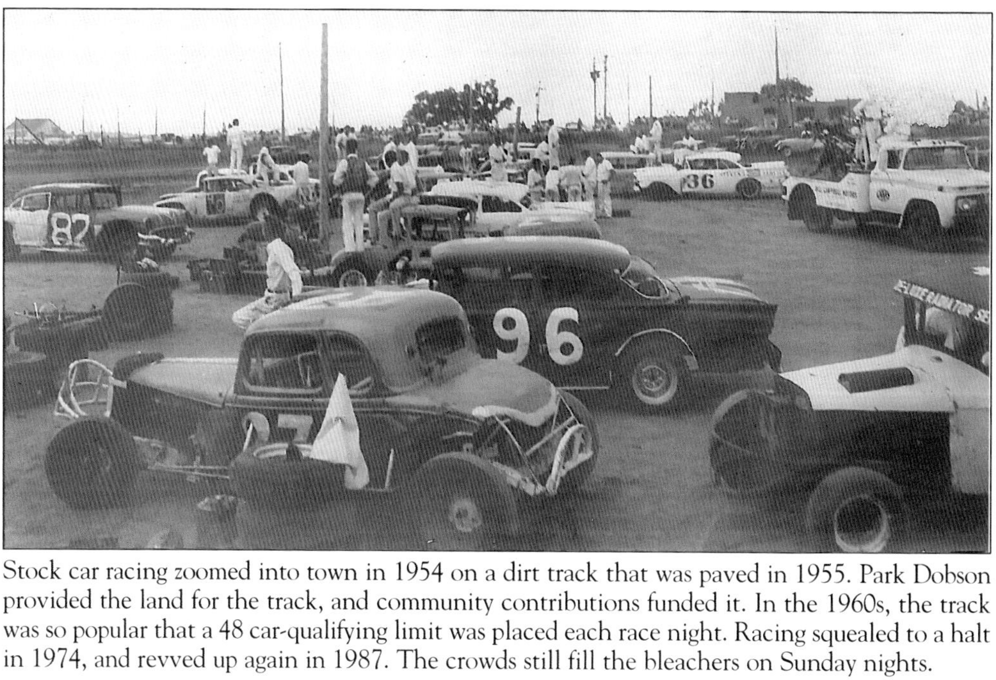

Stock car racing zoomed into town in 1954 on a dirt track that was paved in 1955. Park Dobson provided the land for the track, and community contributions funded it. In the 1960s, the track was so popular that a 48 car-qualifying limit was placed each race night. Racing squealed to a halt in 1974, and revved up again in 1987. The crowds still fill the bleachers on Sunday nights.

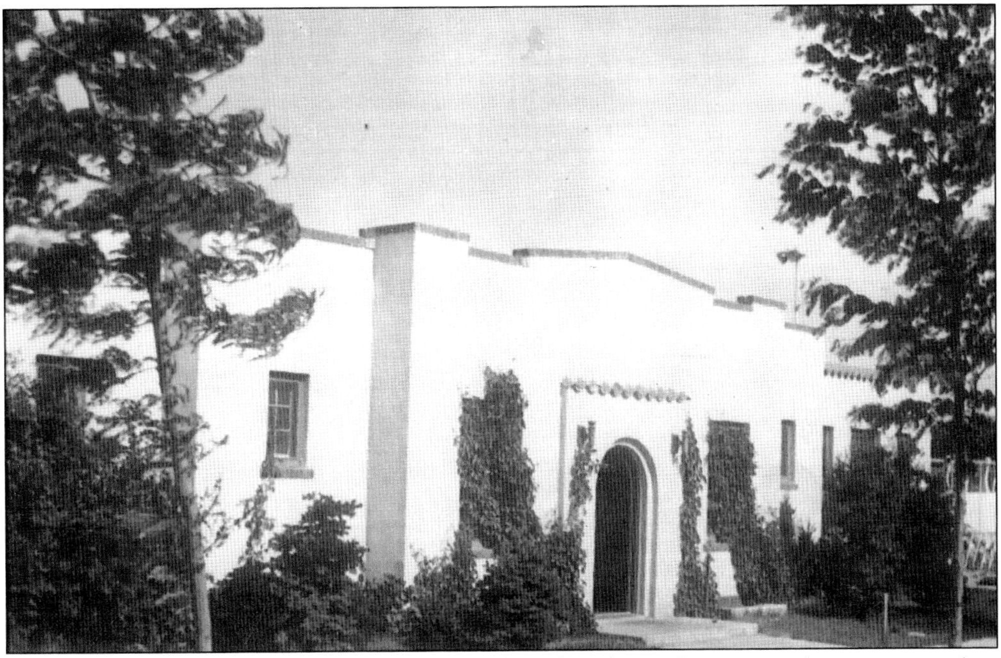

The Alliance Pool was built in 1934 at Eleventh and Niobrara. Large enough to accommodate one thousand bathers a day, it boasted "adequate filtration and no effort spared to insure complete sanitation." When a new modern pool was built in the1970s, the large Spanish style bath house and pool were converted into the Sallows Conservatory. It houses the park office and shop, and a beautiful indoor garden with a pond and birds.

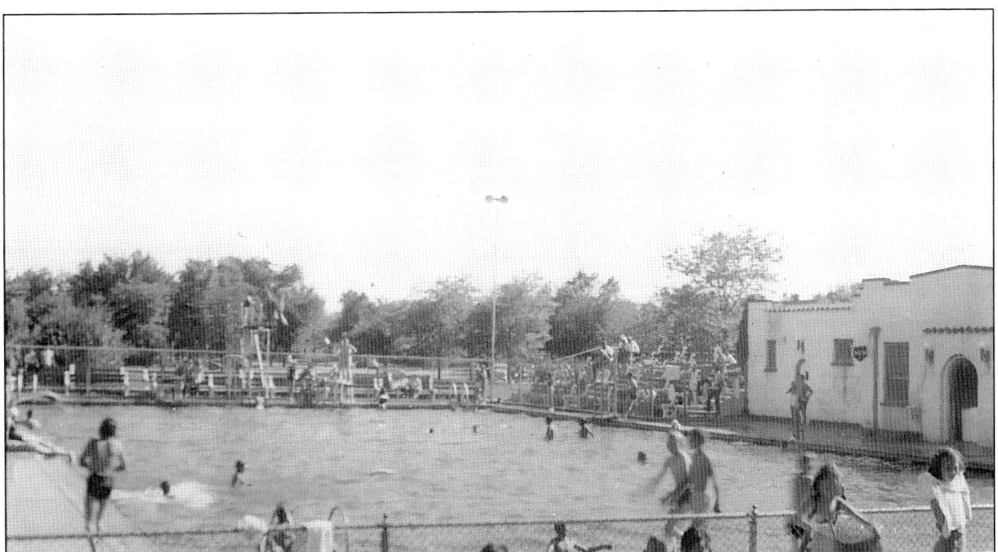

The pool was a popular site for off-duty soldiers during the air base days. Trained lifeguards, swim teams, beauty contests, toddlers' pool, and Olympic-style diving boards all made this an attraction that is still remembered by many. The new pool at Sixteenth and Cheyenne still finds swimmers of all ages basking in the Nebraska sunshine.

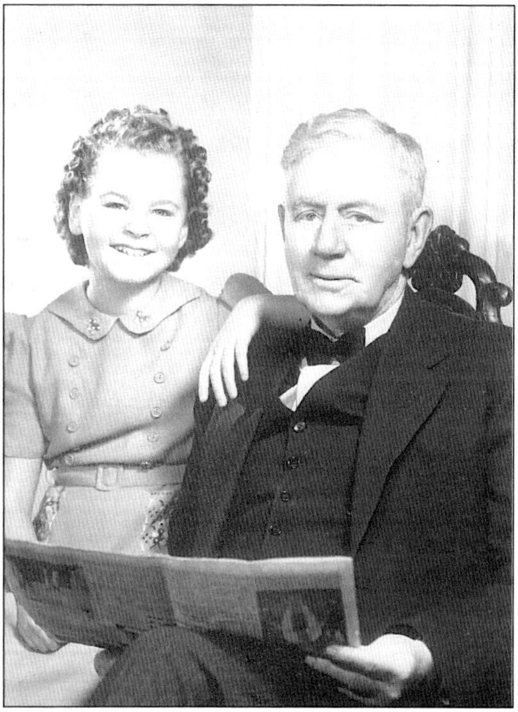

John A. Bower planted many unique flower beds at his daughter's home which caught the eye of city officials. They hired him in 1926 as park superintendent. He will be remembered as the visionary of the park system. Bower passed away in 1941, and his son-in-law Warren Maxwell took over and completed many of the projects. The Bower Park and Ball field, home of the Spartans, at Second and Mississippi, is Bower's namesake.

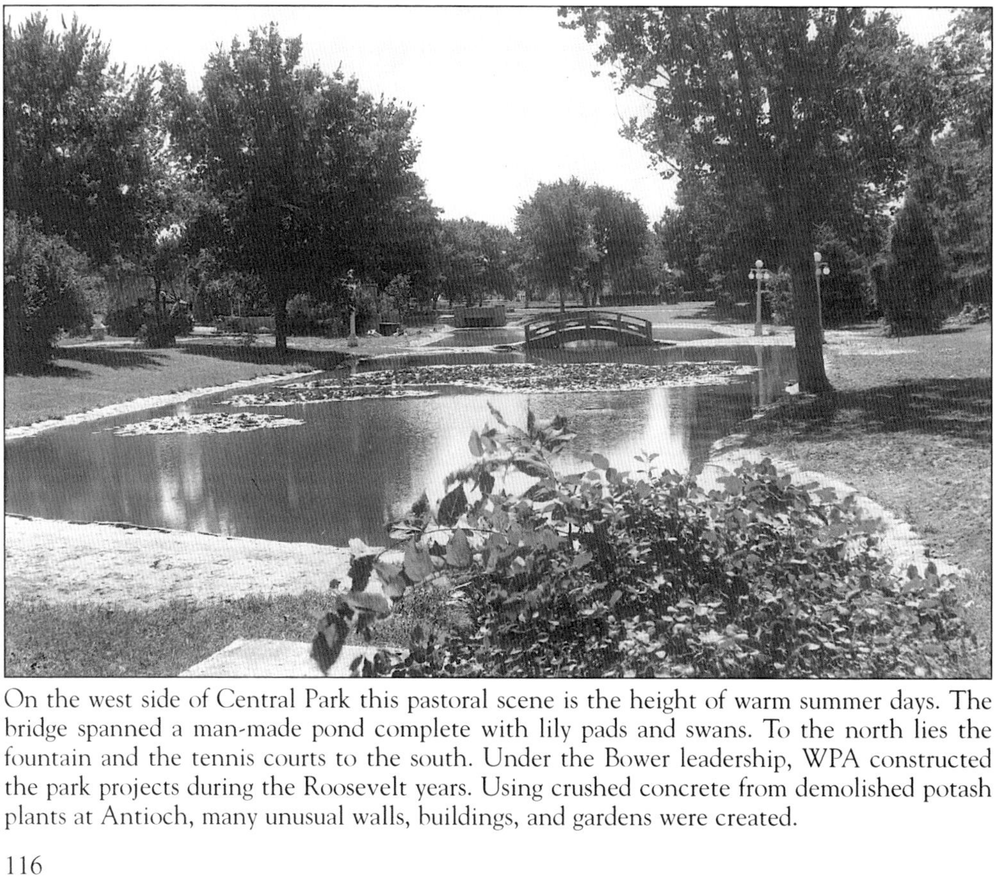

On the west side of Central Park this pastoral scene is the height of warm summer days. The bridge spanned a man-made pond complete with lily pads and swans. To the north lies the fountain and the tennis courts to the south. Under the Bower leadership, WPA constructed the park projects during the Roosevelt years. Using crushed concrete from demolished potash plants at Antioch, many unusual walls, buildings, and gardens were created.

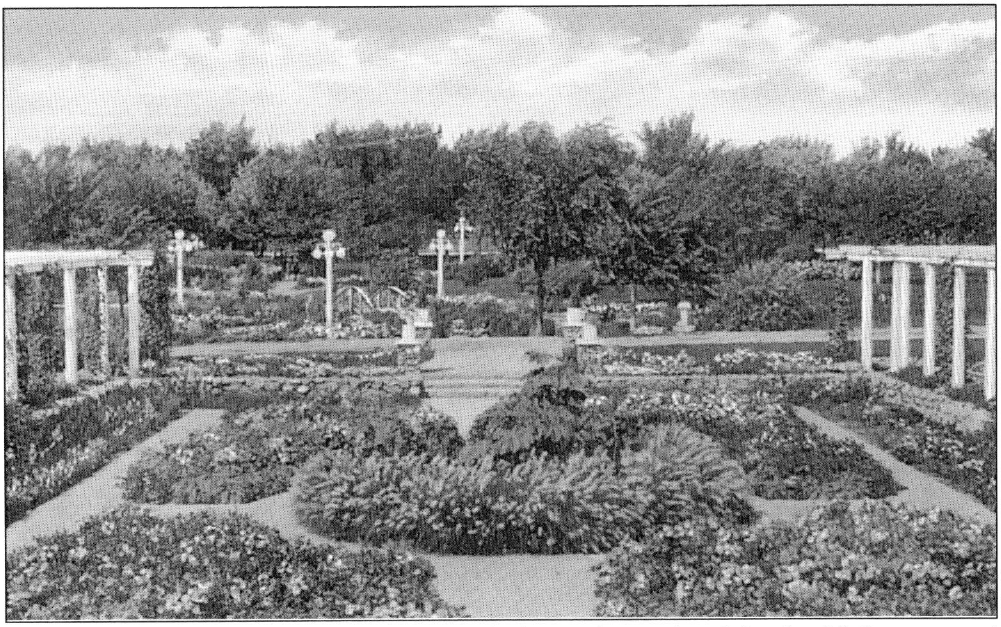

The formal sunken gardens have been described as a "horticultural fairyland." Once an arid cornfield, the sunken gardens were used by Bower to test hundreds of varieties of flowers that were new to the area. Two small pens kept small wild animals as part of a very small city zoo. Flagstone walkways and brilliant floral displays make this the site of many summer weddings.

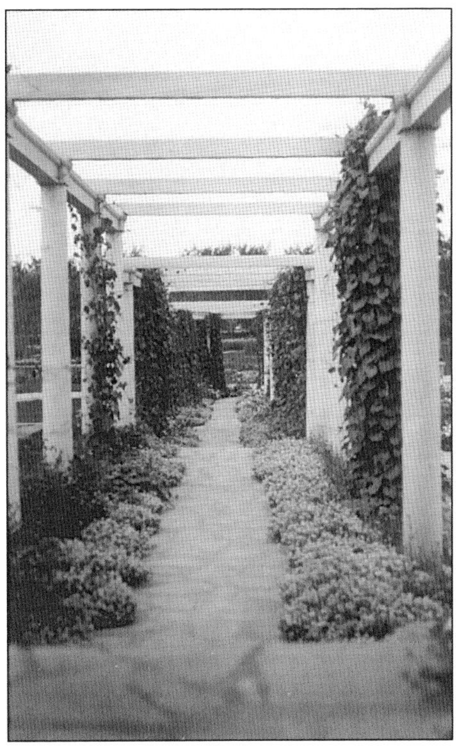

The massive white concrete columns line the sides of the floral walkways on each side of the sunken garden. A wood-vine overhead creates a shady spot for a stroll or children to play in. Bower planted hundreds of shade trees providing cool picnic places throughout the park. The same concrete mosaic forms the retaining walls and steps in the garden.

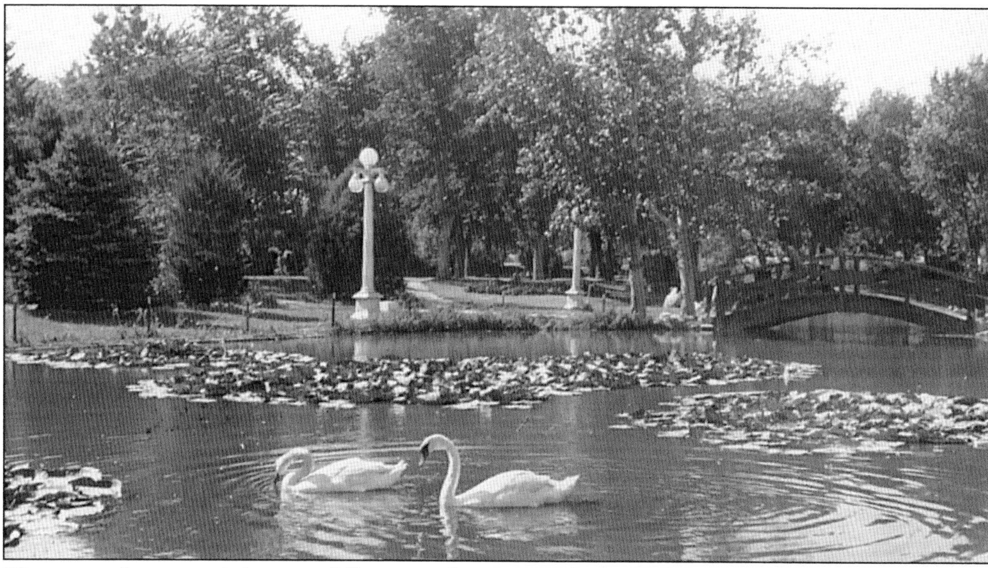

The pair of swans glide gracefully over the water, ducking through lily pads and amusing visitors. They were the symbol of a quiet life. An aviary full of feathered friends sat next to the pond. No longer in use, birds are now a small part of the conservatory. Inabilities to aerate the water caused the pond to be drained. The parks are part of the Public Works Department, and continue to be an asset.

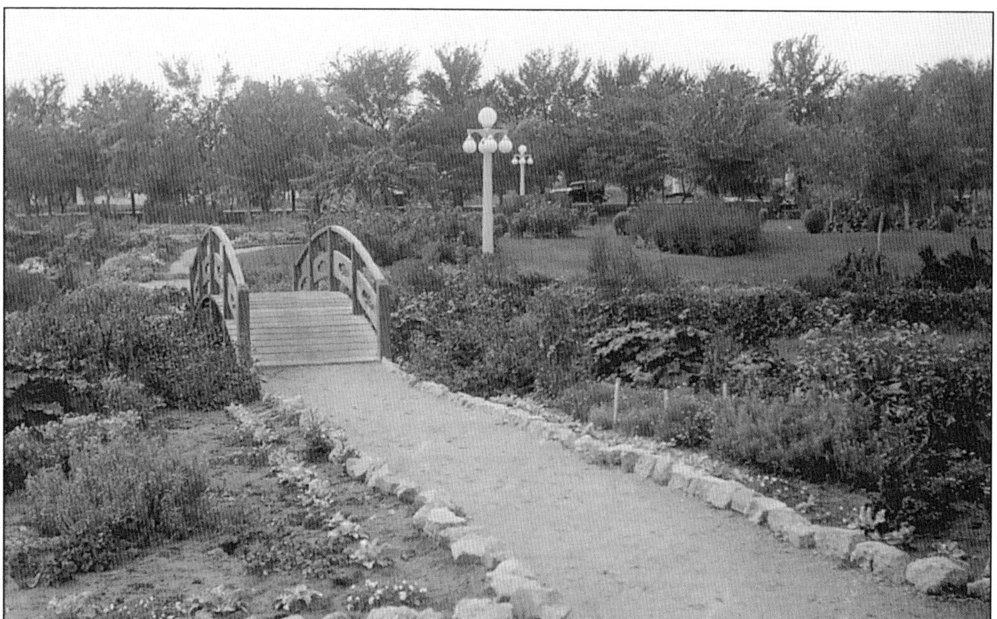

The Japanese-style bridge was used to cross the pond. Rock lined pathways connected various points in the park. From the playground you could follow flowerbeds throughout the grounds. Giant pillars on the north and east marked entrances for automobile paths. These were later discontinued. A local Eagle Scout reconstructed the new bridge in 1998.

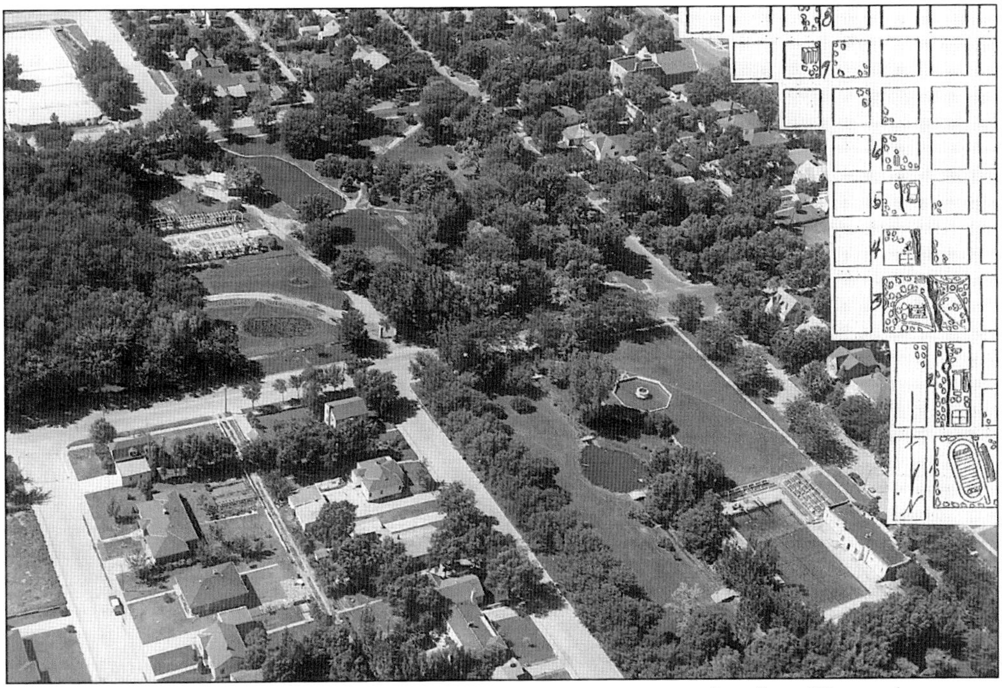

John Bower's dream of connecting recreation sites is apparent in this shot. The parks start at Eighteenth and Box Butte with Laing Lake, go south past the ball fields, swimming pool, tennis courts, pathways, football field, Sallows Conservatory, fountain, central park, Knight Museum, tennis courts, open park, and end at Bower Field and Park. Including the softball complex, the parks contain 135 acres. One man's dream became a community's legacy!

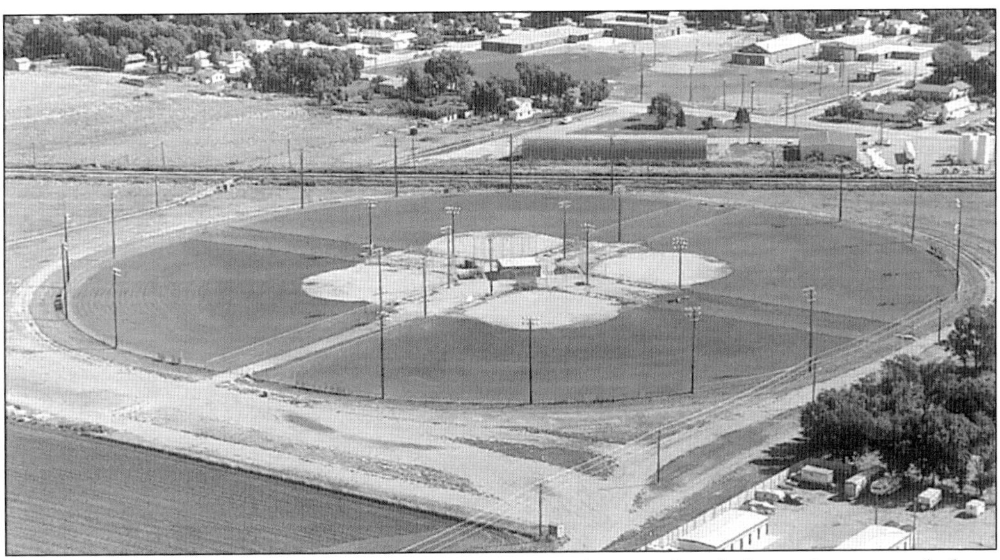

With a need for more ball diamonds, local sports enthusiasts banded together to work for a softball complex which was built in the 1980s with funds raised through community support and grants. The four-plex at Fourth and Cody hosts many tournaments and local leagues. A large concession stand with an announcing booth face electronic scoreboards. In the background you can see Emerson School and the Burkholder Education Center.

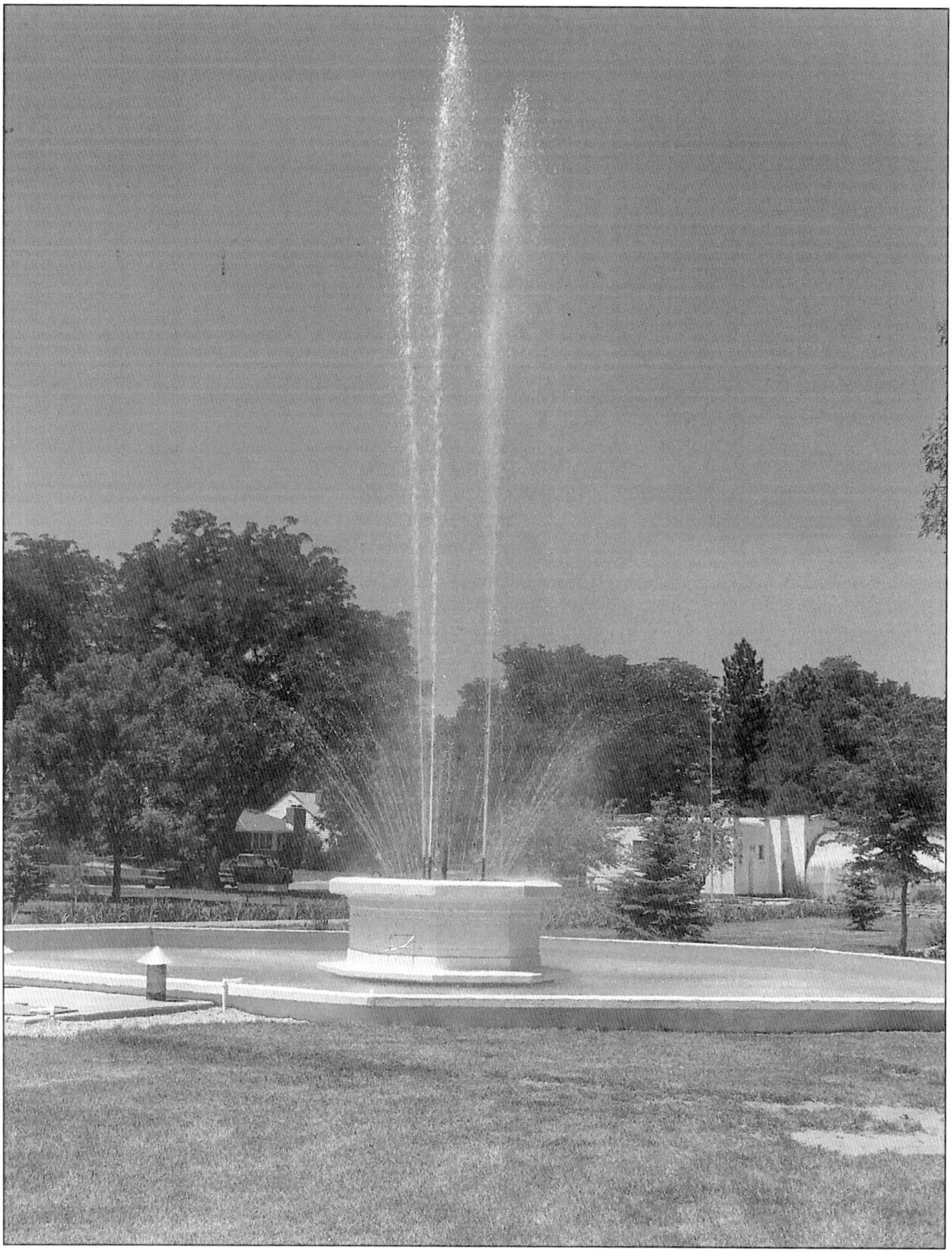

The crowning achievement of the park system is the electric fountain at Tenth and Niobrara. Created in 1935, endless color combinations and water patterns have awed visitors for years. In the 1970s, the fountain needed major repairs, and by 1985 it was nearly inoperable. In 1988, Mayor Eva Knight organized "Coins for the Fountain," where $20,000 was raised by placing quarters side-by-side from the Courthouse to the Fountain. It is also on the National Register of Historic Places.

Ten

THEN AND NOW . . . THE FUTURE OF ALLIANCE

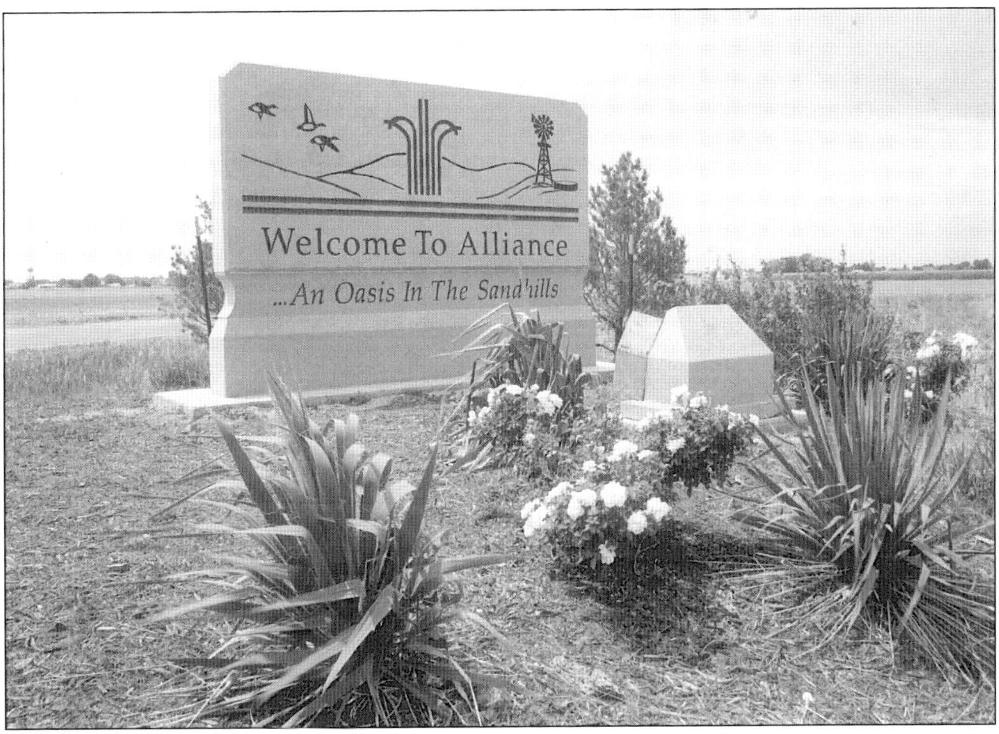

The three inviting entrance signs that welcome one and all to Alliance are located on the east, west, and northeast entries to the city. A design committee, consisting of four Alliance residents, chose granite as the sign's material and formulated the design. Beside the good feelings they evoke, it's worth noting that Keno funds, not tax dollars, paid for them.

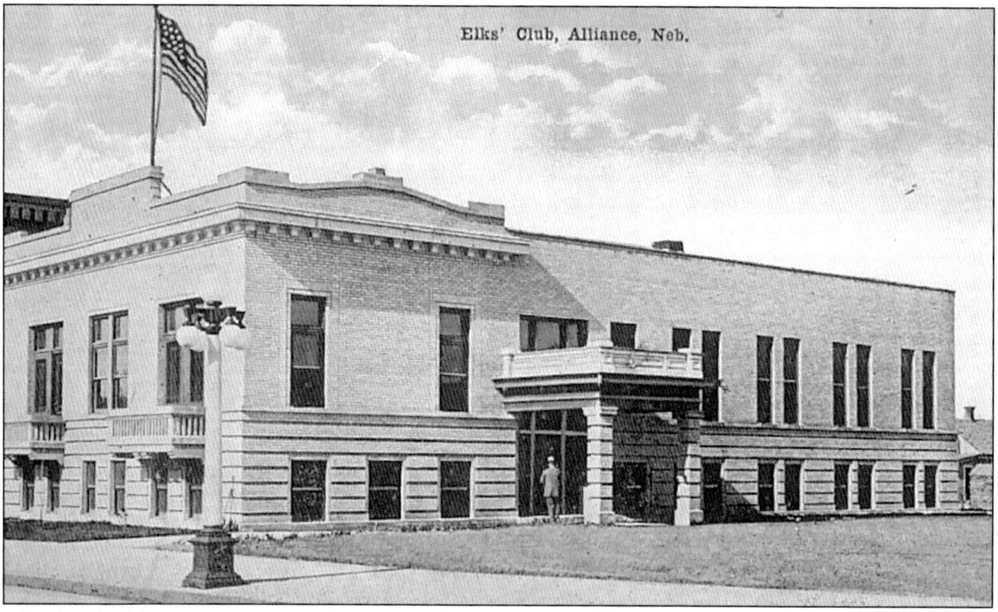

The local Elk's Club was a wonderful social building built in 1912 for $6,000. The original building contained a swimming pool that was later converted to a gym, and then into clubrooms for the use of more than nine hundred members. In 2000, the building was sold and the much smaller Elks group relocated. It will now become part of the post office complex.

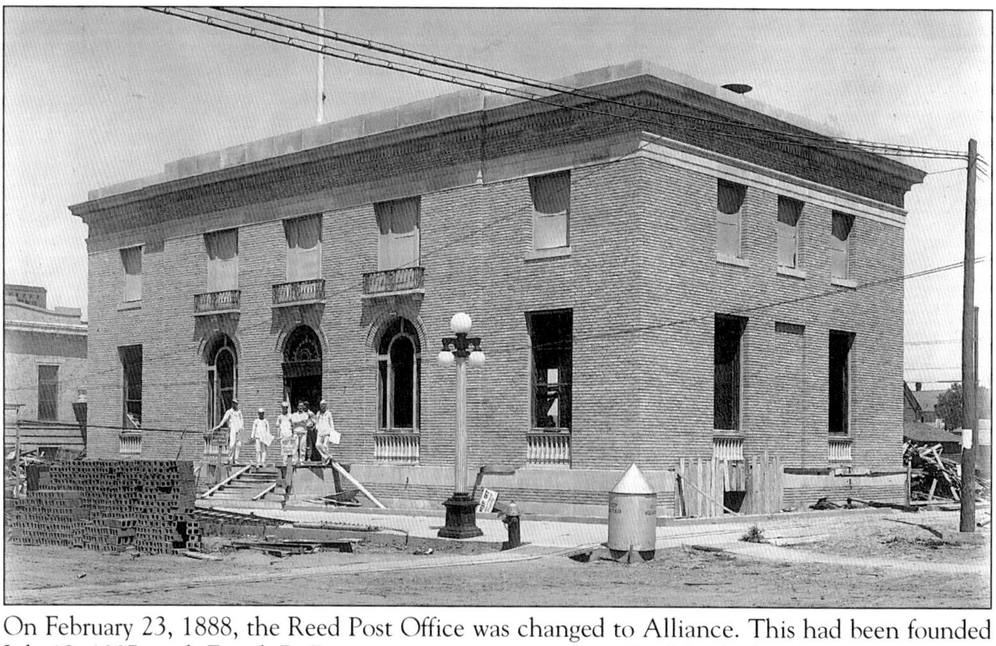

On February 23, 1888, the Reed Post Office was changed to Alliance. This had been founded July 12, 1887, with Enoch R. Patterson as postmaster. Sang Reck built the first post office, and went on to become county commissioner. In 1916, our present building was constructed to accommodate the growing population. Additions and remodeling took place in 1961–62, and the community looks forward to more growth with its merger into the Elks Building next door. Millions of pieces of mail pass through Alliance every year.

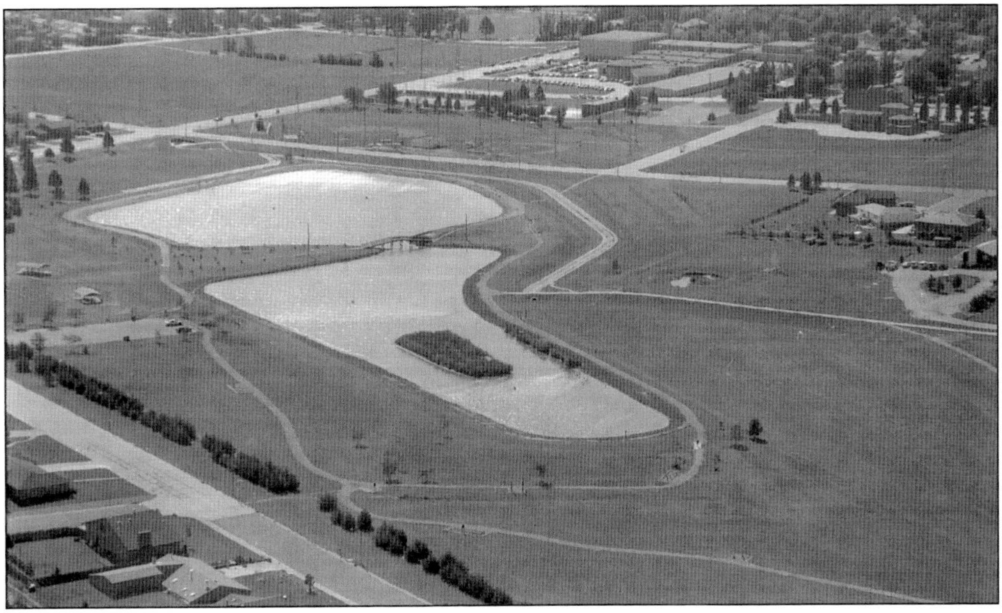

When the concept of a lake was first proposed, it was met with some controversy. The years have gone by and Laing Lake has become a favorite gathering place. Folks come to feed the waterfowl, picnic, fish, take a walk, and play disc golf at the year-round recreation park. This 9.5-acre lake was first created in 1978, and will be used for generations to come.

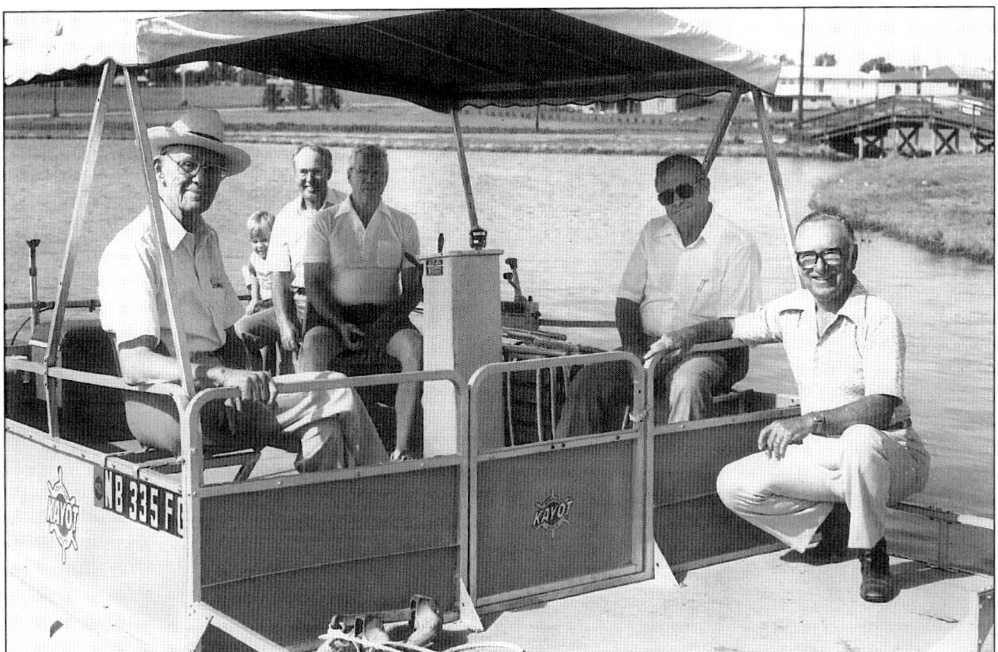

In July of 1982, a pontoon boat provided rides on Laing Lake for the Heritage Days celebration. This seaworthy craft proved its worth when the "maiden voyage" was taken by (L-R) Clyde Sudman, Jeff Kusek (next to his grandfather), Warren Trank, Neil Colerick, Keith Sorum, and Roberts W. "Bob" Laing. Looks like Bob is enjoying his namesake!

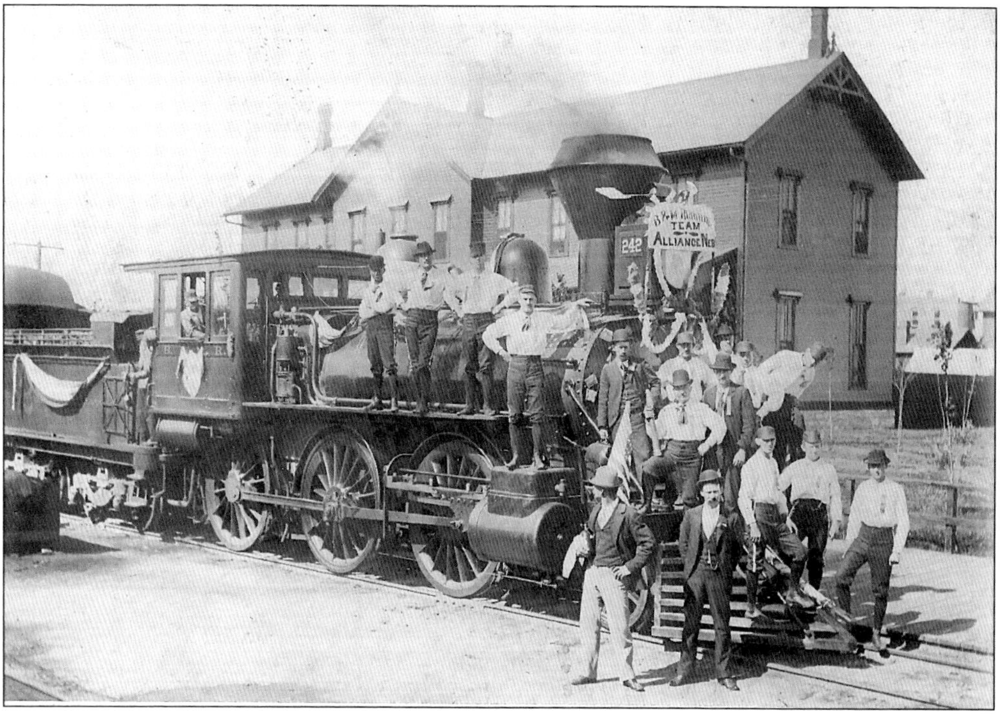

This diamond-stack engine is almost hidden by the members of the Burlington and Missouri River Railroad Running Team. In the background stands the original depot that burned in 1906. This group of men formed the backbone of the industry that caused Alliance to thrive. Combined with the agriculture industry, it has made this a town with a tremendous future.

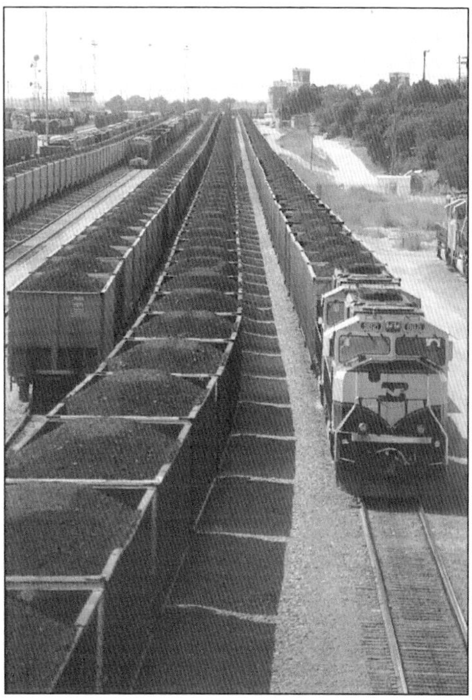

Alliance sees one hundred trains a day, full of coal, the lifeblood of BNSF. The coal comes from Wyoming and heads to points east, supplying many with energy. Alliance and BNSF together do their part in fueling the nation. It is the largest employer in the town, with over 1,800 employees. It has also brought in many independently owned businesses that do contract work, like Swepco and Progress Rail.

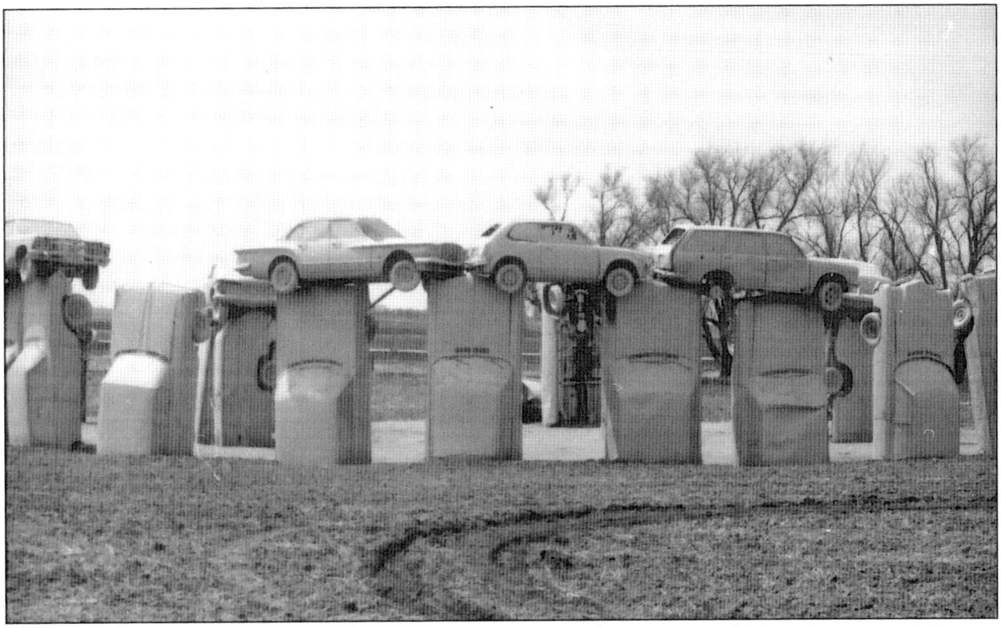

In June of 1987, the Reinders' family reunion spawned a project of folly that turned into a National Tourist Attraction. The vision was that of a replica of Stonehenge, but made out of cars. The size of cars had to be modeled after the large 1950s and 1960s vintage ones. These were close to the size of the original stones. Love it or hate it, Carhenge attracts about 85,000 people to the panhandle, and Alliance, area each year.

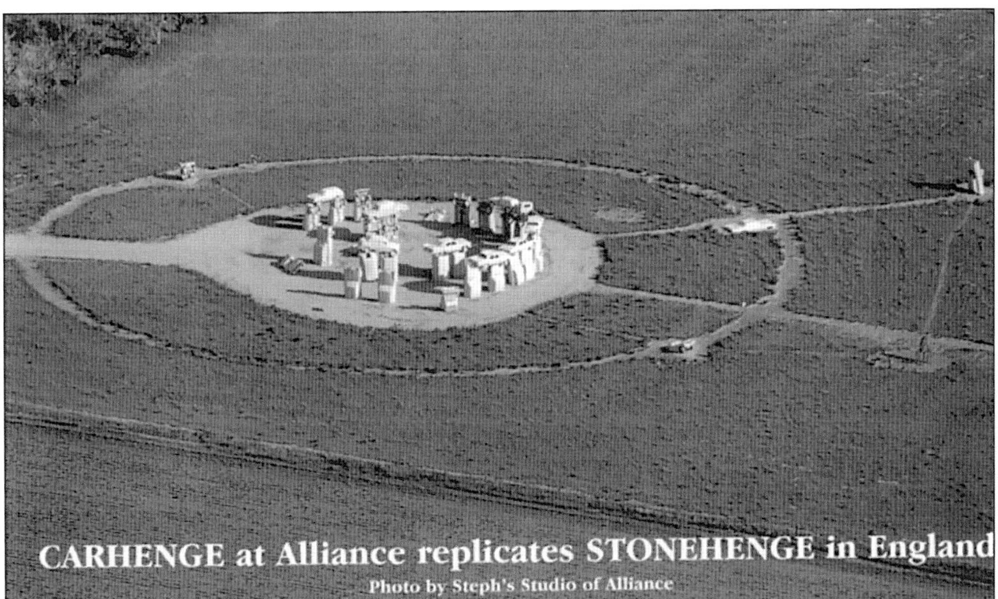

The aerial view of Carhenge gives one the feel for the similarity to "the real thing." Friends of Carhenge is a group that was formed to promote and maintain this attraction. They welcome new sculptures, known as "car art," under the condition that only car parts are used. Comments are welcome, and some of the best received have been from England tourists. They love the American "sense of humor."

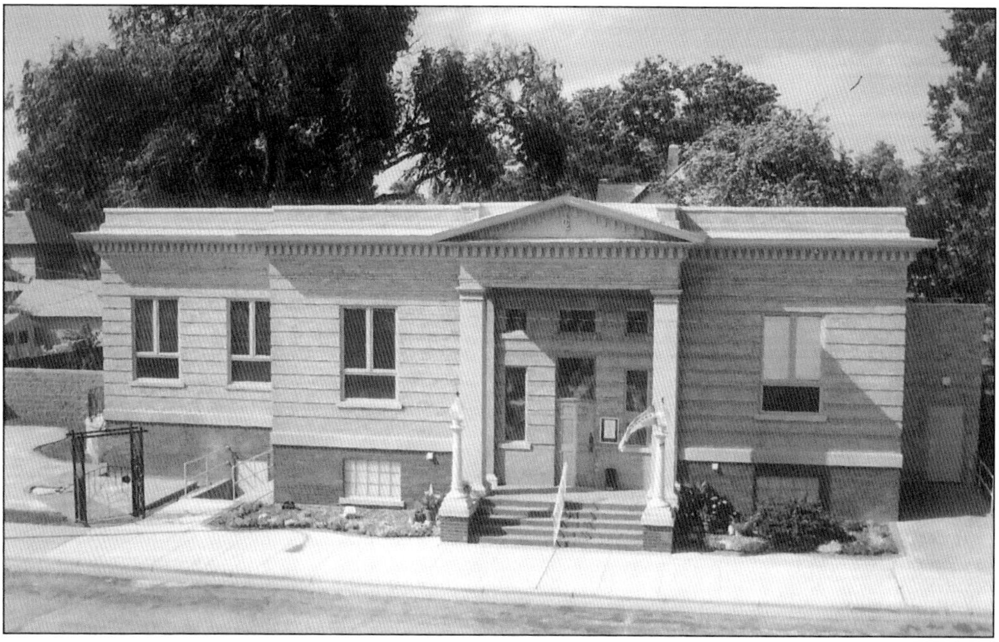

The first library was in the basement of the Phelen Opera House in 1900. A grant from the Carnegie Foundation completed the building in 1911 for $9,850. The possibility of demolishment caused concerned local art patrons to rally, and in 1993 the Carnegie Art Center opened. It has brought a refurbished purpose to an aging legend. Many art shows and classes bring much joy to the community.

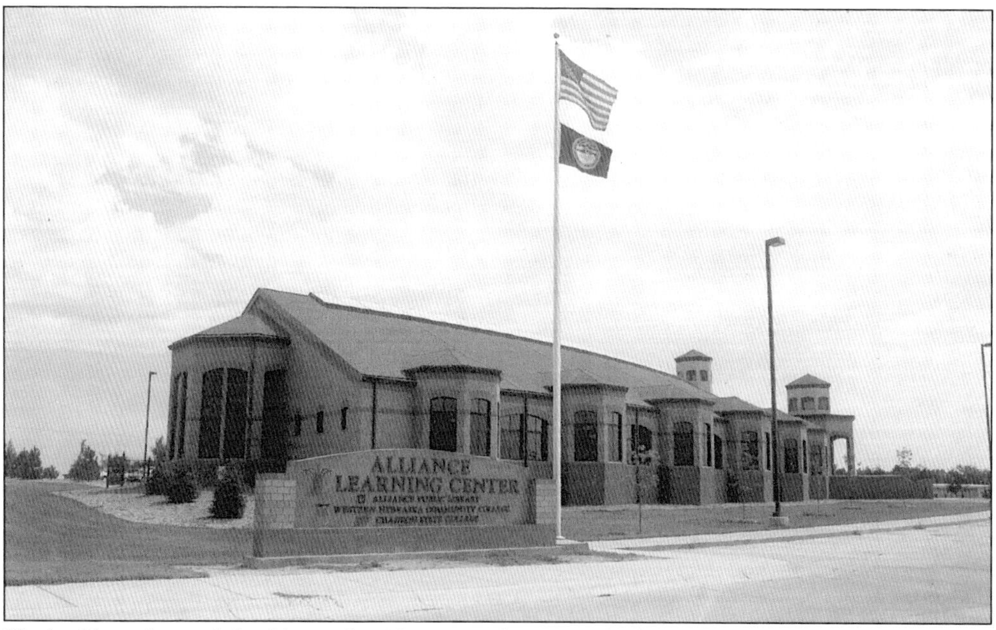

Slagle Clinic housed the library for 19 years, when growth forced the library's move from the Carnegie building. This served Alliance until a bond issue passed to build the Alliance Library and Attendance Center in 1998. Dedicated in 1999, it became a shining example of the faith the Alliance resident's place in our future. It was voted the top NCIP project in Nebraska in 1999.

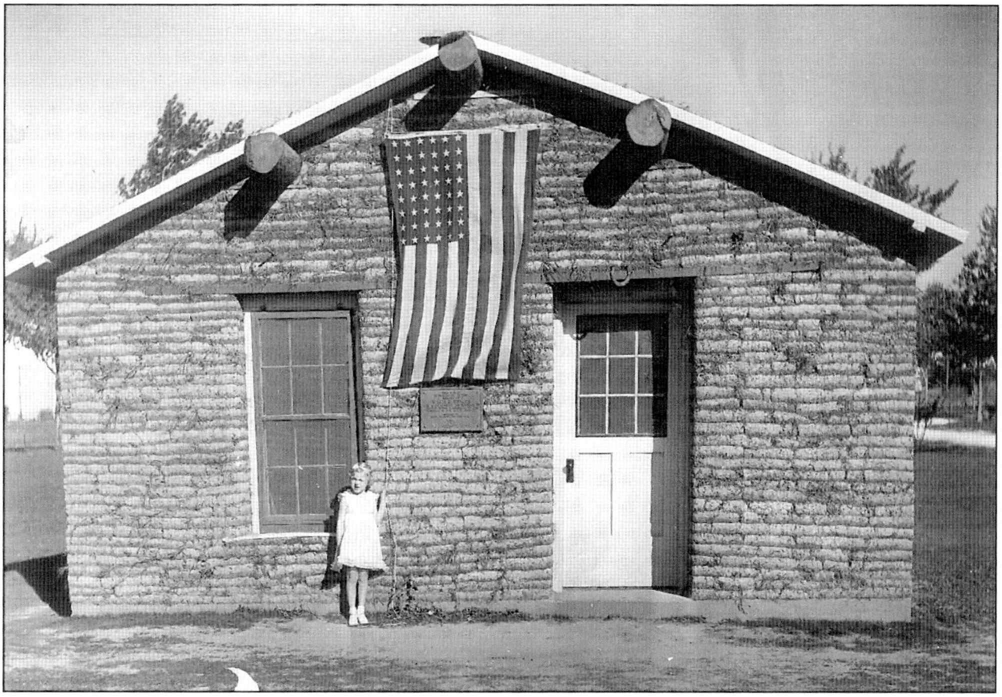

The DAR, with the help of Vera Spencer, chapter regent, and her father, Willis, built a Sod House Museum in 1932. Pictured is her niece Catherine. A flood in 1938 was fatal to the sod, and a new home was needed. Planning started, but the next years were rocky. In 1957, a temporary site was found at 624 Yellowstone in a former air base barracks.

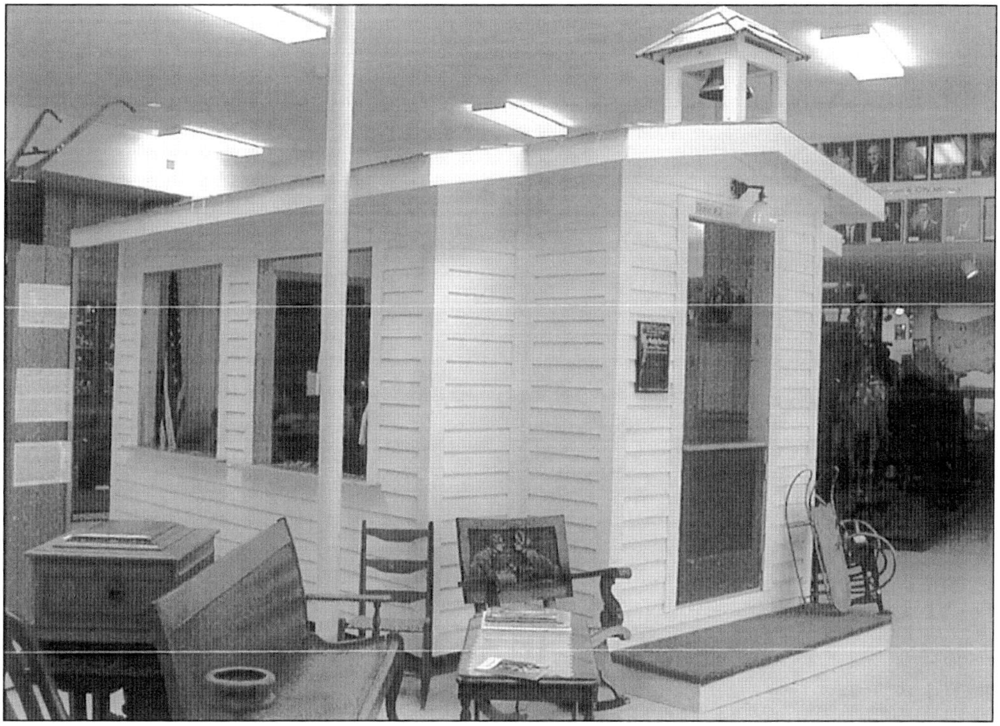

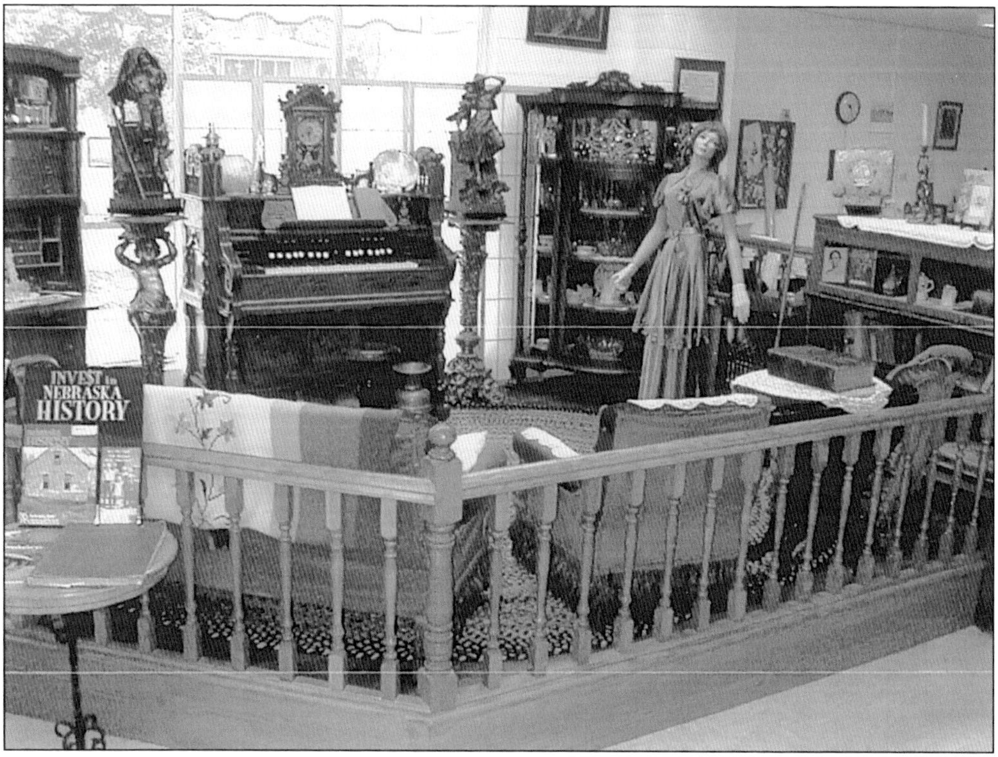

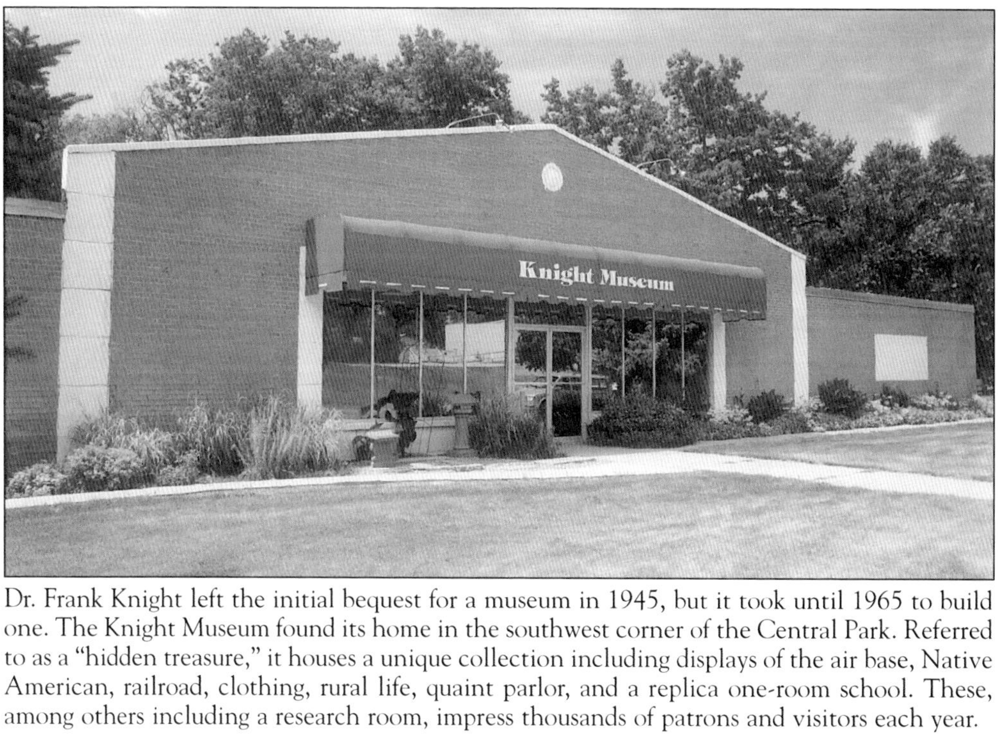

Dr. Frank Knight left the initial bequest for a museum in 1945, but it took until 1965 to build one. The Knight Museum found its home in the southwest corner of the Central Park. Referred to as a "hidden treasure," it houses a unique collection including displays of the air base, Native American, railroad, clothing, rural life, quaint parlor, and a replica one-room school. These, among others including a research room, impress thousands of patrons and visitors each year.